Blas ar Gymr

Gobeithiwn y byddwch yn mwynhau'r arweiniad hwn g[...]
bwyd a theithio wrth iddo eich arwain drwy fyd bwyd [...]

Nod Blas ar Gymru Cyfyngedig yw codi safonau'r diw[...]
Nghymru a hybu defnyddio cynnyrch Cymreig uchel ei ar[...]
ystod y ddwy flynedd ers ei sefydlu mae wedi ennill cydnab[...]
Cymru ymhlith y gorau sydd ar [...]

Taste of Wales

Wir hoffen, daß Ihnen dieser Restaurant – und Reiseführer – Taste of Wales – gefallen wird und daß Sie sich an seiner Gesellschaft freuen, wenn er Ihnen die vielseitige und reichhaltige kulinarische Landschaft von Wales nahebringt.

Taste of Wales Limited ist darum bemüht, die Standards der Nahrungsmittel – und Gaststättenbetriebe in Wales noch weiter anzuheben und die Verwendung qualitativ hochwertiger walisischer Erzeugnisse innerhalb dieses Sektors zu fördern. Seit der Gründung vor zwei Jahren hat Taste of Wales dazu beigetragen, daß die führende Position walisischer Agrarerzeugnisse und der walisischen Küche allgemein anerkannt werden.

Taste of Wales

Wij hopen dat u geniet van deze Taste of Wales restaurant–, spijs– en reisgids, daar het u door het uitgebreide en gevarieerde etenstafereel in Wales neemt.

Taste of Wales Limited beoogt de normen in de voedings– en provianderingsindustrie in Wales te verhogen en het gebruik van kwaliteitsprodukten van Wales binnen de industrie te bevorderen. In de twee jaren sinds de lancering hebben zij bereikt dat de produkten en de keuken van Wales herkend worden als behorend tot de beste.

Taste of Wales – Il Sapore Del Galles

Speriamo che vi piaccia questo ristorante Taste of Wales e il suo cibo e la guida di viaggio, che vi trasporta attraverso l'ambiente gastronomico ricco e svariato del Galles.

Taste of Wales Limited ha come obiettivo il raggiungimento di livelli sempre più alti nell'industria gastronomica e dell'approvvigionamento del Galles, e la promozione dell'uso di prodotti gallesi d'alta qualità in seno a questa industria. Nei due anni trascorsi dal suo lancio, ha fatto sì che ai prodotti e alla cucina gallesi venisse riconosciuto un posto fra i migliori del settore.

Taste of Wales

Nous espérons que vous appréciez ce restaurant Taste of Wales, sa nourriture et son guide gastronomique car il vous donne un aperçu des spécialités culinaires riches et variées du Pays de Galles.

Taste of Wales Limited a pour but d'élever le niveau de la qualité dans l'industrie alimentaire et l'industrie de la restauration au Pays de Galles et de promouvoir l'utilisation de produits gallois d'excellente qualité au sein de l'industrie. Depuis son lancement, il y a deux ans, la société a permis aux produits et à la cuisine du Pays de Galles d'être reconnus parmi les meilleurs.

テイスト・オブ・ウェールズ

皆様にはテイスト・オブ・ウェールズのバラエティーに富むレストラン、特産フード、観光ガイドをご紹介いたしましたが、充分にご満足して頂けたものと存じます。

テイスト・オブ・ウェールズ・リミテッドでは、常にウェールズ地域における食品業界の躍進を念頭においたビジネスを展開しています。もちろん、ウェールズで製造されるハイクオリティーの食品のプロモーションにも積極的に取り組んでいます。テイスト・オブ・ウェールズは、スタート以後の僅か2年間でウェールズの食品、料理がファーストクラスとして認められるまでに貢献しました。

The truth is, I'm not here by chance.

The truth is, nor am I.

RICHARD BINNS

Richard Binns resigned from a successful career in computers in 1980 to become a do-it-yourself publisher with his first book, French Leave. *The success of his first venture into print – it zoomed up* The Sunday Times *bestseller list – led to eight further successful guide books on travel, hotels and restaurants covering both France and Britain. A self-confessed Francophile and 'mapoholic', he marries his enthusiasm and zest for travel with an unflinching honesty when it comes to recommending hotels and restaurants. When not exploring France and Britain he lives in Warwickshire with his wife. He is a regular contributor to* The Sunday Times *and* The Observer.

GILLI DAVIES

Gilli Davies has enjoyed food from many different angles. Married to an army officer, with three children, she has attempted a variety of jobs with each new posting. These range from running a bistro in Berlin to writing A Taste of Cyprus, *a book about the cultural and seasonal dishes of the island. But real home is Wales and from here Gilli finds that journalism gives her the perfect excuse to travel throughout the Principality and discover its new flavours. In 1989 she published her first book about Welsh food called* Lamb, Leeks and Laverbread *and 1990 saw the BBC Wales TV series* Tastes of Wales *which she wrote and presented together with a BBC book of the same name.*

JOHN HOWELLS

John Howells lives in Cardiff, not far from his roots in the Rhymney valley. Mathematics lecturer, church organist and manqué historian, he has written the Bon Appetit *restaurant review column in the* Western Mail *for seven years, as well as a variety of articles for their* Welsh Style *magazine. He has travelled all over Wales, England and Europe, and believes that food in the Principality now compares very favourably both nationally and internationally. He is the Welsh correspondent for one of the British restaurant guides.*

BRENDA PARRY

Brenda Parry is a journalist, wife and mother who left Fleet Street behind after 20 years of covering everything from the Queen's Silver Jubilee to the troubles in Northern Ireland to bring up her small daughter, Angharad, in the Welsh mountains, her husband's homeland. She worked for The Daily Telegraph *for 12 years, and for her last five years with the newspaper wrote a weekly food column. She firmly believes that the people best qualified to judge food and cooking standards are those who have to prepare daily meals. She still writes regularly about restaurants for newspapers and food guides. She is married to Gareth Parry,* The Guardian's *chief reporter.*

CONTENTS

	Page		Page
MAP OF WALES	8	**GILLI DAVIES**	
		RECIPES	46
ANGELA PARRY-LOWTHER,		*First courses/light meals*	46
Director, Taste of Wales		*Main meals*	55
WHAT IS A TASTE OF WALES?	9	*Puddings*	70
		Baking	81
RICHARD BINNS			
MY WALES	11	BRENDA PARRY	
		ON THE GOOD FOOD TRAIL	86
GILLI DAVIES		*South*	87
FOOD IN WALES	20	*West*	93
South	20	*Mid*	98
West	22	*North*	104
Mid	24		
North	26	BRENDA PARRY	
		BECOMING A SUCCESSFUL	
GILLI DAVIES		**CHEF**	113
FIVE FAVOURITES	28		
Cheese	28	**GAZETTEER OF TASTE OF WALES**	
Healthy eating	29	**MEMBERS**	128
Baking	29	*(this gazetteer contains short items on Welsh*	
Lamb	30	*history and legends by John Howells)*	
Seafood	31		
		INDEX	188
GILLI DAVIES			
SHOPPING IN WALES	34		
South	34		
West	38		
Mid	40		
North	43		

Wales

ANGELA PARRY-LOWTHER

WHAT IS A TASTE OF WALES?

As director of Taste of Wales – *Blas ar Gymru*, I should be able to answer that question easily. But it's not as straightforward as you might think. I can tell you what Taste of Wales is *not* about. It's not simply concerned with promoting the old image of Welsh food – the traditional meat dishes, the long-established recipes and so on. The traditional side is, of course, an important part of Taste of Wales. But this food initiative is not based on what Wales's cuisine has produced in the past. Taste of Wales reflects what is happening in the Wales of today, and points the way to the future.

Let's take lamb as an example. Welsh lamb is prized throughout the world for its quality. Today in Wales, chefs are serving locally produced lamb in fresh, imaginative ways – though if you're set in your ways and know what you like, you can still, of course, enjoy Welsh lamb cooked traditionally to time-honoured perfection!

Taste of Wales is all about the best of the old and the best of the new. The emphasis is not on specific dishes or recipes, but on *quality* – quality local produce and quality cooking. On both counts – on the produce and those who make use of it – Wales is very well endowed. In addition to lamb, Wales has a bountiful larder of fresh vegetables, superb seafoods, and cheeses that rival the world's best. And no longer is Wales a gastronomic desert. Talented chefs are working in hotels, restaurants, inns and farmhouses the length and breadth of the country making the best use of what Wales has to offer.

Please don't get the impression that we are only talking about *haute cuisine*. Wales has its gourmet restaurants which stand comparison with the best in Britain. But it also has less elaborate establishments, its farmhouses and its inns, where simple – but superbly prepared – country fare is served. The strength of Taste of Wales is that it embraces both approaches.

The Taste of Wales message is encapsulated in the pages of this book. Its contents reflect the imaginative and creative ways in which local produce is used throughout Wales. But it's much more than a simple

Some of the tasty recipes from the Gelli Fawr Country House, near Fishguard, are featured in this book

cook book. There are sections on regional foods and where to shop, profiles of some of the leading lights on the cooking scene, a recipe section, and a gazetteer of Taste of Wales members where you can enjoy meals which make the best use of fresh local ingredients. There are many hotels, inns and farmhouses amongst that number, so you can also use this book as an accommodation guide when you're on your travels throughout Wales.

And that's not all. We begin the book with a scene-setting introduction by food and travel writer Richard Binns (who is, I'm glad to say, something of a Welshophile and a big fan of Welsh cooking!) and also include a tour of Taste of Wales establishments by Brenda Parry. Television cook Gilli Davies has prepared some tempting recipes for you, while John Howells has enlivened the gazetteer section with anecdotes and stories on Wales and Welsh history.

So, as you can see, this is not just a cook book, but also a guide to travel and the best places to eat in Wales. But if you *really* want to find out for yourself what Taste of Wales is all about, call in at an establishment on your travels which displays our distinctive membership and plaque and enjoy a memorable meal.

BLAS AR CYMRU
TASTE OF WALES

MY WALES

RICHARD BINNS

During the last decade I suspect I've seen more of Britain and France than many other travel or food writers. And because I've published all my own books on these two countries myself, I've probably received more readers' letters than most.

Much-travelled readers frequently comment that they have found French culinary standards have slipped. My answer is always the same: yes, standards and quality are lower; bread, breakfasts, vegetables, soups, puddings, meats and so on are not what they were 20 years ago. I then go on to stress, vigorously, that the real reason why we feel that these standards are lower is because levels of skill and quality of produce have improved so dramatically here in Britain.

Nowhere is this more true than in Wales. At last the Welsh are discovering the latent treasure chest of culinary gems on their very own doorstep. Some of my most enjoyable eating-out treats during the last two years have been meals where I've relished delights such as crispy laverbread, Glamorgan 'sausages' (a cheese-based, three-star winner), *sewin* (sea trout) – both smoked and poached – salt duck with Swansea potato cakes, world-beating Welsh lamb, a pudding concoction with the wondrous label 'Welsh over Welsh with Welsh as well', and Welsh cheeses galore. Can any better a Pencarreg, Llanboidy or Skirrid when served in perfect condition?

Not only are home-based Welsh chefs beginning to make good use of Welsh produce, but so are others. Three Welsh-as-Welsh-can-be chefs are at the forefront of the crusade outside Wales: the master, Stephen Bull, at his restaurant of the same name in London's Blandford Street; Bryan Webb at Hilaire's in the Old Brompton Road, Kensington; and Carole Evans at her pub and restaurant, Poppies at the Roebuck, in Brimsfield, south of Ludlow. How times change: three cheers for such innovative culinary work by Welsh chefs – in both Wales and to the east of Offa's Dyke!

When you are exploring Wales with the help of this book, you will discover some marvellous places, both culinary and scenic. Which brings me on to another of my favourite subjects: maps. Later, I'll have a few words to say about the vital importance of arming yourself with the relevant large-scale maps for every area of Wales you are exploring; and I'll explain some of the more common Welsh placenames. It is absolutely vital to get off the beaten track as much as you can – the only true way of taking in the best of any country. I'll also give you a brief personal insight into the current Welsh culinary scene. But to start with, let me sketch for you my own thumbnail-sized account of Welsh history. It is an essential prerequisite for any visitor to Wales to grasp just how the nation's turbulent history has moulded the character and independence of its people. A mixture of geography and history helps to explain some of the story.

Welsh History:
A Brief Personal Outline

Before the Romans extended their vast Empire across most of northern Europe our islands were inhabited by Celts. It took only a handful of years, after the Roman conquest began in AD43, for the Celts in England to be subdued by the invading armies. But those in the west, in the mountainous refuge of Cambria, were never brought to heel. Some Roman influence was stamped on parts of both the North and South Wales coasts – Segontium, now Caernarfon, was the most important of their forts – but not elsewhere.

The Roman Amphitheatre, Caerleon

The Roman legions governed much of Britain for over four centuries. When they withdrew they left a nation of 'Britons' poorly equipped to defend themselves against the waves of Saxon invaders from continental Europe. The Saxons forced numerous Britons westwards into the natural strongholds of Scotland, Cornwall and Wales. The word 'Welsh' in fact stems from the Saxon word for 'foreigners', *wealas*. It could be said, as H V Morton once claimed, that the Welsh are 'the real Britons'. To be precise he should have made it clear they share that right with the Scots and Cornish. Even today the 'Welsh' would rather be known as *Cymry*, 'fellow-countrymen' or 'comrades', and for their mountainous country to be known as *Cymru*. The Welsh language, *Cymraeg*, is primarily part of an ancient Celtic family. Many Latin words were added to the Celtic base during Roman times – *pont*, bridge, is just one example – and, later, the language absorbed words and phrases from the Anglo-Saxons, Norman French and English. Marvel then at how the proud Welsh language has not only survived but has grown and developed so much. Surely it is a modern-day miracle that the nation's language is today flourishing so strongly and proudly?

The *Cymry* haven't stopped battling ever since the Saxon invaders overran the flatlands of England. In the 8th century Offa, the King of Mercia, built his legendary Offa's Dyke which runs the length of Wales's eastern border, from the mouth of the Dee to the confluence of the Wye and Severn. The dyke, a high earthen rampart up to 60ft (18m) wide, with a ditch some 12ft (3^1/$_2$m) wide on the western or 'Welsh' side, was built partly as a defensive system, but mainly as a demarcation line. Offa was not the first, nor the last, of a succession of English kings to have endless sleepless nights of worry over how to keep the troublesome Welsh at bay!

Chepstow Castle

Offa's Dyke, only visible in some sections of its snake-like path, also plays a part in an 'invisible' way too: for the Welsh, *dros Glawdd Offa* has the same significance as 'to cross the Rubicon' - an irrevocable course of action or, put more bluntly, to burn one's boats!

The four Norman kings – William I and II, Henry I and Stephen – had no better luck at subduing the warring Welsh from 1066 to 1154. During William the Conqueror's reign (1066–87) Norman castle were built at Chester, Shrewsbury, Richard's Castle, Wigmore (both near Ludlow), Ewyas Harold (south-west of Hereford), Monmouth and Chepstow. Later the Normans pushed further west, along both the southern and northern coasts of Wales: castles were constructed at many places, including Cardiff, Carmarthen, Cardigan and Pembroke in the south and at Caernarfon, Bangor and Aber Lleiniog (Aber on the maps, north-east of Bangor) in the north. Fighting was non-stop and all the castle were constantly under siege; the Normans could hardly be said to have dominated the Welsh.

Grosmont, one of the 'three castles' of Gwent

Henry II was the first of the 14 Plantagenet kings who ruled our islands from 1154 until 1485. Of the eight Angevin kings in the Plantagenet dynasty – the other six were from the houses of Lancaster and York – only Edward II and Richard II failed to make their mark as castle builders. This was the age of the numerous and influential Marcher Lords who built a long necklace of castles in the 'Welsh Marches' or Border Country (*Y Goror* in Welsh). Some involved impressive rebuilding of older wooden castles first erected in Norman times: Grosmont was an example, one of the 'three castles' – the other two are White and Skenfrith – north of Monmouth, used as a group to control a huge circle of Border Country.

Cardiff's well-preserved Norman keep

Montgomery Castle, on a superb strategic site high on a spur above the town, was built during the third decade of the 13th century, during Henry III's reign. The important understanding of past history underlines one salient fact: the Welsh, by and large, remained fiercely independent and, most certainly, resisted all efforts by the early Plantagenet kings to overcome Wales.

For the Plantagenets to succeed in a final conquest of Wales meant overcoming the native princes of Wales. Llywelyn ab Iorwerth, Llywelyn the Great, was the first of the independent Welsh princes who managed to unite the entire country in the 13th century against the English invaders. His grandson, Llywelyn ap Gruffudd, or Llywelyn the Last, faced Edward I's vast armies on two occasions. In 1277 four separate English armies overran Wales: one advancing in the north from Chester, a second through Montgomery, a third marched on Brecon, and a fourth attacked Carmarthen. At first Llywelyn retreated to the natural fastness of Snowdonia but, on 10 November, he was forced by the threat of famine to sign a peace treaty. Then followed five uneasy years of submission. But, in 1282, revolts broke out in many differing parts of Wales, culminating in Edward I once again throwing his armies against the fighting Welsh. Llywelyn met his death near Builth.

Edward I reigned from 1272 to 1307. During his time on the throne a host of formidable fortresses were completed in Wales: the border strongholds of Chester, Shrewsbury, Montgomery and St Briavels were all remodelled and strengthened. Three captured Welsh castle were entirely rebuilt: Dolwyddelan, Criccieth and Castell-y-Bere – the latter south-east of Cader Idris, the mountain that dominates Dolgellau; and among a dozen or more brand-new castle constructed by Edward were those at Caerphilly, Conwy (Conway), Harlech, Caernarfon, Beaumaris, Builth, Denbigh and Chirk. Not all this castle building was easy. Edward I was trapped at Conwy Castle shortly after it was completed by an insurgent Welsh force and he had to endure a long siege before help came from his own army. In 1284 Edward I's son was born in Caernarfon; three days later the infant boy was proclaimed 'Prince of Wales'. He was crowned Edward II in 1307, aged 23. His son, Edward III, ruled for 50 years, from 1327 to 1377.

The mighty Edwardian fortress at Caernarfon

The legendary Welsh fighting prowess made its mark in France during the 14th century: first at Crécy, in 1346, where the killing power of the formidable Welsh longbow was felt by the French for the first time; and, 10 years later, at Poitiers. The latter victory came under the leadership of the 'Black Prince', the eldest son of Edward III; alas, this courageous warrior was never crowned a king! In 1415, 69 years after Crécy, the Welsh longbowmen played another vital part in Henry V's spectacular victory at Agincourt.

Henry V was the second of the three House of Lancaster kings, succeeding his father Henry IV, who had ascended the throne after the murder of Richard II, the Black Prince's son, in 1399. That murder, together with a series of hard statutes imposed by Henry IV, proved to be the catalyst that brought another of the legendary figures of Welsh history to the fore: Owain Glyndŵr or Owen Glendower.

In late 1400 Glyndŵr put Ruthin to the torch, in 1401 Conwy Castle was taken, the following year Lord Grey was captured – eventually being released after payment of a massive ransom – and in 1404 Harlech Castle was taken; Glyndŵr was virtually the ruler of Wales. He chose Machynlleth as his capital and he was crowned 'King of Wales' there in 1404. But, within 10 years his influence and rule had crumbled. It has been said Glyndŵr was the 'father of modern Welsh nationalism'.

The unquenchable pride that the Welsh have for their race, heritage and country remains as strong today as it did throughout the 15th century. And it was a Welshman who changed our nation's history so profoundly in 1485 when Henry VII won the throne of England, the first of the incomparable Tudor line of kings and queens. Let me tell you, in two brief paragraphs, his family's story.

In 1420 Henry V married Catherine de Valois, the daughter of Charles VI of France, when she was just 19. Henry died in 1422, one year after their son, Henry VI, was born at Windsor. Henry VI ruled from 1422 to 1461. His reign was a disaster: France was lost; civil war erupted and eventually the House of Lancaster was defeated. In the years that followed Henry V's death, Catherine, his widow, had a secret love affair with Owen Tudor, a Welshman from Plas Penmynydd on Anglesey. Owen, together with thousands of other fierce Welsh fighters, had served under Henry V at Agincourt in 1415.

Catherine bore Owen four children, three of them sons. Their first child, Edmund Tudor, half-brother of Henry VI, later married Margaret, daughter of the Duke of Somerset; the couple's first child, born at Pembroke Castle in 1457, arrived when Margaret was only 13 years old! Their son was to become, in 1485, Henry VII – the first of a legendary dynasty, the Tudors, one which changed and influenced British history in the most profound way. By 1536, in Henry VIII's reign, the Act of Union with Wales was passed. In the centuries since, Wales has played a significant part, in myriad ways, in ensuring that Britain became one of the world's most powerful nations.

Pembroke Castle, birthplace of Henry VII

The Welsh culinary scene today

Cooks in Wales have some super produce to work with: magnificent lamb; excellent beef and quality vegetables; fish and shellfish including *sewin* (sea trout), charr, wild salmon, lobsters, crabs, scallops, cockles, mussels and numerous other treats from trout to sea bass and turbot; and cheeses which I personally rate as good as any from an equivalent 'region' in France.

Two wretched problems persist, however. Ninety per cent or more of the superb sea harvests landed at Welsh ports find their way to Europe – especially to Spain. Far too few Welsh hotels and restaurants make enough use of the bounty trawled in from the seas surrounding Wales; the sooner that failure is put right the better. The other, even more insulting, problem is the one perpetrated by 'cheating' chefs who, instead of using local fresh produce, turn to 'out-of-the-bag' or 'frozen' products, prepared in factories far away from their kitchens. Why don't these chefs have the guts to say, on their menus, that their offerings are not their own?

Though many Welsh people refuse to acknowledge that an authentic Welsh cooking tradition exists there's enough evidence to refute their misguided claims. There have been many noble attempts at documenting traditional Welsh recipes: two of the finest works on 'regional' cuisine which I've ever encountered are Gilli Davies's *Lamb, Leeks and Laverbread* (Grafton Press) and Bobby Freeman's *First Catch Your Peacock*. Bobby published the book, on her own, in 1980. It's now out of print, but I'm crossing my fingers that some publisher will be remarketing this superb book very soon. Bobby's six small pocket books, on various Welsh culinary topics, are however still available from Y Lolfa of Talybont in Dyfed.

Don't assume that Welsh cookery is exclusively lamb, leeks, laverbread, *bara brith* – speckled (fruit) bread – and Welsh rarebit! All the books mentioned above put paid to that lie: they are treasure chests of knowledge on the origins and development of Welsh cooking and they contain scores of well-researched specialities.

More and more Welsh chefs should adopt a small but carefully thought-out repertoire of traditional and authentic Welsh specialities. Candidates could include: *brithyll a chig moch* – trout with bacon; flavoursome Welsh salt duck; simply cooked sewin; the finest version of *cawl* – a soup or broth but, in reality, a 'meal' of meat and vegetables; and *bara mwyar* – a blackberry bread pudding. These, plus many others, would create immense interest for both tourists and locals alike. Many chefs already make a considerable effort in establishing at least some of the traditional Welsh recipes; but I implore all Welsh cooks to have a go! Even the language helps, by bringing a touch of mystery to the tantalizing menu descriptions.

But less of the depressing news of past history. Let me turn to the good news. At last there are signs that the sleeping red dragon is awakening and is making a start at the Herculean task of getting its culinary act together.

In May 1988 Peter Walker, then Secretary of State for Wales, launched 'Taste of Wales', a company formed by the Welsh Development Agency, Mid Wales Development and the Wales Tourist Board. Its aims are simple: to encourage hotels, restaurants, pubs and farmhouses to use and promote the best of Welsh food and to ensure that quality becomes the byword of all food producers and chefs throughout the Principality.

Bravo! The foundations have been laid. Already 'Taste of Wales' has got its teeth into the business of training Welsh chefs at all levels of skill; strong links are being forged with catering colleges and the company is sponsoring the Young Welsh Chef of the Year competition. 'Taste of Wales' is also trying to establish, so that it becomes part of everyday restaurant cookery, a repertoire of traditional Welsh specialities. These dishes, complemented by the liberated style of modern British cooking, could soon earn Wales a culinary reputation far beyond its borders. I cannot stress enough the vital importance of the culinary aspect of a nation's tourism efforts; it is a fundamental cornerstone of any region's or nation's reputation. Let's match the French in terms of pride and skill! Who knows, by the end of the millennium, Michelin could be placing both 'M' and 'star' awards on enough Welsh heads to match the numbers awarded in Scotland and Ireland.

My recent travels in Wales have confirmed that at last the corner has been turned: the red dragon's fire will soon set the culinary world alight!

A delicious piece of cheese, ham cooked with cider, and a loaf baked at Gelli Fawr Country House, near Fishguard

Maps

During the '80s I must have written a million words or more on the topography and culinary scene in both France and Britain. Three observations, more than all the others, capture the heart and soul of what I implore all my readers to do on their travels.

The first of the three introduces this short section on maps: 'The more you run the risk of getting lost, the more certain you are of seeing the real Wales.' I could list many hundreds of examples where large-scale maps will lead you to the very best of rural Wales. Here is a typical quartet: the Llyfnant valley, south-west of Machynlleth; Marsh's Pool, south-west of Llanidloes – access from the 233m spot height in map square 136 9381; the Edw valley, off the Wye valley between Builth Wells and Hay-on-Wye; and the 'Harlech hairpins', only 2 miles east of the town, where the lane climbs up from the Afon

The spectacular Bwlch y Groes mountain road south of Bala

Artro towards Foel Senigl and then north towards Moel Goedog (see the list of Welsh placenames that follows shortly). Is there a more pulsating, more exhilarating vista anywhere in Britain from the road just north of spot height 279?

The second observation demonstrates the 'essential constituent of surprise – one which unfailingly rewards travellers who pocket their prejudices and who travel instead with both open minds and receptive hearts.'

If you follow these two simple pleas and adopt the equally straightforward philosophy of 'enquire, encourage, enthuse and enjoy', I guarantee that Wales will reward you handsomely indeed. Why not put my claim to the test?

I do not expect readers to be 'mapoholics' like me; probably only members of that masochistic breed called 'rally navigators' will understand why I have such a passion about maps. I think I can safely say that in my rally navigating days I must have been driven over every lane there is in the Principality; the only exceptions being the populated valleys and cities in the south and the far coastal areas of Pembroke.

I implore you all: get off the beaten track as often as you can. It is a fact that most of the touring literature and books published by the motoring organizations and the Wales Tourist Board suggest you use both A and B classified roads to see the best of Wales. Fine – as far as it goes! But that's never been good enough for me – or my readers. Desert the main roads and head up as many of the 'yellow' and 'white' lanes that you can – particularly the 'dead-end' roads. Remember, the loveliest parts of any country are more often than not found up roads that, apparently, go nowhere!

To take in the best of Wales use some of the world's finest maps – the ones made by the Ordnance Survey. Their maps, alas, are expensive – but try to use as many as you can for each area you explore. Never begrudge your investment in any large-scale map; used diligently it returns dividends which far exceed the outlay required. I'll describe in detail the maps you should be using in Wales.

The Ordnance Survey (OS) publish many maps. For route planning the Routemaster maps (1 inch to 4 miles) are useful – though I much prefer the Michelin orange '400' series for this purpose (1 inch to 6.3 miles). I suggest you use, as much as possible, the OS large-scale maps. For the best general purpose maps – perfect for the motorist – use the Landranger series (1.25 inches to 1 mile); they highlight just about everything you'll find *en route*.

WELSH PLACENAMES

Map reading is never difficult; don't worry if at first you miss some turnings – you'll soon get the hang of it! In Wales it helps enormously to have some idea of what placenames on OS maps mean; they are normally made up by joining together various word segments. An example: Aberystwyth is *aber* (rivermouth), meaning mouth of the river Ystwyth (*ystwyth* itself means 'winding').

Here are the meanings of the more common terms on OS maps:

aber	rivermouth	*dol*	meadow
afon	river	*dyffryn*	valley
bach, fach	small	*eglwys*	church
ban	high place	*glan*	ashore
bedd	grave	*glas*	green
ben, pen	headland	*hafod*	summer dwelling
betws	chapel	*hendre*	winter dwelling
bont, pont	bridge	*lan, llan*	church
bwlch	pass	*lyn, llyn*	lake
caer, gaer	fort	*mawr, fawr*	large
capel	chapel	*moel, foel*	rounded hill
carn	cairn	*mynydd, fynydd*	mountain
coed, goed	wood	*nant*	brook
coch, goch	red	*pistyll*	waterfall
cors	bog	*rhos, ros*	moorland
craig, graig	crag	*wyn, gwyn*	white
cwm	hollow (cirque)	*ystwyth*	winding
dinas	fort		

FOOD IN WALES
GILLI DAVIES

When Giraldus Cambrensis (Gerald of Wales) travelled through Wales with Baldwin, Archbishop of Canterbury in the 12th century, he noted that 'Almost all the population lives on its flocks and on oats, milk, cheese and butter.' Sounds dull, doesn't it? Well, times have changed and even though these same ingredients still play a part in the Welsh diet, the strength of Welsh food today is in its great variety.

Wales offers a plethora of choice to its hungry visitors, and to help you discover the tastes of Wales, I have given a brief round-up of produce available in each region, so that wherever you travel in the Principality you can be sure of finding the true flavour of food in Wales today.

SOUTH WALES

Caerphilly cheese is as much a rarity in Caerphilly as working coalmines are to the South Wales valleys. It was a favourite with the miners who would take a slice down the pit with them. This, together with a slice of *teisen lap*, or moist cake, fitted snugly into a lunch box. But if fewer men now toil underground, then should we not be happy to find the slag heaps turn green with grass and, in turn, see a growth in the healthier food industry on the surface?

Today modern and traditional foods are produced side by side, and we can witness the much-loved diet of faggot and peas with bread pudding making way for the ubiquitous hamburger. Even the age-old art of baking is seeing a glimpse of the future. Not that you can't still buy a welshcake hot off the griddle in Swansea market or a loaf of bread baked in a traditional 19th-century faggot oven at St Fagans Folk Museum, but every kind of modern loaf is now available – even rolls in the shape of hedgehogs from Sansom's of

Sheltered lowlands in the Brecon Beacons

The cockle pickers of Penclawdd

Newport. It all seems a far cry from those Celtic oatcakes! To eat with your fresh bread why not try some fresh goat's cheese. Up until the 18th century large goat herds provided milk for cheese and there has been a revival in the Abergavenny area.

It's easy to imagine how, out of the poverty of the industrial valleys, came a real appreciation for food for free, and in this southern part of the Principality the coast provides tasty molluscs for those with time enough to gather them. There is still a cottage industry in Penclawdd, on the Gower peninsula, where cockles and mussels are collected and cleaned. Laverbread, that much appreciated seaweed, is boiled and pulped into a dark green gelatinous mass and still eaten by a fair proportion of the population, mainly for breakfast!

The Wye and Usk are famous for their salmon and trout. Richard Llewellyn in *How Green was my Valley* describes so clearly how trout tickling from the rivers meant not only a relaxing few hours for a weary miner, but a good meal for the family too. You'll be lucky to find a brown trout in the rivers these days though; it's safer to visit a fish farm. There you'll find healthy pink fish, reared with the greatest of care, in clean water and fed on a good diet.

Hake used to be the favourite fish in South Wales but now haddock and cod are more likely to be on the wet-fish vans travelling the South Wales valleys. Visit Cardiff market, though, and you'll find an enormous variety of exotic fish. If you just look at the shoppers waiting patiently – or not so patiently – to be served, you will see that South Wales has a large immigrant population. And it's the Chinese, Japanese, Portuguese, West Indians, Italians, Asians, Greek, Polish, and even Egyptians who now bring a diversity to the diet in South Wales. Their demand for unusual ingredients encourages the stores and supermarkets to stock a more cosmopolitan range of food and restaurants now offer dishes from all over the world.

Talking about dining, it's easy enough to think yourself back to medieval Wales and partake in a banquet at Cardiff Castle. Do you fancy a goblet of mead and the odd chicken drumstick to throw over your shoulder? How about some chocolates for after dinner? The Castle Collection made in Newport is certainly worth an indulgence.

The influences of the English who dominated this part of Wales for so much of its history, especially amongst the upper classes and country mansions, are still present near the Hereford border. The

Medieval banquet at Cardiff Castle

Hereford forest has been home to a variety of game for centuries, and deer is again on local menus. But this is farmed deer, and a tender tasty meal it makes.

Gwent is rich in agriculture and as well as the established dairy farming there is a significant growth in market gardening. Down the Wye valley, around Newport, through the Vale of Glamorgan and west to the Gower peninsula market gardening has developed in recent years to the pick-your-own concept offering a wide variety of everyday and more unusual soft fruits and vegetables. Cider is made near Hereford and you can still find the odd cider press tucked away on the farms around Abergavenny. Vineyards face south on the gentle slopes above the river Monnow at Monmouth, where the Romans once grew their grapes. Tintern is also enjoying a revival of the noble vine, for wine. Another vineyard at Pontyclun, Llantrisant, also produces a yearly vintage of Croffta, and I hear tell that the next few years will see the emergence of a number of new Welsh wines in the Vale of Glamorgan, albeit small in production.

No visitor to Cardiff could miss the pungent smell of malt on brewing days. Brains Brewery is responsible for filling the air, and later for quenching many a Welshman's thirst. You can drink Welsh whisky too, blended in Brecon. Fresh springs run from the Beacons and the water is pure enough to drink. Natural healthy water is also being bottled on Gower.

South Wales has been the home of the humbug and you will find locally made boiled sweets, toffee and even handmade chocolates. The Italians are well established in this area, having arrived to cater for the mining communities towards the end of last century. First they set up their cafés and milk bars in the valleys and have now diversified into wholesale ice cream production and the importing of Italian delicacies.

WEST WALES

'Produce for Sale' – these roadside signs are more common than lamp posts in West Wales. And you can buy anything from honey to organically grown vegetables, smoked venison sausages to real dairy ice cream: and this is before we mention the subject of farmhouse cheeses.

A healthy agriculture comes naturally to a region with a mild climate and good soil. The rolling pasturelands of old

Marloes Sands, one of Pembrokeshire's finest beaches

Harvest time

Carmarthenshire and southern Pembrokeshire lend themselves to dairy farming, and the high plateau of northern Ceredigion offers a living to sheep farmers. The central area, from the Cleddau estuary to the west coast, is where the major cereals are grown such as wheat and barley for the traditional raising of cattle. Earlier this century, when daily milk trains took supplies to London, great wealth was made. Since then, the introduction of milk quotas has hit hard and many a dairy farmer has faced financial ruin over the past decade.

Diversification has been the answer and aid from government-based advisory agencies has not only been beneficial to the local farming community but also the host of new arrivals who bought land at a good price when the bottom dropped out of the dairy business. So now there is a new look to West Wales. Established rural families and enthusiastic newcomers are turning their hand to the land and producing food. Good quality food too, some of it reaching outlets nationwide and other products simply sold at the farm gate.

Cheese is a prime example and you can find a superb array of cheeses now made in West Wales. Would you like a traditional Caerphilly or perhaps a farmhouse Cheddar, or how about a goat's or ewe's milk cheese? The variety is endless and you are more than welcome to visit over 20 farms and watch the production, taste the cheese and buy a chunk to take home with you. Dairy farms make cream too, and yoghurt, butter and buttermilk. Some even make real dairy ices, delicious to taste but designed to ruin the waistline!

The fishing industry has seen changes recently. During the past 10 years lobsters have been reseeded in Cardigan Bay, oysters farmed in Carew and even freshwater fish reared in seawater pens in Pembroke Dock. Milford Haven, alas, is a much-diminished port compared to 50 years ago – now only a handful of trawlers dock with their catch and the early morning fish market operates at a tenth of its original size. The fish landed here is mostly sent to other markets where the prices are better. Local fish is available though, best bought as the small trawlers land all along the coast. You'll find a small fish stall in many of the small ports and seaside towns – try Fishguard, or Newquay or wander down to the Parrog at Newport to catch a couple of fresh crabs or perhaps a lobster. Mackerel fishing is a summer sport and provides a tasty bite too.

At Cenarth, not only do you have the chance to see coracle fishing boats in action, whose design hasn't changed in 2000 years, but you can collect fine smoked trout, salmon or the Welsh sea trout, known as *sewin*. If you prefer rainbow or brown trout then look out for a sign on the road and perhaps you can catch your supper fresh from a trout farm.

Fresh poultry is no problem either – chickens, turkeys and ducks are all reared in West Wales, with eggs now being produced from free-range poultry. Organic is not a new theme in this area. Livestock and vegetables have been grown organically for some time and even organic cheese is available.

A day at a watermill is good fun. A number of 19th-century watermills have been lovingly restored to working order, and stoneground flour is available throughout the region. Watch the huge stones grind the corn into healthy stoneground flour, learn about the history of the mill and, best of all, nibble some of the delicious baking on offer.

If you're thirsty, then sample some of the beer that is brewed locally, or perhaps you would prefer sparkling water from local springs. Last, but not least, you simply cannot leave West Wales without a bag of Pembroke potatoes stowed somewhere in the luggage – they are just too good to miss. Never has it been easier to sample a real Taste of Wales, and we must thank not only the good cooks in the region who demand quality fresh food produced locally, but also the visitor who will buy at the farm shop, roadside stall or harbour fish stand, bringing income direct to the producer.

MID WALES

The high hill sheep farming country of Mid Wales

Much of this region is above 1000ft (305m), the main mountain and hill ranges reaching over 2000ft (610m). Moisture falls mainly on the peaks, filling in giant reservoirs and lakes that supply Liverpool and Birmingham with water. It doesn't seem to bother the sheep as they graze in great numbers on the vast expanse of open moorland.

Upland sheep have to be hardy to cope with their tough living conditions; the pure Welsh mountain breed certainly is. It is a small-framed sheep with a warm but not top-quality coat, so the sheep you see in Mid Wales are usually crossbred to suit today's taste. One sheep that is easily recognizable is the speckled-faced sheep from around Beulah, in the Irfon valley.

It is here in Mid Wales that Welsh Lamb Enterprise has established itself and over the past few years the story of lamb in Wales has proved to be one of success. The aim of the scheme is to improve the quality of Welsh lambs on the market by selective grading of the carcasses, so farmers receive a premium for presenting top-quality lamb to the abattoirs. In turn, this quality lamb is passed on to butchers who are proud to

24

identify their meat as Welsh.

If lamb has had a face-lift, then so have a number of other foods in Mid Wales. From a health food point of view, potato crisps have kept their skins on and vegetables are grown without the aid of artificial fertilizers. There is now a firm market for these organic crops and the producers are no longer considered cranks. Organic farming is well established in Mid Wales; in fact some farms, like Brynllys, in Tywyn, run by Gareth and Rachel Rowlands, has never been anything else. Using traditional farming methods of crop rotation and encouraging good herbage, healthy Guernsey cows produce organic milk which is churned into butter or simply drunk as it is! Cheeses made from organically produced milk have proved their worth and to maintain a constant quality many cheese producers adhere to a quality-control scheme administered by the Agricultural Development and Advisory Service (ADAS). A great deal of goat's milk comes from the west of the region; some of it is air-dried in order to distribute it throughout health food shops for allergy sufferers.

Llandrindod Wells had its heyday as a spa town – 'Efficacious in the treatment of gout' was its boast. It still has a healthy air about it, especially for those who drink the spa water that continues to flow on tap at the Rock Park Spa. At the other extreme, those of you with a sweet tooth will enjoy Mid Wales. You will find fudge in Aberystwyth, chocolates in Newtown and honey in Aberaeron. Aberaeron is also the place to pick up fresh mackerel; and you can spend a little time at the Marine Aquarium and the Honey Museum before indulging in the natural refreshment of a honey ice cream.

The Dovey and Mawddach rivers offer the opportunity of freshwater fish and Cardigan Bay has stocks of sea fish enough for everyone. Local fishermen will bring in plaice, brill, hake, monkfish, sea bass, and dogfish, not forgetting the usual herring glut in the autumn.

For a look to the future, check out the latest designs at the Centre for Alternative Technology a few miles north of Machynlleth. Its 10-acre smallholding and vegetable garden are worked organically, providing the centre with meat, eggs and vegetables. The farm also keeps free-range hens, goats, fish, bees, sheep and pigs, and there is an interesting ecological gardening display which shows how to make gardens more attractive to wildlife.

National Centre for Alternative Technology near Machynlleth

Felin Crewi, just outside Machynlleth, is a recently restored watermill and you can see the grinding stones in action as well as displays telling its history. There is a range of flours and baked products available.

Perhaps the best way to enjoy Mid Wales is to stay at one of the many farmhouses that offer accommodation. The food is always good, if rather robust, and you are guaranteed never to feel hungry! If you ever wondered what these active farm housewives did during the winter, a group of them are busy baking traditional cakes and scones. They load their goodies into a trailer and head for the Continent where they do a great job in public relations,

NORTH WALES

With its castles, royal princes and rugged mountains, North Wales is a place for the romantic. It also suits the gourmet as the food is superb. Why? Because there is a great deal of fertile arable land, a fine coastline, good distribution and, most important of all, there are the people. North Walians have a way with food or, to be more precise, they have a knack for business and the two blend well here. They are charming too, and every visitor to North Wales is made to feel very welcome.

Sheep farming is big business throughout the region, with the Welsh Mountain being almost the universal breed. The lower slopes of the uplands are also used for raising cattle, mainly the Welsh Black. This traditional, sturdy, slow-maturing breed of cattle is increasingly being crossbred with continental Charolais and Limousin breeds to give a larger beast which grows more quickly. Dairy farming has boomed over recent years but since the introduction of milk quotas, dairy farmers have redirected their milk yield into other products. Cream, yoghurt, soft and hard cheeses and dairy ice cream are all available locally and are of top quality.

A horticultural industry is well established around Wrexham, with more and more pick-your-own outlets opening each season. Market gardeners are also being encouraged to grow some of the more exotic vegetables and fruit to supply the increasing demand from restaurants and hotels.

Health foods and healthy food are being produced by a number of small firms. Pâtés, quiches, cheesecakes, mustards and non-dairy based products are available locally as well as being sold far and wide. Pizzas and jacket potatoes are new products on sale, no doubt to satisfy the tourists who flock to the this part of Wales the whole year round. In the region you'll find a superb ranges of larder goodies like honey, preserves and sugar-free specialities.

Baking, as ever, is a forte with the Welsh here in the north. Can't you just smell that

In the heart of the Snowdonia National Park

bara brith coming hot out of the oven? There are quite a few new enterprises offering a good range of baking. Beer is brewed in Wrexham and natural spring water bubbles up in Trofarth to find itself bottled. Either one or other of these will be necessary to wash down a delicious quarter-pound of Anglesey fudge or toffee from Llandudno.

Now, let's talk of fish. If the horticulturalists and dairy farmers are clever in North Wales then the fishermen are nothing short of genius. If you enjoy mussels but don't have the time to prepare them, a firm in Penrhyn just outside Bangor will do the dirty work for you. Oysters have been reseeded on Anglesey and in the Menai Strait, and scallops arrive by the sackful into Holyhead. Both the large king and smaller queen scallops are found off the coast. Freshwater trout and salmon farms abound inland. You can catch, gut, smoke or simply buy trout and salmon from a number of small fish farms.

Anglesey is fringed by a beautiful shoreline

Wherever you travel in Wales you are bound to come across a working watermill and North Wales is no exception. Felin Isaf Watermill just south of Llandudno consists of a series of Grade II listed buildings all related to milling. At Pentrefoelas you can see a recently renovated mill in action and buy freshly milled flour.

CELTICA 1991 CYMRU WALES

CELTICA 1991 is a celebration of over 2,000 years of our heritage and a culture that once straddled the whole of Europe.
During 1991 there will be a year-long series of festivals and events that will promote many aspects of this culture. These will include major exhibitions like The Celts in Wales at the National Museum of Wales and events like the World Harp Festival and the Dylan Thomas Festival.
World experts will be giving lectures on various aspects of the lives of the Celts and there will be a series of workshops on Celtic myth and magic.
For further information contact:
Wales Tourist Board, Brunel House, 2 Fitzalan Road, Cardiff CF2 1UY.
Telephone: 0222 499909

FIVE FAVOURITES

GILLI DAVIES

....

This chapter will put and end, once and for all, to the simplistic old image of Welsh food. In addition to its traditional strengths in the fields of lamb and baking, Wales now offers world-class cheeses, superb seafoods and an enticing range of products that reflects today's interests in healthy eating. Even Welsh lamb, that most traditional of dishes, is going through changes resulting from the customer's demands for new lean cuts which form the basis of imaginative dishes. There's much more to Welsh cooking in the 1990s than the traditional Sunday joint, as you'll see from the following descriptions of cheeses, healthy eating, baking, seafoods and lamb.

CHEESES

....

Once an integral part of rural life in Wales, cheesemaking almost came to a halt during the deprivations of the two World Wars. However, it has seen a major revival over the past 20 years and skills and recipes that were once thought to be lost have been dug out of Welsh attics. These, combined with the latest technology and cheesemaking experience gathered throughout Europe, make Welsh cheese some of the best in Britain today.

It was in the late 1960s when the offer of inexpensive land and a desire to escape from the rat race brought a variety of people into West Wales, many of whom took up dairy farming on a small scale. With the introduction of milk quotas in the early 1980s, they turned to cheesemaking as a natural outlet for the surplus milk.

The range of cheeses now made in Wales is extensive, from the smallest cottage industry producing just a couple of cheeses a week to full factory production weighed in tons. And with over 50 to choose from, variety is the key to the success of Welsh cheeses. They are produced from cow's, goat's and ewe's milk, and there is even cheese made from organic milk. Welsh cheeses vary enormously in shape and texture too, from hard rinded to soft and creamy, even brie types, and maybe a blue-veined one soon.

Varieties to look out for are ewe's milk cheeses such as Acorn, Skirrid, Penlon; goat's milk – Pant Ysgawn, Pen-y-Bont, Pumpkin, Senlac, Caron; and cow's milk – Plas Dairy Farm, Llanboidy, Llangloffan, Nevern, Caws Cenarth, Maesllyn, Teifi, Castle Hywel, Penbryn, Nantybwla, T'yn Grug, Cardigan and Pencarreg.

You can buy these cheeses in most good delicatessens, from Wales to London. But best of all, take a trip to Dyfed and visit the farms themselves.

Welsh cheeses are superb

HEALTHY EATING

Eating well in Wales is nothing new – all the local produce is naturally healthy in the first place. Throughout Wales there is environmental awareness, with producers striving to obtain top quality without detracting from nature. Take Welsh lamb for instance. Fattened on the open moorland, it's the original natural product. And in Wales you will find free-range pork and organically produced beef – even cheese from organic milk.

In the early days one of the first organic horticulturalists set up in Lampeter, and this trend has now been followed in other parts of Wales. Organic dairy farming is hardly a new way of life at Rachel's Dairy, Brynllys Farm near Borth; for two generations it has never been anything else. Crop rotation of white clover, cereals and Italian ryegrass or red clover ley provide the pedigree Guernsey herd with herbage to ensure a constant supply of quality milk. Milk, yoghurt, butter and clotted cream are distributed over a wide area from the farm, all organic and absolutely delicious.

If, as a cook, you enjoy the individual flavour and texture that stoneground flour gives to cooking, then don't leave Wales without a visit to one of the many watermills that have been restored to working order. Here you have the chance to buy traditional, even organic natural wholemeal flour, white flour and even semolina.

Mineral waters spring up all over Wales. They are now bottled and distributed throughout Great Britain, so look for Welsh labels when buying a bottle of the bubbly stuff.

BAKING

Baking, based on the Celtic tradition of cooking on a griddle, has always been one of the strengths of the Welsh kitchen. Even today the pancake is a favourite food in the Principality. Oats were the staple crop at one time, and oatcakes, as well as oat gruel, were every-day food. Barley flour and rye were used principally for breadmaking before wheat, the grains being ground at one of the many mills through out Wales, some of which have been restored to working order. Visit the Welsh Folk Museum at St Fagans outside Cardiff where you can see a 'turn-

There's a long-established teatime baking tradition in Wales

of-the-century' brick oven still in use, its glowing embers giving the heat and flavour to traditional bread loaves.

Welshcakes, little fruity griddle scones, accompany many a cup of tea offered to visitors to Wales, as does a slice of *bara brith* or fruit loaf, of which the Welsh are equally proud. But baking in Wales does not just dwell on past glories. Today's bakers can offer every kind of fashionable product. At Sansom's bakery in Newport, Gwent, where the equipment is as modern as any in Britain, up to 2400 rolls are produced an hour. Novelty breads in the shape of hedgehogs, crabs and even dragons are a real favourite with families.

In almost every corner of Wales there are groups of enterprising bakers and confectioners who are combining old and new skills with the best of ingredients to produce a range of baking that is worthy of much praise.

Lamb

Welsh lamb is wonderful! Sheep farmers in Wales produce lamb that is geared to modern taste: it's lean and free of additives – the most natural of products. And top-quality Welsh lamb is now available all the year round.

In spring there are milk-fed lambs on the table in time for Easter, with their delicate flavour and tender flesh. Summer sees the majority of lowland lamb in the shops. Born in the spring this lamb has been reared in the relative shelter of the lowlands and fed on a natural diet of grass. Mountain lambs are born in late spring when the weather is kinder to them. After an initial period in the shelter of the farm, they will spend the summer grazing the high pastures and be ready for market during the autumn.

As to the fine flavour of Welsh lamb, it is achieved by slow maturing on natural pastures and a basic good breed of sheep. Most sheep farmers crossbreed their stock and the resulting lamb has good conformation in the way of size and muscle-to-fat ratio. The housewife won't buy fatty lamb so the farmers are now penalized if they send fat lambs to market.

And this is where the butcher comes in. He realizes that lamb must move away from the Sunday joint image if it is to compete in supermarkets, so it now appears in a whole range of new lean cuts. Have you tasted a lamb steak cut from the top of the leg, or stir-fried fillet? How about a grilled valentine steak or even 'traffic-lights' – meat balls made of lamb and coloured with herbs, paprika and turmeric. Perhaps the most revolutionary cut is boned rolled lamb that has all the flavour but cuts just like a loaf of bread.

Livestock sales at Brecon Market

So next time you buy lamb ask the butcher where it came from, whether it was a mountain or valley lamb, and check to see how lean it is. But most important, make sure it's Welsh.

Seafood

What has happened to the seafood industry in Wales? Decline set in after the war when investment was lacking and the trawler fleets shrank and rusted. Now there is a slow revival. Holyhead has seen massive investment and the deepwater port now operates 24 hours a day, offering an offloading point for trawlers from the Irish Sea. Milford Haven has been slower to come to the rescue of its once-powerful sea-going population. A new icing plant is under construction, but alas, no longer does the 9am train hurry away from Milford Dock full of fresh fish heading for Billingsgate.

Fish such as cod, whiting, plaice, sole, turbot, brill, hake, bass, monkfish and dogfish are still landed in Wales but the markets are better in Fleetwood, Billingsgate and Grimsby, so almost all the catch leaves Wales as soon as it can be packed into refrigerated lorries, heading for a better price. Welsh shellfish fare better. Investment has seen a boom in the mussel and oyster beds, lobsters have been reseeded in Cardigan Bay and crabs and scallops continue to enjoy their natural Welsh habitats.

But the problems are still the same – these crustaceans leave Wales almost as soon as they are landed. Why? Because the Welsh, and the rest of Britain, don't value their fish half as much as the French or Spanish and that's where they end up. Does it matter? Yes, I think it does, and so do many of the restaurants in Wales. With a little persuasion on their part, they have succeeded in capturing some of this Welsh fish before it heads for the Continent.

GOOD FOOD FROM WALES

They make a cheese *in* Wales. It's called Caerphilly.

RIGHT: A SELECTION OF SOFT AND HARD FARMHOUSE CHEESES FROM WALES, ILLUSTRATED BY **OLIVIA BEASLEY**.

ACORN FARMHOUSE EWES MILK CHEESE.
Firm white cheese with a superb aftertaste. Ideal texture for souffle, mousse, soups etc.

LLANBOIDY CHEESE.
Full fat, hard pressed cheese made from the milk of a specialist herd of Red Poll cattle.

Caerphilly is, without doubt, the most famous Welsh cheese. But it's by no means the only one that we produce. In the county of Dyfed alone, we make over thirty different varieties of farmhouse cheese. Many of these cheeses are made by hand in small local dairies, where they owe as much to the character of the milk as they do to the skill of the local cheesemakers. We use cows, goats, ewes and even organically produced milk to give our cheeses a distinctive taste and texture. We also use a selection of home-grown herbs to enhance the flavour and add variety. We even make our own versions of traditional favourites. So don't be surprised if your next Cheddar or Lancashire was made in Wales. Until recently, many of our cheeses have only been sold locally. But they can now be found in selected supermarkets and specialist shops all over the country. So the next time you're out shopping, keep an eye open for them. You'll find a wide variety of excellent cheeses. Including Caerphilly, of course. For more information about Welsh Food, write to The Welsh Food Initiative, Pearl House, Greyfriars Road, Cardiff CF1 3XX.

PLAS DAIRY FARM CHEESE.
Low fat goats milk cheese.
Natural or garlic and herbs.

MERLIN GOATS MILK CHEESE.
A semi-hard, full fat cheese.
Also available with walnuts,
olives and smoked.

PANT-YS-GAWN FARM GOATS CHEESE.
A soft, white creamy cheese.
Excellent as an aperitif or as an
after dinner cheese.

PENCARREG CHEESE.
A soft full fat cheese with a white
mould ripened crust. Made from
organic cows milk.

SHOPPING IN WALES
GILLI DAVIES

Shopping in a strange place can be as rewarding as it can be frustrating. Either you know what you want but can't find it, or else you stumble across something unusual for an unexpected treat.

In this shopping guide to Wales I have tried to highlight some of the best shops in each region, so that as a traveller you can find a good food shop fairly easily wherever you are. Each of the delicatessens mentioned offers a different range of food but they all have the aim of providing the best-quality produce for the customer. Much of their stock comes from within Wales and I have sought out those shops where I feel that the buyers have chosen to promote local produce.

Perhaps the weekly food shop at home is no more than a routine to be endured, but I hope that a trip to one of the many good food shops in Wales will be something of a gastronomic experience.

SOUTH WALES

The pleasure about shopping in South Wales is the choice. You can either head for one of the large markets where you are guaranteed to find stands selling fresh vegetables, local meats, cheeses, and baking products or dive into the smaller streets and seek out the smartest of delicatessens.

On the market front, try *Newport Market* for a start. In this fine Victorian building in the centre of town the stalls are spaciously laid out and the stallholders have the patience of Job. Ask them where their produce comes from and they will delight in a little chat. *Baldock's* is a delicatessen stall not to miss. Here Anne Forde will serve you the most delicious local Glamorgan ham. Not full of preservative, colouring or water, it's the real thing! Anne is an ambassador for all good Welsh foods and as one of the first retailers to seek out and sell Welsh farmhouse cheeses she must be congratulated on her fine selection. She will offer you cow's, ewe's or goat's milk Welsh cheeses from all the best cheesemakers – and tell you all about the history behind the cheeses too. Just around the corner is butcher *Tony Turner* whose meat is too good to miss.

Newport also offers a branch of *Beanfreaks* at 5 Upper Dock Street, who suggest that 'Your health is their business' and will supply a range of whole and healthy foods and products. Cardiff and Cwmbran also have Beanfreaks.

Cardiff old and new – the modern St David's Centre is just opposite the traditional covered market

Catch a bargain in *Cardiff's Covered Market*. It is open every day except Sunday, and the prices are very competitive. You will need an oversized basket, for here you can collect a choice of Welsh lamb and beef from *John Morgan* as well as Welsh bacon from his neighbour. *Mill Farm Dairy* offers a superb range of well-cared-for Welsh cheeses and other dairy products. Good fresh bread and fresh basic vegetables occupy many stalls, but a few now sell the most tempting ready-to-eat snacks such as spicy chicken wings or sweet-and-sour ribs. *Ashton's* marble slabs will catch your attention with their huge multicoloured range of fish, with over 60 varieties from as far afield as Aberdeen, Brixton and Paris. Don't leave this busy covered market without a trip round the upper 'deck' to see the pets.

Swansea Market is very special. Open every day, except Sunday, in a spacious hall in the centre of town, you will get as good a Taste of Wales here as almost anywhere else. Visit the 'casuals' stalls. Tables are rented out by the square foot, and from day to day local producers fill their stall with anything from beetroot out of their garden to cockles and laver which they have collected from the sands on the nearby Gower peninsula. See and smell the speciality breads such as bara brith and teisen lap and nibble on a pancake or welshcake hot off the griddle. *Mavis Davies* will sell you a slice of traditional bread pudding while a good range of healthfood snacks sell fast at lunch time. *Thayer's Ice Cream* do a roaring trade on a hot day and *A Taste of the Tropics* tempts those looking for an exciting fruit or vegetable. *Curds and Whey*, a cheese stall run by John Driver, sells a great range of Welsh farmhouse cheeses as well as organic wholefoods. From March to August look out for *sewin*, the Welsh name for sea trout, or any of the other local fish brought into Swansea harbour. *Coakley Green, Tucker's* and *Smitham's* all compete for the fish trade with superb displays.

Swansea Market

Monmouth has more than its fair share of good food shops. Look out for *Evans of Monmouth*, 26–28 Monnow Street, who offer fine fresh quality fruit and vegetables as well as fish. Higher up Monnow Street, at 64, *Irma Fingal–Rock Food*, is a tiny delicatessen which specializes in a small but select range of farmhouse cheeses – some from within Wales – good wines, local ciders, homemade cakes, a few organic vegetables and good olive oils. *Epicure* is also well worth a visit and *King's Table*, in Beaufort Court, is noted for fine food and its wine selection. Here you can rest your legs, have a cup of coffee or take away a meal for later from a range of homemade temptations such as filled crêpes or pasta. Speciality teas and coffees, as well as smoked and cured meats and even hampers, are on offer here.

In Abergavenny you will find *Vin Sullivan* at 4 Frogmore Street, selling fish, poultry and game. The retail manager, Sam Milburn, used to be a chef, so understands only too well how quality and reliable supplies of produce are important. Traditional chalked boards stand out in the street tempting you within, where the display is breathtaking.

The shop's superb range of fish includes cod, haddock, grey mullet, monk tails, squid, tuna, shellfish, swordfish steak and so much more. Samphire from Essex and laverbread from Swansea jostle for space together with fresh local farmed trout. Welsh honey and ice cream from Carmarthen boost the Welsh products, having attained the high standards of quality demanded by Sam. In the game department you can choose from local venison, rabbit, grouse and pheasants. Unusual bites such as frogs' legs, Bombay duck, snails and haggis, sit on the shelves along with Chinese foods, soups, sauces, Tiptree preserves and all manner of Oriental foods. And if you choose a whole salmon too big to fit in the oven, Sam will even loan you a fish kettle!

Brian's, at 23 Merthyr Road, Abergavenny, recently converted from a traditional family butcher, now offers a fast-expanding range of organically produced goods. Local pork, lamb and beef are to be recommended and there is also a selective range of Welsh cheese, cured meats and sausages, pâté, organic vegetables and locally baked fresh bread.

Abergavenny stands in fertile countryside

Brecon is a thriving market town

Just sniff when you visit Brecon and your nose will lead you to *Top Drawer 2*, right in the centre of the town. The baking is blissful, although the dough is not made on the premises, and fresh crusty loaves, croissants and all manner of savoury and sweet pastries are sold hot from the oven. Twice a week a superb range of patisseries arrive hotfoot from London, pricey but nice. There is also a good range of local dairy products, home-cooked hams and salads, cured meats and sausages, homemade pasta and sauces as well as a range of cheeses, many from Wales. Just down the road is *Top Drawer 1* which sells a range of wholefoods.

Cowbridge in the Vale of Glamorgan is another centre of good food. *Glyn T Jenkins and Son*, established in Bridgend since 1939, have recently opened a branch of their grocery business here at 50 High Street. Grandson Jonathan runs the shop, and although it is still early days he is offering a great range of tempting goodies – home-cured bacons and ham, honey-roast hams, traditional salt Carmarthen hams, local sausages and black pudding, Pembrokeshire laverbread, Welsh pâté, smoked venison from Cardigan and Swansea salted butter on block, as well as lard and goat's milk butter. He also sells Welsh cheese, local cream, Welsh dairy ice cream and goat's milk ice cream, local honey, free-range and deep-litter double yolk eggs; and, if you're not hungry by now, let me tell you about the homemade ravioli with a filling of smoked salmon, garlic, ricotta and prawns. There is a tea room upstairs for those in need of refreshment.

Next door finds another new venture. *Tony Holtam*, 50A High Street, has converted and redesigned the fruit and veg shop to include fish. He is justly proud of his fish supply which comes, whenever possible, from within Wales. Local salmon and sea trout come and go extremely fast as well as shellfish, turbot and halibut. There is an air of luxury to the shop: smart fittings and quality carrier bags, together with an emphasis on personal service, have earned Tony good business.

L'Epicure, the original delicatessen of Cowbridge, at 42 High Street, has a marvellous range of goods, knows its customers well and trades on a wealth of experience. Offering health foods and an off-licence, it completes a High Street full of good shops.

Penarth's delightful Victorian pier

Penarth has, amongst other things, a butcher who specializes in organic meats – *David Lush*, 5 Glebe Street – and a reliable game and poultry dealer, *Charles Saddler*.

Cardiff has a good range of speciality food shops to service its large immigrant population. *Berni's* of Wellfield Road will satisfy your pangs for fresh pasta and homemade pesto sauce. This well-stocked delicatessen sells an extensive range of

A Welsh dresser at the Welsh Folk Museum, St Fagans

Italian specialities. *Wally's*, in Morgan Arcade in the city centre, is an Aladdin's cave of good things to eat. Continental sausages hang from the ceiling and spices fill every nook and cranny. Baskets of Continental biscuits crowd the floor space, with the fresh and smoked meat counter rarely free from a queue of appreciative customers.

Bread, just as your great great grandmother used to make, can be yours to taste if you visit the *Welsh Folk Museum* at St Fagans, just to the west of Cardiff. A 19th-century bakehouse has recently been renovated and fresh bread and bara brith are on sale. *Shelly's*, in Cathedral Road, offers a range of delicatessen goodies with an ever-increasing choice of home-baked savouries. For a really extensive look at Welsh foods, I suggest you pop into the food hall at *Howell's* in St Mary Street; Welsh cheeses feature strongly here.

Throughout Gwent and the Glamorgans, fruit farms will offer you the chance to pick your own fruit. The farm shops are always worth a visit if you need to stock up on homemade jams and honey as well as pre-picked fruit. Some pick-your-own farms have tea shops where you can take a break with a slice of local flavour. Try *Berryhill Farm* at Coedkernew, near Newport.

Goat's milk cheese is sold straight from the farm by Tony Craske at *Pant-ys-Gawn* near Mamhilad. Try his herb-covered fresh goat's milk cheeses, or even his crumbed variety for frying.

West Wales

Shopping at friendly Carmarthen Market

Carmarthen Market opens on Wednesday and Saturday. This is the largest market in West Wales and is situated in the town centre. The *Women's Institute* have an ever-popular stall and you will find local organically grown vegetables as well as a huge selection of exotic ones. Carmarthen ham, traditionally cured by *Albert Rees*, is too good to miss, and lamb as well as other local meat products fill many stalls. Look out for *Raymond Rees's* fish shop for locally caught fish, especially lobsters in season, and sea trout. Mussels and cockles come up from Penclawdd on the Gower peninsula in *Selwyn's* fish van, and you will find laverbread here too. Perhaps most special in Carmarthen Market, though, is *John Savage's* cheese counter. He can offer you at least 25 different Dyfed cheeses, all made from unpasteurized milk with flavours of varying intensity.

Healthfoods and a vegetarian restaurant are to be found at the *Waverley Stores* in Lammas Street, Carmarthen. Local produce, plus organic vegetables, honey, Thayer's ice cream, speciality teas and natural cosmetics and herbal remedies are on sale here.

In Narberth you might be forgiven for thinking that you are in the Deli Centre of Dyfed! This small town has a whole host of good foods on offer. Wander around its characterful streets and sample the wares from the local butcher's, baker's and wholefood stores, ending up with a cup of coffee or meal at Gregory's Restaurant.

In Tenby, *Craig's Dairy and Delicatessen* in the High Street does a good trade with holidaymakers. Here, among the crisps and cans of pop you can find local cheeses, welshcakes, fudge and shortbread. The range of goods varies from gentleman's relish to frozen peas – there is bound to be something here for you! Opposite, *Ben Davies* offers a good range of wines and spirits.

The demand for fresh fish in Wales is so much in decline that Milford Haven, once the major sea-port of Wales, doesn't even have a wet-fish shop. Two fish stands and a couple of fish-and-chip shops must suffice. However, Milford offers a good range of local foods and delicatessen items at *Food For Thought*, Charles Street. Choose from home-cooked ham on the bone and turkey, vegetable pies and quiches, local bread, smoked trout pâté from Pembrokeshire's fish farms, dressed crabs, local cheese, healthfoods, free-range eggs, fresh yeast, spring water, a limited range of fine wines and even cake-decorating kits.

New to Haverfordwest is *Vittles*, a delicatessen at 11 Market Street. Although they are still testing customer opinion, the shop already stocks a good range of Welsh cheeses, homemade quiches, pâtés, homemade sauces and herb butters. Also on sale here are local waters, Upton's ice cream, speciality teas and Pataks Indian foods, as well as a selection of fine wines. I hear that the toasted sandwiches are a dream. Not to be missed at the other end of Haverfordwest in Quay Street is *The Natural Grocer*. Here you will find health foods, herbal remedies, homemade wine kits, herbal teas and a small range of local Welsh cheeses and yoghurts.

The old quay at Lower Fishguard

Reports from Fishguard suggest that the *Women's Institute market* on a Thursday in the town hall is not to be missed! Passing through Newport? Then pop down to the Parrog to visit *The Newport Bay Fresh Fish Shop* for a lobster or crab during the summer months. In Market Street you will find *Bwydydd Cyffawn*, a wholefood shop that specializes in products with Soil Association labels. Choose from a selection of local cheeses, all made with vegetarian rennet, 50 organic wines, local organic vegetables and fruit, speciality teas and dandelion coffee.

Moving on to Cardigan, don't miss The Mews. Gwynne Thomas suggests that he serves 'Simply Good Taste' at the small restaurant within his *Deli Delights*, The Mews. Gather ingredients here for a picnic, select a 'food' present for a friend or take a break and enjoy a cup of coffee and some local baking. Amongst a huge range of specialist items – Jacksons teas, Bonne Maman jams, Bendicks mints and so on – you will find a lot of local products,
including Welsh pesto sauce, rum and marzipan truffles, liver cheese and herb pâtés, wholewheat crust pies with savoury fillings, Welsh shortbread and fudge, bara brith, locally smoked salmon, ham, venison and venison garlic sausage. Opposite, *Go Mango* has a comprehensive range of wholefoods and sells the local Y Felin flour from the mill at nearby St Dogmael's.

If you feel like getting down to the nitty gritty, and actually seeing these local products being made, then ask in any of these delicatessens for the name and address of producers who welcome visitors. Or simply keep your eyes open and follow road-side signs. For example, Leon Downey makes cheese daily at *Llangloffan Farm*, Castle Morris. This is your chance to stroke a Jersey cow, wander around the farm, buy stocks from the farm shop and take a lesson in the basic principles of farmhouse cheesemaking. Thelma Adams offers the chance to see Caws Cenarth, a Caerphilly and farmhouse Cheddar being produced on her farm *Glyneithiniog*, near Newcastle Emlyn.

John and Jenny White, at *Mountpleasant Goat Farm*, Pen-y-Bont, near Carmarthen, offer cheesemaking demonstrations and guided tours of the farm, together with the chance of buying goat's milk cheeses. If you are in the Cardigan area then *Nevern Dairy*, near Newport, offers you the chance to buy and watch cheese and farmhouse butter being made. Teifi Farmhouse Cheese at *Glynhynod Farm*, Ffostrasol, near Llandysul, makes cheeses with unpasteurized milk, using methods dating back five centuries. You are welcome to visit. *Ty'n Grug* Farmhouse Cheese was one of the first farmhouse cheeses to be made in Dyfed and you can see it being produced at an organic dairy farm just outside Lampeter.

Felin Geri Watermill at Cwm-cou, near Newcastle Emlyn, operates in its renovated state. It offers visitors the chance to see a 19th-century flourmill at work, after which they can buy from a large range of fresh baking. There is a small restaurant and lots for the family to see here. *Melin Maesdulais* at Porthyrhyd, near Carmarthen, offers a superb range of flours – it's well worth collecting a bag or two. *Y Felin*, another flourmill which sells stoneground flour, is situated in the pretty village of St Dogmael's next door to Cardigan.

Tregroes Waffle Bakery offers visitors a delight to the eye but a threat to the waistline with its moor-ish soft-butter, toffee-filled waffles. You will find the bakery at The Shop, Tregroes, near Llandysul.

Flour making the traditional way at Felin Geri, near Newcastle Emlyn

MID WALES

Street market, Machynlleth

Throughout Mid Wales, market day alternates so that stallholders can travel between the different towns. These street markets offer a colourful glimpse of local produce with bargains at the cake and bread stalls and some excellent ethnic stalls selling craftwork. Fresh vegetables, often organically grown, fresh fruit in season and herbs are available. Local dairy products are a good buy too. Butter, cheeses and cream can be bought in small amounts which can be very useful if you are self-catering or camping.

Here are the markets to put in your diary: Aberystwyth – Monday, Builth Wells – Monday, Lampeter – alternate Tuesdays, Llandovery – Saturday, Llanidloes – Saturday, Machynlleth – Wednesday, Newtown – Tuesday and Saturday, Rhayader – Wednesday and Tregaron – alternate Tuesdays.

Of course the product to buy in Mid Wales must be lamb. One shop that specializes in the very best quality lamb and the large variety of new cuts, as well as traditional roasts, chops, etc. is *Edward Hamer* at Plynlimon House in Llanidloes. Ask for valentine steaks, 'traffic lights' or a melon roast and you will discover a lean, boneless piece of lamb, easy to cook and full of flavour.

Capers, 26 High Street, Welshpool, sells organic vegetables, local cheeses – including goat's cheese – and wholefoods, healthfoods and herbal remedies, together with Welsh soap. 'Whatever's local and comes our way - we sell!' Capers is also the place to find out what's on locally.

The Mousetrap Delicatessen at 24 Market Street, Newtown, offers a range of cheeses, fruit and vegetables, with local honey and mustard, speciality tea and coffee, together with a range of dried fruits and Oriental sauces. *Mac Beans* in the High Street also has local honeys together with organic vegetables and Maesdulais flour locally milled. Meridan preserves and Zest pesto sauce, both local, are sold as well as organic dairy products. At Lake Mochdre near Newtown in the heart of Mid Wales, *Nettesheim Fish Farm* offers you the chance to wander freely and try your hand at fishing. The shops sells fresh and home-smoked trout.

Llandrindod Wells holds an annual Victorian Festival

Hay Wholefoods, 1 Lion Street, Hay-on-Wye, is a fine advert for all things Welsh. Jan Shrivel and Paul Goldman stock a good range of Welsh cheeses, at least 12, sometimes many more, as well as smoked turkey, venison sausages, organic eggs, home-cooked hams, organic local vegetables and 'the best bread in town' ... or so they say! If you are passing, why not test it for yourself

Established over the past 16 years is *Van's Good Food Shop*, Elmswood, Middleton Street, Llandrindod Wells. Here you will find health foods and wholefoods, all packed on the premises, organic dry goods, plus a selection of Welsh cheeses, spring waters and dairy products. This attractive shop, with its wooden floor, has a rustic charm to it.

Travelling west to the coast, Aberaeron boasts a Honey Museum, *The Hive on the Quay*, and in the light and airy restaurant beside (open summer season only) you can taste a selection of local products cooked with more than a little ingenuity – soused mackerel, potted shrimps, quiches and laverbread pancakes. No one should leave without a large cornet of the delicious honey ice cream.

At *Mesen Fach Farm* at Bethania, near Llanon, you can buy Acorn ewe's milk cheese. It is made from vegetarian rennet and pure sea salt and is a product suitable for people with allergies. Watch the sheep-milking daily at 4pm. If you are moving up the coast to Aberystwyth, then look up Jeff Williams at *The Welsh Cellar*, 19 Pier Street. He sells a range of British and Continental delicatessen goods, with a good smattering of Welsh produce – cheeses, local honey, cold meats, smoked turkey, local vegetarian pâtés, yoghurts, buttermilk, laverbread and locally milled flours. There is a big trade with Italians, Poles and, of course, tourists.

Frosts have two outlets in Aberystwyth: a fresh fruit and vegetable stall in the market hall, and *The Salad Shop* on the corner of Pier and Great Darkgate Street. Originally opened to supply locally grown organic salad stuffs, the shop now sells a plethora of local and imported organic products including meat, vegetables and fruit, as well as local delicacies such as honey.

Aberystwyth grew up around a medieval castle

Borth, centrally located on the grand sweep of Cardigan Bay

Rachel's Dairy at Brynllys, Borth, is one of the most successful organic farms in Wales, specializing in dairy produce. Visitors can enjoy a farm trail and browse around the shop where they will find a range of products including thick golden yellow cream, clotted cream, natural and fruit yoghurt, butter, and soft and hard cheeses.

Hen Efail at Furnace on the road between Aberystwyth and Machynlleth makes a refreshing spot to break for a cuppa. This pleasant restaurant specializes in Welsh teas and the gift shop next door might provide those Welsh souvenirs you need. Machynlleth will tempt you with a wholefood café offering tasty vegetarian snacks freshly prepared on the premises. *Speakes*, a very small delicatessen, has a selection of local cheeses, honeys, mustards and local jams and preserves. *Felin Crewi Working Watermill*, at Penegoes, near Machynlleth, has recently been restored to working order after 40 years of decay. Visitors can see the mill in operation as well as displays telling its history. The shop sells stoneground products, muesli and a range of Welsh baking. Hampers of Welsh produce are also available.

Holgates at Tywyn produce honey and honey products on a national scale. Visitors are made welcome and invited to look round the bee display. *Dorothy Bakery*, in the main street, has a secret recipe for the famous butter bun, and all I can tell you is that it's certainly worth a taste.

A visit to the *Centre for Alternative Technology*, just to the north of Machynlleth off the A487, makes a good day out. Founded in 1975, the centre is completely self-sufficient and it demonstrates new technologies which save resources and cut waste and pollution. A fine range of vegetarian and vegan food made from local produce is on offer.

Popty Dref, which literally means 'The Town's Oven', is situated in the centre of Dolgellau. Your nose should take you there, for the smell of fresh bread is enticing. The shops aims to sell as many

National Centre for Alternative Technology, near Machynlleth

Welsh products as possible and you will find a good range of Welsh cheeses, local goat's milk, free-range eggs, yoghurts, organic oatmeal and flours, Meridan and Welsh Lady preserves, Anglesey fudge and a mouthwatering array of baked products. During the hectic summer months as many as 120 loaves of bara brith are sold in a day! Barmouth offers a couple of small good food shops. *Goodies*, in the High Street, has a range of local products and in this fresh little delicatessen everything on offer looks most tempting.

If you fancy a Taste of Wales but can't quite get to the shops, then why not order a hamper from *Marshall's* of Newtown, tel (0938) 810239, and speak to Trixie Porter.

NORTH WALES

Markets are a great attraction with visitors throughout North Wales. They take place throughout the week, guaranteeing an outing for the tourist and chaos in the car park!

Don't miss *Llangefni's Indoor Market* on Anglesey on a Thursday morning. Be early though, because the popular *Women's Institute stall* which sells top-quality home cooking is always sold out by 11am. In the height of the summer season three fish vans hover outside the market selling everything fishy from mussels and cockles to plaice, lobster and crab. At *The Whole Thing* in Field Street you can find wholefoods, sourdough and rye bread, yeast-free soda bread, wholemeal and granary, all baked locally. Goat's milk, pulses, nuts, grains and health remedies as well as a range of vitamins are also available. *Golden Dairy* produces mozzarella cheese and David Williams of Plas Farm on Anglesey now sells his soft cheeses through *Safeways*.

Beaumaris has a good range of small specialist shops along its lively Castle Street. *Gavin Shaw* has fine wines; the *Nuthouse* offers wholefood; *Castle Bakery* has bread and cakes; and don't miss the *Seafoods Fish Shop* and *Denbigh Ices*.

Beaumaris's Castle Street shops are close to one of Wales's finest medieval fortresses

Anglesey Sea Zoo, at Brynsiencyn, is too good to miss. Take the family and spend some time peering into the oyster hatchery and the lobster beds. Learn about the sea life around the north coast of Wales and the fish you are likely to catch, eat or swim amongst! Don't leave without some local specialities from the shop which also sells game, shellfish, smoked fish, laverbread and delicatessen items.

Penrhyndeudraeth has a good deli called *G M and M Edwards*. It has a fine range of Welsh cheeses and butter, also pasta, teas, honey, jams, vinegar and coffees. The sauces vary from Lotus Chilli to Hoi Sin, which will certainly bring a zing to your cooking. The wines are well selected with special ports, sherry and champagnes. The Edwardses also have an outlet at Portmeirion. *Joe Lewis* in the High Street, Porthmadog, will supply you with local salmon, mackerel and lobsters, although much of his fish comes from Manchester market. Local organic vegetables, free-range eggs and up to 66 cheeses fill his chilled cabinets.

Cadwalader's Ice Cream is famous in Criccieth and the locals boast that it is the best in the world – certainly a recommendation to try it. Pwllheli has a Continental delicatessen called *Siop Caws*. Run by Lisa Filippi, daughter of Andreas who runs the Pompei Restaurant, this delicatessen is buzzes at lunch when hot pizza arrives from dad! A good range of Italian dishes is available as well as some excellent Welsh cheeses.

Caernarfon's claim to good food must be squeezed into the tiny *Just Natural* wholefood shop at 4 Pool Hill. Homemade herb bread, quiche, pizza, filled rolls, apricot and apple slice, felafel burgers and spinach savoury roll are all popular at lunchtime. Also on offer are herbs and spices, nuts, grains, and healthy beauty-care products.

Bala boasts a fine bakery, *Berwyn*, whose bread travels far and wide – look out for it. If you fancy a bite in Llanberis, then go to Mikes Bites, the in-place with the climbing fraternity.

In Upper Bangor, I suggest you visit *Jones and Hunt*, who supply the region with a superb range of organic vegetables and wholefoods. Bangor offers *The Delicatessen* at 2 The Arcade, Wellfield Centre, and *Pantry Pangwern* in Waterloo Street. These two delis supply the town's needs, and for fish why not visit *The Fish Shop* at Port Penrhyn. This is run in conjunction with a mussel farm and its large range of fresh fish comes from near and far. Prices are very competitive: look out for local scallops, crab, lobsters and oysters amongst the shellfish.

Whatever you do, don't miss a trip to Llanrwst to *Blas Ar Fwyd*, 25 Heol yr Orsaf. It's a wonderful speciality food shop and I defy anyone not to lick his or her lips at least once while visiting! Deiniol and Chandra Dafydd have provided Llanrwst with this gastronomic emporium of fine foods and wines. You can buy Continental cheeses, local dairy products, spring water,

Llanrwst's historic stone bridge

Cottage Delight jams and a range of homemade jams, chutneys and marmalades. The shop also sells lots of pasta, coffee, honey, herb teas, wholefoods (including organic), soya, rice flour, pulses and dried fruits. And that's not all! This outstanding place also stocks locally smoked salmon and trout, home-cooked ham and turkey. Its pâté, barbecued turkey legs, chickens, quiches and salads supply the lunch trade, while fruit tarts and lemon, carrot and eccles cakes tempt the sweet-toothed. The wine list makes a good read, with a choice of 240 wines listed, together with a fine selection of fortified wines, spirits and quality beers.

Baking is the speciality of *Sigwr a Sheis*, at 25 Watling Street, in Llanrwst. Here you can pick fresh cakes and confectionery from the shelves or order a luscious, freshly made dessert for your dinner party at home. Just up the road you can catch your own fish at *Conwy Valley Fisheries*, Rowen, near Conwy. Also visit the *Smokehouse* where you can view fish rearing and growing pools, and have your own fish smoked. Here you can choose from a selection of smoked meats and a range of other good foods, mainly Welsh in origin.

Melin-y-Foelas, at Pentrefoelas, is a recently renovated watermill which gives you the chance to buy stoneground flours. *Briwsion Bakery* operates in the old school house; on your travels through North Wales you will no doubt come across some of its traditional, splendid baking, for the bakery supplies many delicatessens.

Llandudno Junction boasts a very fine fish and game merchant, David Nigel Jones at *The Old Abattoir* in Builder Street. Whatever you buy in the way of fish, it's sure to be fresh unless David Nigel has smoked it – his salmon is famous. He supplies mainly the catering trade, but

44

The promenade, Colwyn Bay

retail customers are always welcome.

Speroni's at 13 Conwy Road, in Colwyn Bay, is a deli with a touch of Italy about it. Popular with the lunch trade, you can buy local Patchwork pâtés, baking from Briwsion, homemade salads, cold meats, pies, quiches and cheeses.

Flint Delicatessen in the town of the same name has a limited range of healthfoods plus cheese, cold meat and luxury sandwiches on offer. In Mold look out for *Tim's Fish Shop*. There is also a good range of speciality foods at *W R Roberts and Son*, with jams, teas and a chilled deli counter. Pop into *Mold Health Foods* for your herbal remedies.

Anne Owen, Love Lane, Denbigh, is the fifth generation to run a fine food store in the town. She took over from her father 17 years ago and the business has gone from strength to strength. Known for miles around, this is the place to come for Welsh speciality foods such as mustards, Welsh butter and yoghurt, honey, cakes, cheeses, Welsh Hill Bakery products and wholefoods together with teas, coffees and herbal remedies. 'Increasingly we offer Welsh foods and if people ask, we try to find whatever they want,' says Anne.

Just out of Denbigh on the Pentrefoelas Road be sure to visit *Broadleys Farm Shop and Tea Room*. Morris and Joan Griffith are champions of Welsh produce and they can supply you with local wild venison, pheasant, trout, mountain lamb, speciality sausages, Welsh cheeses, farm butter, honey, lemon cheese and, of course, a full range of Denbigh ice cream, which is made on the adjoining farm. If there is anything you could add to Joan's list of local specialities, she'd love to know about it.

At 23b Well Street, Ruthin you will find *Maguire's Delicatessen*, a tiny shop full of good things. There are local pâtés, cakes, pies, quiches and vegetable burgers, together with fresh laverbread, trout, hams and local beef, cooked on the premises. The freezer contains maize-fed chickens, guinea fowl, prawns and scallops. Welsh cheeses feature well here too.

Llangollen stands in the lovely Vale of Dee

Llangollen boasts a very glamorous food shop, *James A Bailey*. Again there is a good range of desirable eatables, many local, like the baked products and chocolates, plus speciality teas, mustards and good things to give as gifts. If I have a criticism, it is to see farmhouses cheeses cut into portions and sealed in plastic.

In Wrexham fresh fish is sold at *Peter Evans*, 2 Henblas Street. The increase of Chinese, Japanese and Asians in the population has brought a much wider range to this fish shop. Expect to find squid and cuttlefish along with the local tastes for cod and haddock. *The Butcher's Market* in the High Street offers a range of fresh local produce and *M A Evans* has a range of cheeses, incorporating some Welsh, together with English and Continental. There is a health food shop close by.

RECIPES
GILLI DAVIES

I have gathered together a tempting range of recipes which I think perfectly expresses what Taste of Wales is all about. The recipes are grouped into four categories – first courses/light meals, main meals, puddings and baking. Within this chapter you'll find everything from old favourites to imaginative new creations, nourishing dishes to recipes prepared with the lighter touch. Don't forget the Taste of Wales philosophy – always use fresh ingredients for the best results. And thank you to the talented cooks throughout Wales who have shared some of their secrets with me – and now you, the reader – on the following pages. Happy cooking!

FIRST COURSES/LIGHT MEALS

LAVERBREAD WITH BACON

Let's start with a recipe for a traditional Welsh breakfast. Laverbread, the seaweed collected off the Pembrokeshire coast, is still a favourite with the Welsh and this is how to prepare it.

1lb (450g) prepared laverbread
lots of freshly ground black pepper
2oz (50g) oatmeal
4 rashers bacon
4 slices bread

Serves 4

Divide the laverbread into four portions, season well with black pepper and coat with oatmeal.

Dry fry the bacon so that the fat runs, remove it from the pan when crisp. Add the laverbread cakes and fry in the bacon fat until crisp and golden. Toast the bread and serve the laverbread cakes on top garnished with the rashers of bacon.

LAVERBREAD ROULADE

Here is another recipe using laverbread. Margaret Rees finds that this dish is always popular in her restaurant, The Cobblers, at Llandybie.

1lb (450g) laverbread
4 eggs,
separated nutmeg
zest of 1 orange

Serves 4

Mix the laverbread and egg yolks together with seasonings. Whisk egg whites until stiff and fold into mixture. Pour into a lined swiss roll tin and bake for 10–12 minutes in a moderate oven. Turn on to a sheet of parchment paper and roll up immediately. Leave until cold or freeze at this stage.

Serve as it is, with a sauce or as Margaret suggests, topped with some marinated wild salmon.

Mushrooms with White Wine and Rosemary

This recipe is typical of Kate Scale's ingenuity and flair. As well as preparing gourmet meals for the attractive self-catering Rogeston Cottages in Portfield Gate, Haverfordwest, she is a highly successful cookery demonstrator and inventor of recipes, especially with a slant towards healthy eating.

1oz (25g) Welsh butter
1 onion, thinly sliced
1 clove garlic, crushed
1lb (450g) mushrooms, button or sliced
1 teaspoon dried rosemary
¼ pint (150ml) dry white wine
salt and black pepper
garnish – chopped parsley or chives
Serves 2–4

Heat the butter and sweat onion and garlic for 2 minutes in a large saucepan without browning. Add the mushrooms and rosemary, cover and cook gently to extract the juice from the mushrooms. Add the wine, boil uncovered until reduced to a syrupy glaze. Season to taste.

Serve in individual ramekins as a starter or in soup bowls for a light lunch, garnished with chopped parsley or chives and accompanied with hot garlic bread or french bread.

Chestnut and Mushroom Pâté

Here is another clever idea from Kate Scale. It is a pâté, aimed at vegetarians, which could be used as a starter or for a light lunch.

1oz (25g) butter
1½ lb (750g) mushrooms, roughly chopped
1 teaspoon fresh sage, chopped
1 clove garlic, crushed
15½oz (439g) can chestnut purée (natural)
2oz (50g) wholemeal breadcrumbs
1 tablespoon soy sauce
2 tablespoons brandy
pinch each of nutmeg and chilli powder
salt and pepper
1 tablespoon chopped chives
Serves 6–8

Melt butter in a large frying pan. Sauté mushrooms until golden with the sage and garlic. Remove mushrooms with a draining spoon to a food processor or liquidizer. Reduce any remaining liquid to a syrupy glaze, add to mushrooms and all remaining ingredients, except chives.

Purée the mixture until smooth, season to taste with salt and pepper, turn into a serving dish, sprinkle with chives and chill until required.

Serve with warm toast and a salad. For a change accompany with Cumberland or cranberry sauce.

Leek and Goat's Cheese Parcels

Soft fresh Welsh goat's cheese can be as mild as cream cheese and infinitely less fattening. For this recipe I have used plain goat's cheese and mixed it with chopped walnuts before rolling it into a leek. The honey vinaigrette adds just a little sweetness to the dish.

2 medium-sized leeks
4oz (100g) fresh goat's cheese
2oz (50g) walnuts, chopped
1oz (25g) raisins, soaked in sherry for $1/2$ hour

For the dressing
3 tablespoons walnut oil
1 tablespoon white wine vinegar
1 teaspoon runny honey
salt and freshly ground black pepper
Serves 4

For the dressing, put all the ingredients into a wide topped jam jar. Shake well to blend.

Peel off any muddy outer skins of the leeks and wash under cold running water. Keep the leeks whole and plunge them into a large saucepan of boiling water. Boil the leeks for 8 minutes, drain and immediately run under the cold tap. This will cool them quickly and also maintain their bright green colour.

Peel the layers off the leeks, tearing them as little as possible. Reserve the best 8 layers and chop the remaining leeks finely. Mix the chopped leeks, goat's cheese, walnuts and raisins and divide the mixture into 4 portions. Wrap each portion in 2 leek layers, making a parcel shape. Arrange the leek parcels on a serving dish.

Spoon some dressing over each parcel.

Leek and Potato Pie

Here is a colourful and filling way to use Pembrokeshire potatoes, which combines their excellent flavour with finely sliced leeks. It is also ideal for vegetarians, and tastes very good with added grated cheese.

1lb (450g) peeled potatoes
12oz (350g) leeks, finely sliced or chopped
salt and pepper
4oz (100g) butter
Serves 4

Heat the oven to Gas Mark 4, 350°F, 180°C.

Slice the potatoes paper-thin and put in a bowl of cold water. Stir them around to lose the starch then drain and pat dry. Grease a shallow dish and put alternate layers of potatoes and leeks, seasoning each layer and dotting with butter, leaving about 1oz (25g) of the butter to cover the top.

Cover with foil and cook for $1 1/2$ hours, removing the foil for the last $1/2$ hour to brown the top. Either serve the pie in the dish or turn out on to a plate, flashing under a grill to brown the underside.

Leek and goat's cheese parcels

Cucumber and Cream Cheese Mousse

This recipe was given to me by Joan Downey who, together with her family, produce Llangloffan farmhouse cheese on their farm at Castle Morris, North Pembrokeshire.

½ cucumber
salt
8oz (225g) cream cheese
1 small onion,
finely grated pepper
pinch of dry mustard
¼ pint (150ml) chicken stock
2 level teaspoons gelatine
¼ pint (150ml) double cream
Serves 4

Peel cucumber and dice it. Put pieces into a bowl, sprinkle liberally with salt and leave for 30 minutes.

Beat together cream cheese, onion, seasoning and mustard. Pour stock into pan, sprinkle over the gelatine and dissolve over low heat, then beat the stock into cheese mixture.

Drain the cucumber and add to cheese. Whip cream and add to the rest of the ingredients. Put into small pots and leave to set.

Mrs Downey suggests that you might like to substitute yoghurt for the double cream if you think the cream may be too rich for your constitution.

Gooseberry Sauce for Mackerel

The flavour of really fresh mackerel is unique. If you are spending your summer holidays around the coasts of Wales then why not hire a small boat and go mackerel fishing – it's the best way to be sure that they are straight from the sea.

Here is a simple but delicious way to cook and serve fresh mackerel. After preparation, season and score each fish across 2–3 times to ensure even cooking. Place over a hot grill and cook both sides until crisp on the outside and the flesh is set.

Gooseberry sauce is the perfect foil to counteract the richness of mackerel.

1lb (450g) gooseberries
¼ pint (150ml) water
1 level teaspoon arrowroot sugar to taste
Enough for 4

Simmer gooseberries with the water until tender, then sieve. Blend the arrowroot with a little cold water and add to the purée. Heat to boil, stirring until it thickens.

Season and sweeten to taste.

Leek Crackers

Evelyn Hawksley of Edderton Hall at Forden, near Welshpool, describes her cooking as British with French influence. Here is one of her recipes.

2 x 6in (15cm) lengths of leek
8 queen scallops
small quantity of chives, blanched

For the mixture
peppers – 1 red, 1 green, 1 yellow
1/4 pint (150ml) dry sherry
1oz (25g) butter
Serves 2

Push out centres of leeks so that only one layer remains. Push 4 queen scallops into the centre of each and tie up each side with a blanched chive, to look like a cracker.

Make a *mirepoix* (mixture) of red, yellow and green peppers, simmer in dry sherry till soft and reduce by one third. Strain, arrange peppers in a circle on warm plate and return juice to pan. Reduce again, and thicken with butter. While sauce is cooking, place leek crackers in a sieve which fits over pan and cover so that they steam for about 5 minutes and the juice goes into the sauce. Put them in centre of peppers and pour sauce over the top.

Yoghurt Cheese with Fresh Herbs

There is something very satisfying about making your own soft cheese. Whether you serve it as a dip or perhaps rolled into pancakes or spread on crispbread, yoghurt cheese is a most useful ingredient to have in the fridge.

1 pint (600ml) natural yoghurt
freshly ground black pepper
1 tablespoon thin cream or top of the milk
1/2 clove garlic, crushed with salt
1/2 tablespoon chopped parsley
1/2 tablespoon chopped dill
1/2 tablespoon chopped chervil

Line a colander or strainer with muslin or a double J cloth. Stand it over a bowl. Tip the yoghurt into the sieve and tie it up with string so that it forms a bag. Lift it out of the colander and leave it to drain overnight, tying the string to a tap over a sink.

The next day, tip the drained curds from the bag into a bowl. Beat until smooth, adding pepper and the cream or top of the milk. Fold in the crushed garlic with most of the chopped herbs, keeping some back to scatter over the top.

Pile into a small dish, level off with a knife, and sprinkle the remaining herbs on top. Chill for an hour or so before serving.

ANGLESEY EGGS

Here is a traditional Welsh dish that would suit vegetarians. Whether for Sunday supper, a light lunch or as a starter for a main meal, this recipe is the perfect answer.

8 eggs
1½lb (750g) potatoes
6 medium sized-leeks
1oz (25g) butter

For the sauce
1oz (25g) butter
1oz (25g) plain flour
½ pint (300ml) milk
3oz (75g) grated cheddar
salt and pepper
Serves 8 as a starter, 4 as a light meal

Hard boil the eggs and boil and mash the potatoes. Cut the leeks into rings and cook in salted water for 10 minutes. Add the leeks to the potatoes with the butter and mix thoroughly.

For the sauce, melt the butter in a small saucepan, stir in the flour and add the milk. Stir as the sauce comes to the boil. Add most of the cheese and seasoning.

Fork the potato mixture around the sides of an ovenproof dish or individual dishes and put the halved eggs in the middle. Pour over the cheese sauce, sprinkle with the remaining cheese and bake in a hot oven Gas Mark 6, 400°F, 200°C for 15–20 minutes until the top is golden. Serve piping hot.

LOVAGE SOUP

At Tyddyn Perthi Farm at Tan-y-Maes, Port Dinorwic, Mrs Barbara Lewis and her daughters will tempt you with a menu that is imaginative and interesting. Much of the produce is local, if not produced on the dairy farm itself. This is one of Barbara's recipes.

1oz (25g) butter
¾lb (350g) onions, sliced
4 level teaspoons chopped fresh lovage
1oz (25g) plain flour
1 pint (600ml) good chicken stock
½ pint (300ml) creamy milk
fresh lovage leaves for garnish
Serves 4

Heat butter, add sliced onions and chopped lovage leaves. Sweat for 5–10 minutes. Add flour and cook for 1 minute. Add stock slowly and then milk, cover and simmer for 20 minutes. Purée and serve, with fresh lovage leaves as garnish.

Lovage soup

GELLI FAWR CRAB

Anne Churcher and Frances Roughley fell in love with Gelli Fawr Country House at Pontfaen, near Newport, Pembrokeshire, on sight and became the owners in the autumn of 1987. They aim to make guests feel at home and Frances cooks unusual and creative dishes based on local produce. Here is how Frances serves her local crab.

2 crabs with white and brown meat removed
6oz (175g) mushrooms
1 teaspoon fresh ginger
1 tablespoon butter
¼ pint (150ml) sweet sherry
5 tablespoons whipping cream
salt and pepper
¼ pint (150ml) béchamel sauce with
   1 tablespoon spiced honey mustard
2oz (50g) Nevern cheese, grated
Serves 2

Oil crab shells. Cook mushrooms and ginger in butter for 3 minutes, add sherry and reduce until all evaporated. Add cream and cook for 2 minutes. Season and place in crab shells or small individual oven dishes.

Place some brown and some white meat on top of each shell or dish. Pour on béchamel sauce and sprinkle with cheese. Heat in oven until brown and hot, and serve with brown bread.

NEVERN CHEESE AND RED WINE PÂTÉ

8oz (225g) Nevern cheese, grated,
   or any well-flavoured farmhouse Cheddar
2oz (50g) soft butter
½ teaspoon Tabasco
½ teaspoon raw onion
2 teaspoons chilli and ginger mustard
4fl oz (100ml) red wine
pecan nuts (shelled)

Place all ingredients except wine and pecan nuts in food processor and process for 1 minute. While running, gradually add red wine.

Place in piping bag with star nozzle and pipe in small rosettes on Bakewell paper and place a strip of pecan nuts on top. Open freeze and then pack in box.

To serve, defrost for 1 hour and serve with a salad of all green: pepper, lime, lettuce, kiwi and green apple.

Main Meals

Eileen's Raised Game Pie

This is real pub food – just what you would expect if you stopped at the renowned Griffin Inn, Llyswen, Powys, for a bite.

For the filling
1 pheasant, plucked and drawn
1/2 teaspoon thyme
2 bay leaves
1 level dessertspoon salt
24 black peppercorns
1 large carrot, chopped
1 stick of celery, chopped
1 large onion, chopped
10oz (275g) assorted cooked meats diced, i.e. chicken, ham and whatever game is available
5fl oz (150ml) red wine
1 tablespoon mixed fresh herbs or 1 teaspoon dried herbs

For the pastry
4 1/2 oz (120g) lard
5fl oz (150ml) water
12oz (350g) plain flour
1/2 teaspoon salt
1 egg yolk
beaten egg to glaze
Serves up to 12

The day before you make the pie, put the pheasant in a large saucepan with the herbs, seasoning and chopped carrots, celery and onion. Add enough cold water to cover and bring to the boil, simmer until tender (about 1 1/2 hours). Leave to cool in the liquid.

Strip the flesh from the pheasant carcass, and reserve the pheasant stock. Combine the chopped pheasant to the other chopped cooked meats in a large bowl. Pour over the red wine and stir in the herbs. Cover and leave overnight in a cool place.

To make the pastry case, grease a loose-bottom 6in (15cm) round tin and dust with flour. Melt the fat over a gentle heat. Bring the water up to the boil. Take off the heat and tip in the sieved flour with the salt. Stir thoroughly to combine then make a well in the dough and pour in the melted fat and egg yolk. Beat hard to make a dough and continue to knead into a smooth ball, keeping warm.

Roll out three-quarters of the pastry into a large circle and line the tin. Spoon the filling into the case. Roll the remaining pastry to make a lid. Seal the edges with cold water. Design a pattern on the lid if you like and make 1/4 in (6mm) hole in the centre. Glaze with beaten egg.

Bake for 15 minutes at Gas Mark 6, 400°F, 200°C, then turn down to Gas Mark 3, 325°F, 160°C, for another 1–1 1/2 hours.

Meanwhile, reheat the pheasant stock and boil hard to reduce to about 10fl oz (300ml). When the pie is cooked pour the warm stock through the hole until full. Leave to cool.

Serve the raised game pie cut into slices, with a side salad and relishes.

Trout wrapped in bacon (see page 58)

Trout with lemon, butter and caper sauce (see page 58)

Trout Wrapped in Bacon

This recipes comes from traditional rural Wales – local trout, possibly poached, sitting in a dish wrapped in fat bacon from last year's family pig. For those who hate bones, why not take them out of the trout before you start. First gut the fish and clean under cold running water. Cut off the head, tail and fins. Open out the split fish and spread it flat, skin side up. Press firmly along the centre back of the fish to loosen the backbone, then turn the fish over. Starting at the head end, ease away the backbone with the tip of a knife, removing as many of the small bones as possible at the same time. Your trout is now spineless and ready to cook.

4 good-sized trout, brown if possible, otherwise rainbow
1 tablespoon chopped chives
4 good slices of lemon
salt
freshly ground black pepper
8 rashers smoked streaky bacon
Greek yoghurt mixed with a little fresh grated horseradish or chopped parsley

Serves 4

Heat the oven to Gas Mark 4, 350°F, 180°C.

Clean, gut and bone the trout if you prefer (see previous instructions).

Put some chopped chives and a slice of lemon in the belly of each trout together with salt and pepper. Wrap each fish in two rashers of bacon. Lay the fish side by side in a baking dish and bake for 15–20 minutes until the bacon is crisp on top and the trout flesh cooked and flaky.

Serve the trout with the sauce.

Trout with Lemon, Butter and Caper Sauce

What could be better than fresh trout for a healthy meal?

4 trout
3 tablespoons Nevern butter (or another good farm butter)
1 lemon
1 tablespoon capers
dill, lemon and lime to garnish

Serves 4

Brush trout with a little melted butter and bake in medium oven at Gas Mark 4, 350°F, 180°C for 15–20 minutes.

Remove zest from lemon, blanch and cool. Cut off pith and slice in thin slices. Melt butter, add lemon slices and capers and heat through.

Place trout on serving dish. Pour over sauce and garnish with zest, dill and lemon or lime wedges.

Pembrokeshire Lamb Pie in Hot Water Crusty Pastry

Here is a traditional Welsh recipe from Jane Gratton at the excellent Bryngarw Guest House, Trefin, for minced lamb pies which would have been sold at the autumn hiring fairs throughout Wales. These pies were called Katt Pies at the Templeton Fair in Pembrokeshire, which took place every year on 12 November. Did they use cats in the recipe, one wonders!

hot water crust pastry using 1lb (450g) plain flour
1lb (450g) minced lamb
4oz (100g) currants
approx 4oz (100g) brown sugar
salt and pepper
stock
beaten egg or milk, to glaze

Serves 4

When pastry is cool enough to handle make into small pastry cases, smaller than veal and ham pies. Keep back a quarter of the pastry for lids.

Arrange layers of lamb, currants, sugar, salt and pepper and moisten with stock. Cover with pastry lids, and glaze.

Bake in a hot oven Gas Mark 6, 400°F, 200°C, for 10 minutes, then reduce to moderate heat Gas Mark 4, 350°F, 180°C, for about $1\frac{1}{4}$ hours.

Fill with remaining stock before serving hot.

Potted Lamb Lemonato

Here is a clever idea from Welsh Lamb Enterprise. After preparing this first recipe, you can use the leftovers to produce a good pâté.

2 large onions, chopped
2 cloves garlic, crushed
2lb (900g) shoulder Welsh lamb, boned and cubed with fat, skin and gristle removed
$\frac{1}{2}$ cup oil, for frying
14oz (400g) can tomatoes
2 lemons, sliced and de-pipped
2 bay leaves
2 teaspoons coriander seeds, crushed
1 small pot natural yoghurt
1 teaspoon salt
$\frac{1}{2}$ teaspoon black pepper
$\frac{1}{2}$ teacup desiccated coconut, browned under grill (optional)

Serves 6

Brown onions, garlic and lamb in the oil and drain off excess oil. Chop tomatoes and add to pan with lemon slices, bay leaves, coriander, yoghurt and seasonings. Bring to boil, then reduce to a very low heat, cover and simmer for 1 hour, checking occasionally to ensure liquid is reducing but meat is not sticking to pan (add some juice from tomato can if necessary).

When cooked remove lemon peel (the inside will have cooked away) and bay leaves. Serve hot with potatoes, carrots and beans. Sprinkle browned coconut on top or reserve for use with pâté.

Lamb Pâté

Using leftover cooled lamb lemonato from the last recipe, mince twice or process until smooth. Put pâté mixture into dish and pour on a thin layer of melted unsalted butter. Decorate with toasted coconut and a slice of lemon. (If you want to freeze the pâté, omit coconut until just before serving.)

Serve the pâté at room temperature on hot toast, canapés, rye biscuits or in sandwiches. It is also delicious sliced, with salad.

Lamb Steaks with Rosemary

4-8 boneless loin steaks of Welsh lamb
salt and pepper
3 dessertspoons oil
2oz (50g) Welsh butter
4 tablespoons Madeira or sweet sherry
1 tablespoon rosemary, finely chopped
3 tablespoons double cream
Serves 4

Season the meat. Heat the oil and 1oz (25g) butter. Fry the chops briskly for 5–10 minutes on each side. Arrange the meat in a serving dish and keep hot. Add the remaining butter to the pan together with the sherry, rosemary and cream. Boil the sauce up for a minute or two and pour over the lamb steaks.

Serve immediately with fresh vegetables or a crisp salad.

Clwydian Medieval Lamb

Bryn Awel offers accommodation in a farmhouse on a 35-acre (14-hectare) working farm on the outskirts of the picturesque market town of Ruthin, conveniently based for the North Wales coast, Snowdonia and Chester. Your host, Mrs Beryl Jones, is an award-winning cook and this is one of her recipes.

4 lamb steaks or chops
juice of 2 oranges
1 glass mead
oil for frying
1 onion
1 tablespoon Dijon mustard
4 tablespoons mint sauce
seasoning
1 tablespoon cornflour
¼ pint (150ml) stock
Serves 4

Marinate the lamb in the juice of 1 orange and the mead for a few hours. Remove from the marinade and cook gently in oil in a frying pan until golden brown. Add the onion and cook gently until soft. Place in a casserole dish with the marinade juices, mustard, mint and seasoning.

Blend the cornflour with the remaining orange juice and stock and add them to the casserole. Place on the cooker and simmer at a low heat for 1 hour. Serve on a meat dish garnished with watercress or parsley.

Note: If mead is not available, white wine with a spoonful of honey is fine.

Mussels in a savoury choux pastry case (see page 62)

Mussels in a Savoury Choux Case

Kim Mold sells his mussels under the label mytti mussel from Penrhyn Harbour on the Menai Strait. Kim purifies, cleans and debeards the mussels, so all the customer has to do is cook them.

For the filling
4lb (1.75kg) fresh mussels in their shells or
   12oz (350g) shelled, cooked mussels
1 large onion, chopped
1 clove garlic, chopped
sprigs of fresh parsley
1 tablespoon crushed coriander seeds
8fl oz (225ml) dry white wine
4fl oz (100ml) water
freshly ground black pepper
5fl oz (150ml) double cream
1 tablespoon finely crushed parsley

For the choux pastry
5fl oz (150ml) water
2oz (50g) butter
salt and pepper
3oz (75g) flour
2 eggs
1/4 teaspoon English mustard
Serves 6

Scrub the mussel shells and put them in a large saucepan. Add the onion, garlic, parsley, coriander, wine, water and seasoning. Cover and cook over a high heat until the shells open, shaking the pan from time to time – this takes about 5 minutes. Take care not to overcook the mussels or they will toughen. Discard any shells that refuse to open.

Strain the liquid from the mussels into a small pan and boil well to reduce to about a wineglassful. (If you are using cooked shelled mussels, simply combine the onion, garlic, parsley, coriander, wine, water and seasoning and boil to reduce, then strain.)

Add the cream and parsley, stir to blend, then cool. Shell the mussels and add them to the cream sauce.

For the pastry, place the water, butter, salt and pepper in a saucepan and bring to the boil to melt the butter. Take off the heat and add all the sifted flour at once. Stir until the mixture is smooth and comes away from the sides of the pan. Cool for 5–10 minutes. Gradually beat in the eggs, beating hard until the mixture is smooth and shiny and keeping its shape. Add the mustard.

Either use one 10in (25cm) flan dish or 6 large ramekins or individual heatproof serving dishes and spread a layer of pastry around the edge, about 1/2 in (1cm) thick.

Pre-heat the oven to Gas Mark 7, 425°F, 220°C. Bake the pastry in a hot oven for 10–15 minutes or until risen and golden brown. Allow another 10 minutes for the large flan dish to cook.

To serve, reheat the mussels in the sauce and spoon into the middle of the cooked pastry. Serve at once.

BLAS AR GYMRU VENISON

In my search to find Welsh food over the past few years I have made some remarkably good friends, busy people who will always give me some of their time, offer me a taste of this and that, but most of all divulge some of their innermost secrets! Pat and Merion Dally of Blas ar Gymru at 48 Crwys Road in Cardiff are such people and their generosity has now extended to sharing their recipes with us all. Their restaurant offers a very special warmth and charm with excellent traditional food and Welsh wines.

3lb (1.35kg) piece haunch of venison

For the marinade
½ pint (300ml) claret
¼ pint (150ml) port
1 medium-sized onion, sliced
2 carrots, sliced
8 peppercorns
1 bayleaf

To complete
½ oz (15g) lard
1oz (25g) butter
2 onions, finely chopped
¼ pint (150ml) venison stock
salt and pepper
½ oz (15g) flour
3 tablespoons double cream
Serves 6

Make sure the butcher has covered the meat with a layer of barding fat and has tied the haunch into a neat joint using thin string. Put into a deep, non-aluminium bowl with all the marinade ingredients. Cover and leave to marinate for 3 days in the fridge.

When ready to cook, set the oven at Gas Mark 3, 325°F, 160°C. Heat the lard and half the butter in a heatproof casserole. Add the onions and cook slowly until softened. Lift the meat out of the marinade and drain thoroughly. Add to the onions and cook over a high heat until brown on all sides. Strain the marinade and add the liquid to the casserole with the stock and a little seasoning. Bring to the boil.

Cover and cook gently for 2½–3 hours until tender. Near the end of the cooking time, mix the remaining butter and the flour to a paste and whisk into the bubbling venison juices. Cook, stirring gently, until the sauce thickens. Taste the sauce for seasoning and stir in the cream just before serving the meat thickly sliced.

ESCALOPE OF PORK PANTYSGAWN

Pantysgawn is a soft goat's cheese that makes a good addition to well-flavoured pork. I like to use Sker free-range pork from Porthcawl.

4 good-sized escalopes of pork
4oz (100g) Pantysgawn goat's cheese with garlic and herbs (substitute any cream cheese with garlic and herbs)
wholemeal flour, seasoned
2 eggs, beaten
fresh wholemeal breadcrumbs
2oz (50g) butter
2 tablespoons sunflower or rapeseed oil
garnish – sliced tomato and sprigs of mint

Serves 4

Insert a sharp knife along the side of each escalope to make as big a pocket as possible. Spread a teaspoonful of the cheese evenly in each pocket, and press the edges together gently.

Dip each escalope in the seasoned flour and the egg, then coat in breadcrumbs. Repeat this process along the pocket openings to prevent the cheese escaping. Chill the escalopes until ready to cook.

Heat the butter and oil in a heavy based frying pan until foaming. Add the escalopes, and sauté for 3 minutes on each side, until the outside is golden. Drain on absorbent paper.

Serve the escalopes immediately, garnished with sliced tomato and mint. Accompany with new potatoes and courgettes with tomatoes, or savoyard potatoes and a tomato salad.

ANGLESEY SEA ZOO

MONA SEAFOODS LIMITED

Freshly baked food in a new 100 cover licensed restaurant beside the award-winning Sea Zoo. Fresh and smoked seafood to eat or take away – seafish quality award holders for 3 consecutive years.

The Oyster Hatchery, Brynsiencyn, Anglesey LL61 6TQ
Tel: (0248) 430411 Fax: (0248) 430213

Bringing Fresh Welsh Food to the Fore!

WELSH LAMB
DELICIOUSLY DIFFERENT

Wales has for centuries enjoyed a reputation for producing the best lamb in the world. When you see the Premium Quality Welsh Lamb symbol at a butcher's shop or supermarket, it's your guarantee that the lamb on sale is the finest example of this great tradition, it's quality and taste unequalled.

If you would like a Welsh Lamb consumer pack and a list of your nearest stockists, please write to Welsh Lamb Enterprise, Brynawel, Great Darkgate Street, Aberystwyth, Dyfed. SY23 1DR

PREMIUM QUALITY WELSH LAMB

Rack of Lamb with Rosemary

1 teaspoon fresh rosemary
3oz (75g) garlic-flavoured cream cheese
2oz (50g) brown breadcrumbs
1½–2lb (675-900g) best end of neck lamb, skinned and chined

Serves 4

Chop the rosemary finely and mix with the cream cheese and breadcrumbs. Press this mixture together with a palette knife and spread over the skin side of the lamb.

Put the rack of lamb in a roasting tin and cook in a hot oven Gas Mark 7, 425°F, 220°C for 30 minutes, or a little longer if you don't like your lamb pink.

Serve the lamb, cut down between the rib bones, either as single cutlets or doubles.

Lamb with Asparagus

Every spring the market gardens of Gwent grow a healthy crop of asparagus. This is a good way to combine fresh asparagus with Welsh lamb.

1½lb (750g) fresh asparagus
1½lb (750g) boned shoulder of lamb, cut into fat-free cubes
2 medium-sized onions, sliced
1 tablespoon oil
1oz (25g) butter
1 tablespoon flour
¼ pint (150ml) double cream
salt and pepper
lemon juice (optional)

Serves 4

Cut each stem of asparagus into two, putting the thicker bottom ends in a pan of boiling water. Boil for 3 minutes before gently laying the tips on top of the stems and continue cooking for another 15 minutes or until the asparagus is cooked.

Meanwhile, heat a heavy based casserole, or frying pan, and brown the meat and onions in the oil and butter (frying with oil stops the butter from burning).

Stir in the flour and about ½ pint (300ml) of the asparagus liquid. Bring this to the boil and simmer the lamb very gently for about an hour until tender. If the sauce becomes too thick add more asparagus liquid.

Remove the asparagus tips carefully from the cooking liquid and keep on one side. Liquidize the stems with a little liquid, then sieve to make sure there are no stringy bits left. Mix the purée with the cream, and when the lamb is cooked stir this into the casserole, with salt and pepper to taste, and a dash of lemon juice if you want to sharpen the flavour.

Serve the lamb and asparagus on a serving dish, with the asparagus spears around the outside, accompanied perhaps by some new potatoes or rice.

Ham cooked with Cider

Abergavenny was at one time a major apple-growing area and the locals still have a taste for cider. Here is a recipe that suits them well.

2½–3lb (1.25–1.5kg) joint of ham
1 large onion studded with cloves
1 lemon
2 tablespoons brown sugar
1 pint (600ml) dry cider
½ teaspoon ground mace
3 tablespoons crisp breadcrumbs
1 teaspoon mustard

For the sauce
1oz (25g) butter
1oz (25g) plain flour
½ pint (300ml) ham stock
2 sticks celery, chopped
2oz (50g) raisins
freshly ground black pepper
Serves 6–8

Place the ham in a large saucepan with the onion, lemon and a teaspoon of brown sugar. Add the cider and enough water to cover the joint. Bring to the boil and simmer gently for 1–1½ hours. Allow the ham to cook in its liquid then remove and peel off the skin. Keep the stock.

Mix together the remaining brown sugar, mace, breadcrumbs and mustard. Press into the ham fat and moisten with a little stock. Put the ham in a baking tin, pour in ½ pint (300ml) stock and bake at Gas 5, 375°F, 190°C for 20–25 minutes.

To make the sauce, melt the butter in a small saucepan and stir in the flour. Gradually add the ham stock, and then all the other ingredients. Stir well, bring to the boil and simmer for 10 minutes.

Chicken St Fagans

8 boneless chicken breasts
1 clove garlic
6 oz (175g) laverbread
1 pint (600ml) Croffta white wine
4oz (100g) diced onion
4oz (100g) sliced white mushrooms
1oz (25g) butter
4oz (100g) flour
6fl oz (175ml) double cream
salt and pepper
6oz (175g) peeled prawns
Serves 8

Flatten the chicken breasts with a heavy wooden spoon. Crush the garlic and add to the laverbread. Spread this over the chicken breasts and roll them, securing with a cocktail stick. Poach breasts in the wine with onions and mushrooms for 20 minutes. Remove the breasts from the stock and keep warm.

Blend the butter and flour together with a palette knife and add it in little bits to the hot stock. Bring to the boil and whisk hard until the sauce has thickened and is smooth. Add the cream and season the sauce to taste. Pour over the chicken breasts and garnish with prawns.

Great cooks cook on Gas.

British Gas
Wales/Cymru

Each new generation bears all the family characteristics.

Baron Philippe de Rothschild judged them worthy of his name.

Puddings

Hazelnut and Honey Syllabub

Something naughty, nutty but terribly nice is just what you'll get from the Hive on the Quay at The Old Wharf in Aberaeron. Try this recipe.

2 tablespoons clear Welsh honey
1/2 pint (300ml) double cream
3/4 pint (450ml) medium-sweet white wine
2oz (50g) hazelnuts, roasted (rub together to remove some of the skins)

Serves 4

Have all ingredients and equipment at room temperature. Place honey and cream in bowl. Gradually add wine, whisking continuously to a light foam. Fold in the prepared nuts and pour into individual goblets. Chill slightly.

Decorate with whole nuts and serve with fingers of shortbread or crisp biscuits.

Elderberry and Apple Soufflé with Port

Out and about in the autumn? Then why not gather some elderberries and make this delicious pudding created by Kate Scale of Rogeston Cottages, Portfield Gate, Haverfordwest.

12oz (350g) elderberries (stripped weight)
12oz (350g) dessert apples, peeled, cored and sliced (Kate suggests using Cox's Orange Pippin, Worcester or Granny Smith apples)
2 tablespoons lemon juice
2 tablespoons water
3oz (75g) caster sugar
3 large eggs, separated
1 tablespoon gelatine
4 tablespoons port
1/4 pint (150ml) whipping cream
1/4 pint (150ml) fromage frais or Greek yoghurt

Garnish

2oz (50g) toasted almonds, finely chopped
a few fresh elderberries
1/4 pint (150ml) whipping or double cream, whipped

Serves 4–6

Prepare a 6in (15cm) soufflé dish; tie a double band of foil or greaseproof paper around the outside, to stand 2in (5cm) above the rim.

Place elderberries and apples in a pan with the lemon juice and 2 tablespoons water. Cover and simmer until soft for approx 10–15 minutes. Leave to cool. Purée fruit, sieve to remove seeds – there should be approx 8fl oz (225ml).

Place caster sugar and egg yolks in a large bowl, whisk with an electric beater, or in a food mixer, until thick and mousse-like. Dissolve gelatine in port in a small bowl over simmering water, stir into the fruit purée. Lightly whip the cream and fromage frais or yoghurt together, fold into the mousse with the fruit purée. Whisk the egg whites until fairly stiff, fold 1 tablespoon into the mixture to lighten, then fold in the rest lightly.

Turn into the prepared soufflé dish, chill until set (approx 2 hours).

To serve, carefully remove band of foil or greaseproof, press almonds around the side. Decorate the top with fresh elderberries and whipped cream. (This completed dish will freeze.)

Variation: Omit port and replace with apple juice or water if preferred. To reduced the fat content, all the cream could be substituted with fromage frais or Greek yoghurt.

SAUCEPAN OATY CRUMBLE

Here are a couple of quick, crunchy, crumble toppings from Kate Scale, who also supplied the previous recipe. She suggests that you use fresh fruit in season and alternate the top layer.

3oz (75g) butter or margarine
2oz (50g) sunflower and/or sesame seeds
4oz (100g) jumbo oats
2oz (50g) wholemeal flour
3oz (75g) soft brown sugar
½ teaspoon mixed spice (optional)

Melt butter in a saucepan, add seeds and fry gently for 1 minute. Remove from heat, stir in the oats, cool slightly. Mix flour, sugar and spice and add to oat mixture.

Sprinkle on top of 1–1½lb (450–750g) prepared fruit (cook hard fruits partly beforehand).

Bake at Gas Mark 4, 350°F, 180°C for 20–30 minutes until golden brown.

NUTTY CRUMBLE TOPPING

This is the second of Kate's delicious toppings.

6oz (175g) granary breadcrumbs
4oz (100g) ground hazelnuts
3oz (75g) demerara or soft brown sugar
3oz (75g) butter or margarine
1 teaspoon ground coriander, cinnamon or chopped crystalized ginger
1oz (25g) flaked almonds

Mix breadcrumbs, hazelnuts and sugar together in a large bowl and rub in butter. Alternatively, place all together in a food processor, taking care not to over-process or butter will melt.

Spread mixture over 1–1½ lb (450–750g) prepared fruit in a shallow ovenproof dish. Sprinkle on spice or chopped ginger, according to taste and the fruit used. Top with flaked almonds.

Bake at Gas Mark 4, 350°F, 180°C, for 25–30 minutes until the top is brown and fruit bubbling.

ICE CREAM WITH FRESH PEACHES

Denbigh Farmhouse ice cream is delicious. Made from full cream milk with added cream, it is definitely a dairy ice. This is a recipe devised by Joan Griffith who runs the Broadley's Farm Shop, Denbigh, next to the farm where the ice cream is made.

4 fresh ripe peaches
1 tablespoon brandy
1 teaspoon almond essence
sugar to taste
ice cream (enough for 4)
¼ pint (150ml) whipping cream
Serves 4

Skin the peaches and crush the fruit with a fork and rub through a sieve. Put the peach purée into a saucepan with the brandy and almond essence, sweeten to taste with sugar and heat slowly until warm but not boiling. Pour over portions of ice cream. Pipe whipped cream to decorate and sprinkle with chopped almonds and wafer biscuits.

For your copy of the Welsh Country Holidays brochure, contact: Welsh Country Holidays, Ladywell House, Newtown, Montgomeryshire, Wales SY16 1JB. Telephone: 0686 626965.

Welsh Country Holidays

WALES

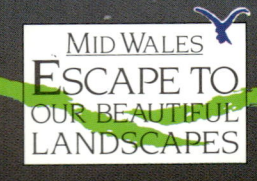

MID WALES
ESCAPE TO OUR BEAUTIFUL LANDSCAPES

Strawberry Roulade

This is a smashing summer recipe from Antoinette Hughes, a talented cook and head of a domestic science department at a North Wales agricultural college. Although the dish looks quite substantial, it's in effect as light as a feather.

whites of 4 large eggs
6oz (175g) caster sugar
1oz (25g) flaked almonds
1 teaspoon cinnamon

For the filling
8fl oz (225ml) whipping cream
8oz (225g) fresh strawberries
3 tablespoons strawberry or orange liqueur

Serves about 6

Pre-heat the oven to Gas Mark 5, 375°F, 190°C. Line a 13in x 9in (32.5cm x 22cm) swiss roll tin with Bakewell paper.

Place egg whites in clean, grease-free bowl and whisk until standing in stiff peaks. Reserving 1oz (25g) of sugar, add remaining to the whisked whites a tablespoon at a time, whisking after each addition. Continue to whisk until thick and shiny.

Spread meringue into lined tin. Sprinkle over the flaked almonds. Mix together reserved sugar and cinnamon and sprinkle over almonds. Bake for 10–12 minutes or until firm to touch. Turn out on to sheet of Bakewell paper and leave to cool.

Whip cream until soft peaks are formed, then whip in liqueur. Spread flavoured cream over meringue and top with sliced strawberries.

From one long side, roll up the meringue and transfer to serving dish. Chill and decorate with a few slices of strawberries just before serving.

STICKY TOFFEE PUDDING

Lynda and Nigel Kettle run an imaginative and welcoming farm hotel at Ty'n Rhos Farm, Seion, not far from Caernarfon. Here is one of Lynda's puddings that always goes down well with her guests.

2oz (50g) butter
6oz (175g) granulated sugar
1 egg, lightly beaten
8oz (225g) plain flour
1 teaspoon baking powder
½ pint (300ml) boiling water
6oz (175g) stoned dates, chopped
1 teaspoon bicarbonate of soda
1 teaspoon vanilla

For the sauce
1½oz (35g) butter
2½oz (60g) brown sugar
2 tablespoons double cream

Serves 4

Grease an 11in x 7in (28cm x 17.5cm) cake tin. Pre-heat oven to Gas Mark 4, 350°F, 180°C. Whisk butter and sugar till light and fluffy. Add eggs and flour and blend till smooth.

Pour boiling water over the dates, add the bicarbonate of soda and vanilla and blend into the batter. Pour the mixture into the prepared tin and bake for 40 minutes.

To make the sauce, melt the butter, add sugar and cream and simmer for 3 minutes.

Cut the hot pudding into squares and cover with the sauce. Place under a hot grill until it bubbles on top and serve immediately.

SPICED PLUM TART

Yet another delicious recipe from Lynda Kettle of Ty'n Rhos Farm using plums in season and a mixture of yoghurt and sour cream.

5oz (150g) shortcrust pastry
8in (20.5cm) fluted flan tin, at least 1½in (3.6cm) deep
3–4lb (1.5–1.75kg) plums, stoned and halved
2 egg yolks
5fl oz (150ml) yoghurt
5fl oz (150ml) soured cream
1oz (25g) caster sugar
1 teaspoon cinnamon
2 tablespoons demerara sugar

Serves 5

Make pastry using as little water as possible. Leave to rest for ½ hour at room temperature. Line flan tin with pastry and chill for ½ hour. Bake in oven at Gas Mark 7, 425°F, 220°C for 10–12 minutes.

Arrange plums, cut side up on pastry. Whisk egg yolks, yoghurt, soured cream and caster sugar together. Pour over and around the plums. Mix cinnamon with demerara sugar and scatter on top of flan. Bake at Gas Mark 4, 350°F, 180°C for about ½ hour until filling is set.

Best served cooled.

Tarten Driog (Treacle Tart)

Here is another traditional Welsh recipe from the Blas ar Gymru restaurant in Cardiff.

For the pastry
225g (8oz) plain flour
100g (4oz) butter or butter and lard mixed
water to mix

For the filling
10oz (275g) golden syrup
7oz (200g) fresh white breadcrumbs
juice and rind of 1 large lemon
1oz (25g) demerara sugar
glacé cherries to decorate
8in (20.5cm) loose-based deep flan tin

Serves 6

Roll out the pastry on a floured work surface and use to line the flan tin, reserving the trimmings for the lattice. Chill while making the fillings. Set the oven at Gas Mark 6, 400°F, 200°C.

In a bowl, mix together the syrup, breadcrumbs, lemon juice and rind. Spoon into the pastry case and sprinkle with demerara sugar. Cut the pastry trimmings into long strips and arrange in a lattice on top of the tart. Cut the cherries in half and place cut-side down in the lattice diamonds. Bake for 30–35 minutes until pale golden. Unmould and serve warm.

Blackberry Bread Pudding

This autumn pudding of bread soaked in blackberry juice is wonderful, especially when the puddings are made individually so that you get to eat one all on your own!

8–10 slices thin, day-old bread, crusts cut off
juice of 1 orange
4–6oz (100–150g) caster sugar
2lb (900g) blackberries
1 tablespoon Cassis liqueur

Serves 6

Rinse a 1½–pint (900ml) pudding basin or 6 small ramekins with cold water. Cut a circle of bread to fit the bottom of the basin or ramekins and some wedge-shaped pieces to fit around the sides. Press bread firmly to line the basin so that there are no gaps. Keep a few slices of bread to cover the top.

In a small saucepan heat the orange juice and sugar, stir to dissolve. Add the blackberries and cook for a few minutes. Take off the heat and strain about 5fl oz (150ml) of the fruit juices.

Pour the fruit and remaining juices into the bread-lined bowl. Arrange the remaining bread over the fruit and cover with a saucer (or coffee cup for the ramekins) that fits snugly into the top of the bowl. Place a weight (I use a tin of baked beans!) on top of the sauce and leave overnight.

Next day turn the blackberry pudding out on to a large serving dish. Add the Cassis to the reserved blackberry juices and pour over. Serve with lashings of thick pouring cream.

SEE WALES THE WELSH RAREBITS WAY

Welsh Rarebits is a collection of 35 hotels and a group of farmhouses spread throughout Wales. It's a refreshing antidote to the standardised hotel chain. Welsh Rarebits is all about individuality, warm welcomes, character and service that comes with a strong personal touch.

How can we say that? All Welsh Rarebits hotels are small and personally owned, which goes a long way to explaining their high standards and distinctive characters. And all are hand picked for inclusion in the Welsh Rarebits scheme.

Bodysgallen Hall, Llandudno, one of Wales's leading country house hotels

The characterful Griffin Inn, Llyswen, close to the river Wye

There's no likelihood that you will confuse one Welsh Rarebits hotel with another. The Welsh Rarebits collection includes luxury country houses, old coaching inns, cosy farmhouses, converted mansions and historic houses - something for all tastes and pockets.

One of the few common features shared by all Welsh Rarebits hotels is value for money. Another is fine food. Wales's top chefs work at some of the hotels. Most are members of Taste of Wales.

Ty'n Rhos near Caernarfon is renowned for its food

Good fare at the Castle Hotel, Trecastle

Discover the *real* Wales by following the Welsh Rarebits trail.
For a copy of our free colour brochure please contact
Welsh Rarebits, EuroWales, Montgomery, Powys SY15 6HR.
Tel (0686) 668030. Fax (0686) 668029.

MUESLI

On a warm summer's evening, nothing could be nicer than a bowl of refreshing homemade muesli. Use all the fresh fruit in season and add yoghurt or fresh cream – whatever your waistline dictates.

1 pint (600ml) plain yoghurt or a mixture of yoghurt and single cream
Welsh honey to taste
1 tablespoon rolled oats
nuts to taste
lots of fresh fruit

In a large bowl, mix the yoghurt, cream, honey, oats, nuts and chopped fruit. Stir well to blend and chill.

Should there be any left after supper, serve it for breakfast!

MONMOUTH PUDDING

This recipe is similar to queen of puddings but I like to serve it in individual dishes so that everyone has their own little meringue to dip into.

grated rind of 1 lemon
2 tablespoons caster sugar
1oz (25g) butter
15fl oz (450ml) milk
6oz (175g) fresh white breadcrumbs
3 egg yolks
4–5 tablespoons raspberry jam or 4oz (100g) fresh seasonal fruit

For the topping
3 egg whites
3 tablespoons caster sugar
Serves 4

Add the lemon rind, sugar and butter to the milk and bring to the boil. Pour this mixture over the breadcrumbs and leave to stand for 15 minutes. Stir the egg yolks into the cooled bread mixture and spoon into 4 ramekin dishes. Spread a layer of jam or the prepared fresh fruit over the top.

For the meringue topping, whisk the egg whites till stiff, fold in the sugar, then swirl over the top of the ramekins.

Bake at Gas Mark 6, 400°F, 200°C for 10 minutes until crisp but not too brown on top. Serve at once.

APRICOT AND ARMAGNAC PUDDING

This recipe is similar to the French clafouti – fruit batter, in effect.

½ pint (300ml) skimmed milk
4 eggs, lightly beaten
2 heaped tablespoons plain flour
pinch salt
1oz (25g) soft brown sugar
4 tablespoons Armagnac
1½lb (750g) ripe apricots
freshly grated nutmeg
1oz (25g) unsalted butter
soft brown sugar (small quantity)
Serves 4–6

Pre-heat the oven to Gas Mark 5, 375°F, 190°C. Make up the batter. Using a liquidizer, add the milk, eggs, flour, salt, sugar and 2 tablespoons of Armagnac and whisk for a minute until smooth. Leave the batter for ½ hour.

Butter a 10–12in (25–30cm) flan dish. Stone and slice the apricots, arrange in the dish and spoon over the remaining Armagnac.

Stir the batter again and pour over the apricots, grate a little nutmeg on top and dot with remaining butter. Place on a hot baking sheet, bake for 40–45 minutes until just set and golden brown. Sprinkle with a little extra soft brown sugar. Serve warm with cream or Greek yoghurt.

Hazelnut and honey syllabub (see page 70) is the perfect way to end a meal of lamb steak with rosemary (see page 60)

Bara brith (see page 82) and welshcakes (see page 83)

BAKING

GELLI FAWR LOAF

Here is the recipe for Frances Roughley's marvellous mixed loaf which she makes at the Gelli Fawr Country House Hotel at Pontfaen, near Newport, Pembrokeshire. Serve it as an accompaniment to a main meal, with cheese, or just eat it on its own.

First make up 3 individual 1lb (450g) batches of bread dough:
1 – using blown flour, to which you must add 2 teaspoons of turmeric;
2 – using white dough;
3 – using white dough to which you must add 1 teaspoon chopped chives or mixed herbs.

3 tablespoons tomato purée or marmite
chopped walnuts or dried apricots
egg – to glaze
sesame seeds (optional)

Place the 3 prepared doughs in separate bowls to rise. Turn on to floured board, stacking the doughs on top of each other. Roll out into a large rectangle 24in x 12in (60cm x 30cm). It doesn't matter if the colours merge.

Spread the dough with 3 tablespoons tomato purée or marmite or sprinkle with chopped walnuts or dried apricots. Roll up like a swiss roll. Cut into 4 loaves. Glaze with brushed egg and sprinkle with sesame seeds.

Place in a greased loaf tin, cover and leave to rise for about 30 minutes. Bake at Gas Mark 6, 400°F, 200°C for 30–40 minutes.

BRYNGARW SEMOLINA ALMOND SLICE

This recipe from Jane Gratton at Bryngarw Guest House, Trefin, North Pembrokeshire, is always popular with all their visitors.

shortcrust pastry for base
apricot jam or any home preserve
4oz (100g) ground semolina
4oz (100g) self-raising flour
4oz (100g) caster sugar
4oz (100g) margarine
1 egg, beaten
$1/2$ teaspoon almond essence
flaked almonds

Line a swiss roll tin with short crust pastry. Spread over a layer of jam. Sift semolina and flour into a basin then add sugar. Rub in the margarine.

Add beaten egg and essence and mix to a stiff consistency. Roll this out on to the jam, using pastry trimmings to make a lattice on top. Sprinkle flaked almonds on top.

Bake at Gas Mark 4, 350°F, 180°C for 20–30 minutes.

BARA BRITH

Bara brith *literally means 'speckled bread' and was traditionally prepared at the end of the weekly bake. This recipe is used at the restored Felin Geri Watermill at Cwmcou, Newcastle Emlyn.*

1lb (450g) sultanas
12fl oz (325ml) milkless tea or orange juice
2 beaten eggs
4 level teaspoons baking powder
2 teaspoons mixed spice
1lb (450g) wholemeal flour
10oz (275g) demerara sugar
2 beaten eggs
milk

Soak the sultanas overnight in the tea or orange juice. Sift the baking powder and mixed spice into the flour and add to the sultanas with the sugar. Mix well and add eggs and sufficient milk to give a soft dropping consistency.

Divide the mixture between 3 greased and lined 1lb (450g) loaf tins and bake for 1–1½ hours at Gas Mark 3, 325°F, 160°C.

YOGHURT CAKE

Rachael's Dairy at Brynlls Farm near Borth produces organic yoghurt which must be good for us, even when we combine it with a few more fattening ingredients in this recipe for yoghurt cake.

6oz (175g) salted Welsh butter
6oz (175g) soft brown sugar
2 eggs
2 teaspoons finely grated lemon rind
8fl oz (225ml) natural yoghurt
8oz (225g) plain flour
½ teaspoon bicarbonate of soda
2 teaspoons baking powder
pinch of salt
icing sugar

Cream the butter and sugar till light and fluffy. Add eggs one at a time, stir in the lemon rind and yoghurt. Sift flour, bicarbonate of soda, baking powder and salt and fold into the cake mixture until well blended and smooth.

Bake in a 1lb (450g) prepared cake tin at Gas Mark 4, 350°F, 180°C for about 35 minutes or until the top of the cake is firm to pressure from a finger. Cool for 5 minutes then turn on to a rack. Dredge with icing sugar and eat while still warm.

The soft sponge is delicious if served with a bowl of fresh stewed fruit.

Chocolate Delight

Naughty but nice is the only way to describe this recipe, by Linda Whiticase of Highgate Farm, Newtown.

12oz (350g) rich tea biscuits
8oz (225g) margarine
4oz (100g) coconut
2 eggs
6oz (175g) soft brown sugar
2oz (50g) sultanas
6oz (175g) cooking chocolate

Serves 4

Place all the ingredients except chocolate in a medium-sized saucepan. Mix over low heat for 5–10 minutes. Spread on a swiss roll tin and cool in fridge for 1 hour.

Melt the chocolate in a basin over low heat or in the microwave and spread over the base. Cut immediately into fingers or squares.

Store in the fridge.

Pikelets

Perhaps you've come across Welsh pikelets in a bakery, thick and warm, piled high and studded with currants or coated with sugar.

2 eggs
$1/2$ pint (300ml) milk
3oz (75g) melted butter
4oz (100g) self-raising flour
2oz (50g) currants (optional)

Makes about 1 dozen

Beat the eggs with the milk and melted butter. Add the flour and beat to a smooth batter. Stir in currants.

Heat a griddle or heavy-based frying pan and lightly oil. Drop dessertspoons of mixture on to the griddle. Lightly brown one side, then turn over to brown the second side.

Serve hot with butter and a sprinkling of sugar to taste.

Welshcakes

These traditional little scones, no more than a moist mouthful, are wonderful. This recipe belongs to Meudwen Stephens of Upper Trewalkin Farm, near Llangorse in the Brecon Beacons.

8oz (225g) self-raising flour
pinch of salt
pinch of mixed spice
2oz (50g) margarine
2oz (50g) lard
3oz (75g) sugar
3oz (75g) currants and sultanas, mixed
1 egg

Sift together flour, salt and mixed spice. Rub margarine and lard into the mixture to resemble breadcrumbs. Add sugar and mixed fruit. Mix in egg to form a soft dough. Roll out to $1/4$in (5mm) thick and cut into 2in (5cm) rounds.

Bake on a hot griddle or a heavy-based frying pan. Grease with a little lard. Fry until lightly browned on both sides. Place on cooling trays to cool.

Serve sprinkled with caster sugar or spread with butter.

Quick Wholemeal Bread

This loaf is nutty and delicious – and good for you too. If you can, use flour from Y Felin Mill at St Dogmael's, just outside Cardigan in Dyfed.

2lb (900g) wholemeal or granary flour
4oz (100g) cracked kibbled wheat
1oz (25g) Welsh butter
1 teaspoon salt
1oz (25g) fresh yeast or dried equivalent
¾–1 pint (450–600ml) tepid water
1fl oz (25ml) Welsh honey or molasses
milk or beaten egg, to glaze
sesame seeds or poppy seeds
Makes 3 x 1lb (450g) loaves

Mix flour and wheat in a large bowl, rub in butter, stir in salt. Dissolve yeast, if fresh, in a little of the water (or if using a fast-acting dried, scatter over flour mix). Add yeast with the molasses or honey to the flour mix, adding enough water to give a moist dough.

Knead dough well for approximately 10 minutes – dough should be fairly wet. Cover and rest for 20 minutes in a warm place, until doubled in size. Knock back dough, mould into loaf tins, cover, and leave to rise for 30 minutes.

Pre-heat oven to Gas Mark 8, 450°F, 220°C. Brush loaves with milk or beaten egg, sprinkle over sesame or poppy seeds. Bake for 15 minutes then reduce oven to Gas Mark 4, 350°F, 180°C for a further 30 minutes or until risen and brown (bread should give a hollow sound when tapped underneath). Cool on a wire rack out of the tins.

Sesame Bread Buns

Lynda Kettle of Ty'n Rhos Farm Hotel near Caernarfon gave me this recipe for 20 delicious little sesame bread buns, which she says are just the right size to go with a bowl of homemade soup.

12oz (350g) stoneground brown flour
12oz (350g) stoneground wholemeal flour
1 packet easy-blend yeast
2 teaspoons salt
1½ fl oz (35ml) cooking oil
15fl oz (450ml) warm water and milk mix
beaten egg
sesame seeds

Toss the two flours together, mix in yeast and salt. Swirl in cooking oil, add warm liquids and mix to a soft dough, kneading well. Cover and leave to rise until doubled in size.

Grease a 20-hole Yorkshire pudding tin. Dividing dough into small egg-sized pieces, roll into a ball with palm of hand. Place into tins, brush with egg and scatter with sesame seeds. Leave to rise until well puffed up then bake in hottest setting of oven for 10 minutes.

Look out for Wales' best kept secret.

Prysg, Purely for pleasure.
NATURAL MINERAL WATER, FROM WALES

Prysg - Maesycrugiau, Pencader, Dyfed SA39 9DJ. Tel: 055 935627   Fax: 055 935444.

ON THE GOOD FOOD TRAIL
Brenda Parry
Dolgellau, September 1990

It was a daunting challenge to write a second guide in two years to the best restaurants in Wales, but as Chris Keenan from Swansea's premier restaurant put it, 'the food scene is literally bubbling over in the Principality.' And so it is. Any thoughts I might have had about covering old ground were quickly dismissed as I sampled the fruits of Wales in restaurants from Anglesey to Pembrokeshire, presented in tiny bistros, grand hotels, pubs and tea rooms, in ever new and exciting ways which are becoming the hallmark of Welsh cuisine.

If last year I struggled to find enough first-class restaurants amongst our members to feature in the guide, this year's problem has been in deciding who to leave out. It proved particularly difficult in North Wales, where good restaurants abound, although it wasn't easy in any of the regions where I found not only superb new restaurants, but many old favourites, forever striving for the increasingly high standards being demanded by Taste of Wales, by the Wales Tourist Board and, not least, by visitors who are flocking to Wales in their thousands on gourmet holidays.

Yes, our secret has been discovered by serious 'foodies' not just from the rest of Britain, but from all corners of the globe. Our restaurants are rightly enjoying the patronage of Americans, Australians, the Japanese and people from all over Europe. Only a few years ago visitors to Britain would not bother with Wales, not only because it was a long way from London, but also because they had heard the food and hotels were not all they might be. Today, like those of us who have the good fortune to live here, they are enjoying the culinary revolution that is quite literally taking Wales by storm.

For the convenience of residents and visitors who need at least four trips to Wales to fully appreciate the range and skill of our chefs, I have divided the country into four regions: South, West, Mid and North Wales, taking you through some of the most magical countryside before stopping for lunch, tea or that most special meal of the day, dinner, followed by relaxation in one of our fine country house hotels, farmhouses or cosy inns.

SOUTH WALES

The South Wales region is the most difficult to define in restaurant terms. While it includes our major cities and the bulk of the population, it is far from top of the pops when it comes to eating. However, there are some very good restaurants in both town and country, but they don't abound as they do in the north. Two stand out in my mind as being extra special - the Crown at Whitebrook and Keenan's in Swansea; two very different establishments with very different styles of cooking, but both achieving remarkable standards with superb local produce.

The *Crown*, once a pub and now a restaurant with rooms, was taken over by Roger and Sandra Bates nearly three years ago. It nestles in wooded countryside just 5 miles from Monmouth on the Gwent-Gloucestershire border, providing an ideal base for exploring this lovely unspoilt area. It's comfortable, cosy and friendly and, what's more, Sandra Bates's French cooking is quite some of the best I've sampled. She works almost single-handed in the kitchen producing fine French food daily, using the very best of Welsh produce supplemented with overseas specialities as supplied by Vin Sullivan. Go to any good restaurant in Wales, or for that matter throughout the British Isles, and you will hear Vin Sullivan's name mentioned. He supplies all the finest things that any good restaurateur cannot immediately lay his hands on, from fresh herbs to quails' eggs, lobster, smoked salmon, the best cheeses and, of course, tip-top fruits and vegetables.

SUTCLIFFE CATERING

Contract Caterer Supports Taste of Wales

One of the biggest contract caterers in the Principality, Sutcliffe, joined forces with Taste of Wales to help boost the demand for local produce. Its commitment to buying Welsh foodstuffs, backed with the strength of its bulk food purchasing, will be a boost to local food producers and also a major contribution to the quality image of food and catering in Wales.

Mr Simon Malloy, operations director of Sutcliffe Catering Wales said: "To get the best foods to our customers we are committed to buying local produce. We have always used Welsh butter, cheeses, meat and mineral water and together with Taste of Wales we are looking forward to supporting Welsh food producers even more."

The company masterminded a Special Taste of Wales Day – a spectacular culinary extravaganza to introduce more Welsh produce and dishes on its menus.

The celebratory lunch-time feast included offering customers delicacies from all over the Principality and incorporated a competition for its staff to ensure they were fully aware of the Welsh produce available and encourage them to use more local produce.

Based in Cardiff Business Park, Llanishen, Sutcliffe manages 46 catering units in South Wales which provide more than 1 million meals a day.

"Having a leading contract caterer like Sutcliffe giving its commitment to purchasing Welsh foodstuffs will help give Welsh produce the recognition it deserves," said Mr Christopher Pollard, Chairman of Taste of Wales.

The scenic Wye valley

But let's go back to the Bateses, who use tip-top quality everything to produce meals from fine breakfasts to exotic bar snacks and superb dinners. For such a small place, with its pub-style dining room, I thought the large menu was adventurous – on further inspection it seemed downright pretentious. In the event, dinner was one of the best I sampled anywhere in Wales – here, deep in the countryside, is an extraordinarily fine French chef, and on top of the imaginative French cooking there is not a choice of salad or vegetables: you get both.

To start I had a delicately flavoured and perfectly textured mussel soup with delicious green samphire grass and chunks of homemade bread. To follow came *mousse de brochet homard* – a mousse of pike topped with a mousse of lobster and served with a sauce made with Ricard and white wine. It was beautifully presented and came with a selection of crunchy vegetables and a salad of mixed leaves with a light vinaigrette dressing and pine kernels. Alternatively I could have had poached local salmon with a sauce of cream and brandy, fresh maize-fed chicken sautéed in butter and served in a cream, lime and tarragon sauce, with a crab mousse; or fillet steak covered with chopped mushrooms, tomatoes, onions and Roquefort cheese, baked in pastry and served with a red wine, cream and horseradish sauce, to mention but a few examples.

The pudding menu was equally impressive, but ever mindful of my increasing waistline I opted for the house sorbet, which was so beautifully presented and so delicious, I wished I was spending a week in this delightful *auberge*. The wine list here has to be seen to be believed – it is both long and exciting with a good choice of half bottles and bottles under £10.

Keenan's, owned and run by chef Chris Keenan, is a downtown restaurant in Swansea, hard by the city's magnificent Guildhall and located between an ice cream parlour and an Indian takeaway in the busy St Helen's Road district. From the outside it's just another of many restaurants in this street, but it's very much the one where serious 'foodies' eat. Walking inside is like walking into a colonial bar with overhead fans, elegant peach and green décor and lots of pine panelling and wrought-iron work. The mere surroundings suggest that this is a very special restaurant.

Very special usually means very expensive, but Chris Keenan cooks a mean two-course lunch for just £7.95 and a three-course dinner plus coffee and mints is just £18.95, with a speciality dinner of

Swansea's new Maritime Quarter

four courses, which might include lobster and fillet steak at £23.95. For me this is Wales's best city restaurant, with its relaxed atmosphere, excellent food and reasonable prices. Just a little example of Chris's cooking – the £7.95 lunch menu offered a choice of melon and avocado with a strawberry and elderflower dressing, salmon mousseline in a vermouth sauce served in a pastry shell or a sauté of mushrooms in soured cream and paprika, all beautifully presented. These were followed by noisettes of lamb *en croute*, mushrooms, tomatoes and a little garlic served with a tarragon *jus-lie* or a selection of fresh fish with a light mustard seed sauce served with fresh pasta noodles; and the helpful staff insisted that it was no trouble to serve the pasta noodles with a cheese sauce for my small daughter, who by this time had had her fill of fine Welsh fare.

She was very keen to try the next-door ice cream parlour which Chris had recommended, but was more than satisfied with ice cream à la Keenan. Chris assures me dinner time is even better! I only wish I worked at the Guildhall, then I could lunch at Keenan's every day.

The other lunch place in Swansea is Kate Taylor's *Green Dragon Bistro* where you can enjoy a truly Welsh experience of cawl or cockle and mussel pie followed by loin of pork with apple and Calvados in winter; or, in summer, sorrel soup or Pembroke oysters, followed by fresh local *sewin* (sea trout) with hollandaise or sea bass with laverbread and lemon. There's some very good French cooking too, but apart from special evenings, the restaurant, in the heart of Swansea, is only open for lunch.

The old bridge across the Usk at Crickhowell

But to get away from the cities again, *Ty Croeso* at Llangattock, near Crickhowell, is exactly what it says it is: 'The House of Welcome'. The feeling of warmth and friendliness the minute you go into this old stone house, which was once an infirmary for a workhouse, lets you know all is going to be well. Kate and Peter Jones do not pretend to run the grandest of establishments, but they are certainly running a happy ship in this delightful setting overlooking the canal and Crickhowell beyond. Although it's not terribly far off the Head's of the Valleys Road, it sits high above the beautiful Usk valley with ever-changing views of the Black Mountains. Even though it's some distance away, on a fine evening you feel you could almost reach out and touch the famous Sugar Loaf from the restaurant balcony.

Kate, who has a long catering background, is always there with a welcome and husband Peter, who teaches science in a local comprehensive, is invariably about in the evenings and at weekends when the hotel is at its busiest. The food, served in the airy and pleasant dining room with flowers from the garden, and also in the big friendly bar, is far from *haute cuisine*, but it's good and imaginative with a definite Welsh flavour. Try the local goat's cheese deep fried in breadcrumbs served with a raspberry sauce, followed by loin of pork steak with cider and apple and lots of fresh local vegetables; or perhaps lamb chops cooked with rosemary, garlic and cream; or local trout with hazelnuts and dill. If you stay at Ty Croeso then you must sample their Welsh breakfast of bacon, laverbread, Glamorgan sausage and tomato – delicious.

Cardiff's magnificent Civic Centre

And so back to the city, this time Cardiff, the capital of Wales, where there are an increasing number of good restaurants. Unfortunately I have room to write about only two, which is sad because more merit comment, but the two I visited are a must for anyone going to Cardiff or indeed living there.

The Armless Dragon in Wyvern Road, beyond Cathays, and De Courcey's at Pentyrch couldn't be more different and yet I can wholly recommend both. While De Courcey's is grand and stylized, the *Armless Dragon* is a mixture of so many styles and tastes that it's difficult to define. My young photographer companion described it as 'wacky' which seems as good an adjective as any.

From the outside of this backstreet restaurant it could be an Indian, a Chinese or perhaps a health-food restaurant; the cooking however is easier to define - it's excellent. Fresh fish abounds and you can choose the way it is cooked and which sauce you prefer. For instance, on the night we went the choice of hake, red snapper or monkfish was offered grilled, poached, pan fried, deep fried, baked with garlic and tomato, seasoned or fried with spicy tomato and red pepper sauce, *Bonne Femme* (with cream and mushrooms) or *Orientale* (in a lightly curried cream sauce with prawns). There's a standard menu offering the various cooking methods and some regular items, but a blackboard posts the daily choices of whatever is best and fresh from the local markets. Some of the fish comes from Paris or others, like the red snapper, from the Caribbean. Even the fillet steak comes with a choice of three sauces: red wine, garlic and mushroom, or peppercorns, brandy and cream. But vegetarians needn't despair – there's something for you too. My colleague chose a courgette, lentil and mushroom dish in a cheesy sauce, just one of David Richards's many concoctions for the non-meat and fish eaters.

With its red table cloths, pot plants and some thought-provoking art on the walls, this is the sort of restaurant we would all love to have just round the corner where

WALES TOURIST BOARD PUBLICATIONS & VIDEOS

WALES: HOTELS AND GUEST HOUSE GUIDE 1991 £2.50

A comprehensive guide to over 300 hotels, guest houses and farmhouses in Wales.

WALES: BED & BREAKFAST GUIDE 1991 £2.50

Guide to budget accommodation in Wales, featuring over 500 hotels, guest houses and farmhouses, all with one thing in common - they offer bed and breakfast at an all inclusive price of £16.00 or under per person per night.

WALES : SELF-CATERING GUIDE 1991 £2.50

Guide to over 250 self-catering properties in Wales, including cottages, flats and chalets, caravan holiday home parks and touring caravan and camping parks.

All publications include 5 mile to the inch full colour maps of Wales.

WALES TOURIST MAP 1991 £1.45

A real best-seller. Detailed 5 mile/1 inch scale, also includes a wealth of tourist information, town plans, suggested tours and information centres.

NOTE: All prices quoted include postage and packaging. *Please indicate clearly video format required when ordering. For copies of the above guides/videos write, enclosing the appropriate remittance, to Wales Tourist Board, Dept. TW, Distribution Centre, Davis Street, Cardiff CF1 2FU.

WALES: CASTLES AND HISTORIC PLACES 1991 £6.95

This full colour guide is a joint publication produced by the Wales Tourist Board and Cadw: Welsh Historic Monuments. More than 140 sites are covered in the extensive gazetteer, including castles, abbeys, country houses, Roman and prehistoric remains - all regularly open to the public. An historic introduction sets the scene, and 12 pages of maps help visitors to plan their routes.

THE WONDER OF WALES VIDEO (VHS)* £10.50

A new 24 minute video encapsulating the breathtaking beauty and myriad attractions of Wales. Narrated by Siân Phillips, the film features prominently the cultural and architectural heritage of Wales and includes the most recent visitor attractions in the Principality.

HERITAGE OF A NATION (VHS/BETA)* £10.00

Narrated by Richard Burton, this 25 minute video presents the Heritage of Wales from prehistoric times through to the present day. Wales as a holiday country is vividly depicted with some memorable sequences.

SOUTH WALES VALLEYS VIDEO (VHS/BETA)* £10.00

'The South Wales Valleys' (approx. 15 minutes) is a lively short presentation of the culture and heritage of the area.

BWRDD CROESO CYMRU
WALES TOURIST BOARD

you can chat, relax and enjoy really first-class cooking.

De Courcey's offers a different atmosphere. You can just glimpse the wonderful timber building – that was shipped from Sweden in 1894 – from the M4 as you drive east from Cardiff. Its history is interesting and varied, but today the former Tyla Morris House is De Courcey's, one of the most elegant restaurants in the south.

Thilo and Patricia Thielmann, who describe the splendidly restored house as homely, have to admit it is rather grand to be described so but, despite its elegance, the Thielmanns are constantly smiling and ever willing to advise on food and wine. The table settings are a joy to behold, as are the dishes when they arrive in the subtly lit dining room with tiny vases of fresh flowers on every table and beautiful arrangements of flowers all around the room.

Although I have come to the conclusion that it's nice to have vegetables served on the plate, the silver tureen of green beans, carrots, courgettes and tiny new potatoes in their skins, presented in the middle of our table, looked very good indeed, as did almost everything at De Courcey's. A starter of avocado, melon and strawberry with an infusion of fresh tarragon looked almost too good to eat as did the smoked meats *hors d'oeuvre* platter. Dare I say the baked brill on fresh pasta with a sweet-and-sour capsicum purée wasn't as good as I had anticipated – the fish lacked sheen and was chewy, but the sauce was delicious and the vegetables excellent. My colleagues enjoyed scollops of beef in three different sauces and a ragout of seafood in dry white burgundy. Never have I enjoyed a more delightful and delicious tasting summer pudding made in an individual mould. The fresh fruit sorbets were equally beautiful and good and the rhubarb and ginger creme brûlée was just right.

Cathays Park, Cardiff

West Wales

Cwm Tudu, one of the loveliest coves on Cardigan Bay

West Wales, with its magnificent coastline and gently rolling hinterland, struggles against all odds to support a flourishing catering trade in an area where the native population is so small. True, the region has long been a favourite with holidaymakers, but even with an extended holiday season that increasingly offers winter weekend breaks for over-stretched city dwellers, many hoteliers and restaurateurs are hard pressed to makes ends meet. Despite this, West Wales's restaurants are renowned for their fine sea food, their concern for special dietary needs and extremely competitive prices.

I could have been in French *auberges* as I sampled seafood platters presented with great panache and skill by chefs who, a few years ago, had never handled a lobster or dreamed of the opportunity of laying their hands on such a fine harvest from the sea. Even though much of our fine shellfish still finds its way to Paris and the markets of Europe, on the west coast at least, many chefs have ensured their pick of the catch by going down to the harbours themselves and bartering with the fishermen.

My journey west took me first to the *Park Hall Hotel*, a handsome Victorian villa overlooking Cardigan Bay at Cwm Tudu, just south of New Quay. Newcomers to the hotel business three years ago, Chris and Peter McDonnell are now fairly established as excellent hosts, producing fine local specialities for the table. Since the last guide they have built on an elegant conservatory which they use as the dining room, giving more space in the cosy bar and lounge for the pre- and after-dinner drinks and chats.

Chris, a florist, does most of the cooking herself and only wishes she could find a chef who would work to her own self-imposed exacting standards. She believes that every meal should be a special occasion. 'If people are paying to come here it's because they expect something special, as I do when I go out to eat,' she says. Most of the business here is residential. There are just five beautifully appointed bedrooms, all *en suite*, and more often than not they could do with double the number, although Chris concedes such an extension would drastically alter the intimate character of the hotel.

Chris and Peter are still attending courses at catering college, and both believe they have a lot more to learn. With a philosophy that says 'we must please our guests', they are on the right tracks. When I dropped by for lunch, as I headed for Pembrokeshire, I was offered mustard and mushroom soup with either a seafood platter – gleaming mackerel caught that morning and marinaded in olive oil, lemon juice and a bay leaf – or quiche with salad. I opted for the seafood platter expecting a small plate of shellfish. I was stunned by what arrived – a huge silver platter with lobster, green-lipped mussels, prawns and cockles arranged with edible flowers and served with a sharp, creamy dip and a beautifully arranged salad. What a way to start my journey west. The platter was enough to serve four and in the end Chris helped me out, insisting that I had to make room for the sweet – raspberries topped with a mixture of cream and yoghurt sprinkled with demerara sugar. The recipe had been given to Chris by a guest.

She tends to stick to John Tovey's recipes for her soups, such as cream of watercress and courgette and rosemary, but uses her own skills and imagination to serve organically grown local vegetables and the excellent meat and fish she obtains mainly from local sources or Vin Sullivan of Abergavenny. Favourites are whole baby salmon with gooseberry sauce, rack of Welsh lamb and leek and walnut quiche. I always want to stay at Park Hall – it's that sort of place where you book for a night and stay seven, not least to have a full Welsh breakfast served in your room. A word of advice: it's always best to book here.

But onwards along the coast to Pembrokeshire and to *Gelli Fawr* at Pontfaen, near Fishguard. It would be nice to keep Gelli Fawr a secret for a favoured few, but the secret is long since out and the lovely old country house hotel's fame has spread way beyond Offa's Dyke and into Europe.

Strumble Head near Fishguard

There's nothing grand or pretentious about the grey-stone farmhouse-style buildings; if anything some of the rooms are rather worn – a touch of faded splendour here and there, but you don't go to Gelli Fawr for the wallpaper and the plumbing, you go for the fine food and the contagiously relaxed and friendly atmosphere. A snack in the bar is an indication of what goes on in Frances Roughley's kitchen – homemade seafood pie, deep fried prawns with various mayonnaise dips, 'miser's feast' (potatoes, cheese, garlic and cream) or lentil rissoles with cucumber, yoghurt and mint. What Frances describes as 'The Seafood Experience' – a whole $1^1/_2$-pound lobster, a dressed crab, tigertail prawns with garlic and mayonnaise tartare dip, prawns with mayonnaise dressing and deep-fried crispy prawns served on a bed of salads, herbs and flowers plus new potatoes and a selection of salads and hot Gelli Fawr loaf with Nevern butter – requires a day's notice. The waiting must be 24 hours of sweet delight.

But given I had had ample seafood for lunch I succumbed to Cardigan Bay crab as a starter before tucking into beef and kidney pie in the most delicious puff pastry, which came with a selection of vegetables including potato galettes, deep-fried crispy leeks, beetroot and perfectly cooked cabbage. The whole thing would have served a family.

My nine-year-old who accompanied me on the tour of this region is always happy to choose from long exciting menus, but she was overjoyed when Anne Churcher, Frances's partner, produced the 'Hello younger guest' menu, which included properly produced nursery food from wicked Welshburgers to lovely lasagne or a bowl of homemade soup. I am assured the wicked Welshburger was much better than my humble hamburgers – perhaps I had better change the name. It really doesn't matter whether you are seven or 70, your every need is catered for *chez* Anne and Frances. The three-course dinners, at just £12.75, represent stupendous value with no extra charges for the loaf of very special Gelli Fawr bread.

Only five minutes along the road from Gelli Fawr is *Tregynon Country Farmhouse Hotel*, a traditional stone farmhouse with low oak beams, Welsh dressers and grandfather clocks – the town-dweller's dream of a country farm where comfort and cooking are the top priorities. The hotel was established as a rural retreat 10 years ago by Sheila and Peter Heard,

Porthgain's sheltered harbour

themselves escapees from the pressures of city life. Mrs Jane Cox, a professional woman from the Midlands and a former guest, runs the kitchen now, taking on board Sheila's many skills and bringing in new ideas of her own. Healthy eating is a priority here and every attempt is made to use produce which is additive and preservative free, much of it coming from surrounding farms. But if you think healthy eating is boring, then I suggest you try a meal at Tregynon Farm, which might include oak-smoked gammon ham, smoked in their own smokehouse, or local trout with a prawn and white wine sauce, or the vegetarian stuffed pancake. Frequently cooked by Peter, this latter treat is a light and frothy wholemeal pancake, stuffed with chopped nuts, cottage cheese, apple, celery and spice.

Since dinner had been pre-booked the following evening at Jemima's, I decided to make a surprise call on Annie Davies at the *Harbour Lights Restaurant*, Porthgain. Nobody could be better placed than Annie to corner the local fish market, for local fishermen come ashore just yards from her door. I never seem to strike lucky here - either they are closed or just closing, which should be a lesson to me and every potential diner to book in advance.

However, I was able to have a chat with this most charming of Liverpudlians in the true Cilla Black mould. She had worked in the property market in London before opening up the Harbour Lights, falling in love with and marrying a local farmer and then giving birth to twins. In between all this activity, she and her sister have established a reputation for being the best seafood restaurant in the area.

Opening times can be pretty erratic – 'that's one of the perks of being your own boss, Sweet,' says Annie – but looking at her menu and being well aware of the high standards of cooking in this tiny harbour outpost, I will book and get there one of these days to sample the laverbread and cockle crustade, or the mussel chowder followed by the whole Dover sole with fresh herbs grown in her mother-in-law's window boxes, or one of the special vegetable dishes created by Annie's sister. 'She's a vegetarian herself and cooks really yummy things. I do them too, but she's better in that area,' says Annie, who is busy preparing for the evening as I wait for National Breakdown to come and recharge my battery. It was one of those occasions when I wouldn't have minded if they had left me there until morning, even if I do find Porthgain just a little eerie. But then we had Jemima's and Ramsey House to look forward to.

Ramsey House is a smashing little guest house in St David's, where we stayed but didn't have a chance for dinner. Hard by St David's Cathedral, Sandra and Mac Thompson have taken Taste of Wales to their hearts. Sandra has researched old and new Welsh cookery books and produced her own very special brand of Welsh cuisine, using all the best available Pembrokeshire produce. She regularly makes 'Dragons eggs' (Welsh-style beef olives), Monmouth pudding and smoked trout pâté. She wouldn't let us leave without trying her Sunday rice pudding – even though it was Wednesday I would certainly go back for more. Sunday rice pudding, incidentally, is a rice and egg custard tart. The pastry said a lot about Sandra's cooking.

And so to *Jemima's* for dinner. Notwithstanding all the Beatrix Potter associations – Jemima's is on Puddleduck Hill at Freystrop, south of Haverfordwest – the thing that will forever stand out in my mind at this restaurant is the wholemeal bread and the melt-in-the-mouth yeast buns.

St David's Cathedral

Wolfscastle Country House Hotel between Fishguard and Haverfordwest

Ann Owston, who hails from Pembrokeshire, cooked for many years with her sister at Gibson's in Cardiff before the call of the west took her home. Her small, neat restaurant serves freshly prepared local food. The tiny pink cottage is a bit off the beaten track, but well worth seeking out for the small but interesting menu, which often includes duck, chicken with tarragon sauce or the dish I tried and enjoyed, sea bass cooked in a spinach parcel and a vermouth sauce. And the vegetables that night were all from Ann's own garden. The menu changes daily, offering a choice of at least four starters and main courses as well as a good vegetarian selection. You must read the wine list carefully here with notes by Ann's daughter, Wendy, who clearly not only knows a thing or two about wine but is more than anxious to impart her knowledge.

To end our tour of the west, we spent a night at *Wolfscastle Country House*, a greystone house that seems to have changed little for years. The dinner menu was not altogether exciting, and yet in the 1950s-style dining room with its beautiful flower arrangements and tinkling piano we enjoyed good English fare. There may have been little suggestion of anything overtly Welsh on the menu, but quite clearly the excellent vegetables were locally grown and many of the dishes inspired by local produce. The Sussex beef casserole with Guinness, port and ale was the real thing, as were the baby carrots, crisp cabbage and cauliflower. Pudding was a mousse of apricots with Cointreau in a delicious orange sauce, and the service, despite the large restaurant being quite full, was absolutely charming. At breakfast time there was excellent homemade muesli followed by free-range eggs and particularly good bacon.

Mid Wales

The river Wye near Builth Wells

Here beats the secret heart of Wales – mile after unspoilt mile of countryside with lakes and hills and a gentle tranquillity that comes with centuries of isolation from big cities and major trunk roads. You have to make a real effort to get to this remote area of Wales, but one which is truly worthwhile for a weekend or more in Britain's best rest and relaxation country.

It is perhaps a little unfair on long-established hotels to dwell on a new one, but it is interesting to note that Sir Bernard Ashley has chosen this area just north of Brecon for his latest multi-million pound venture – *Llangoed Hall*, a superb country house hotel that within months of opening its doors last June won the *Good Hotel Guide's* award as the best newcomer of the year.

A glimpse inside reveals why. This has got to be the finest hotel in Wales – the house, the décor, the gardens, the staff and, for our purposes, particularly the food. How gratifying to find such a fine house with food that does it justice. But then Sir Bernard, or B A as he is known to his staff, would not sink £3$^{1}/_{2}$ million of his personal wealth into something without ensuring that it was the best. As a sure indication that he was well pleased with the result, he held his wedding reception here.

He had looked long and hard for the right place in which to fulfil his dream of recreating the perfect Edwardian country house. One flight over Llangoed Hall in its derelict state in 1988 was sufficient to convince him that this was the perfect house in the perfect setting. Less than two years later the hotel of his dreams was winning awards. The hall is believed to have been built on the site of the first Welsh parliament. It was designed in 1913 by Clough Williams-Ellis, the creator of Portmeirion. He incorporated into his design part of a Jacobean mansion built on the site in 1632. It was a fine example of an Edwardian country house, but years of neglect had taken their toll when Sir Bernard took over with the intention of recreating the elegant house-party scene of the '20s.

I suspect what he has done is create an even more stylish way of living, but whatever, a week here would set up any high-powered businessman or woman for dealing with another pressured year. It is like walking into a different world – a world of friendly informality, of comfort, luxury and concern. The staff blend in with the elegant surroundings, doing everything they can to ensure a memorable visit.

But I digress, I am here to write about the food, which is served in the sumptuous Laura Ashley-style dining room, with its high-backed yellow and blue upholstered chairs and magnificent views across the lawns. It is good to go to a fine hotel where the cuisine is of a standard to match the beautiful surroundings. The appointment of Mark Salter, previously chef at Cromlix House in Scotland, back in January was an indication of the standards that would be expected in the kitchen. He immediately went into action appointing his staff and finding the best suppliers of fine food. One of his first tasks was to supervise the planting of a large and formal herb garden just outside the kitchen window and, beyond it, a vegetable garden, both of which were producing by June.

The lunchtime menu at £17.50 is short, with only two choices at each course, but excellent. We enjoyed cream of artichoke soup with chicken quenelles followed by fillets of lemon sole with char-grilled scallops, deep-fried courgettes, saffron potatoes and a tomato and basil sauce; and rosettes of Welsh lamb with kidneys, ratatouille, potatoes dauphinoise and a rosemary sauce. Both dishes were served with their vegetables on the plate. I am so tired of those crescents of vegetables with the same selection whatever meal you have selected. Salter's way means you not only

Sumptuous Llangoed Hall, near Llyswen

Stop off at the Griffin, Llyswen

get the vegetables that best complement your meal, you also get them the way the chef chooses to present them.

A pudding of caramelized apple tart with vanilla ice cream sounded fairly ordinary, but was extremely good and the selection of British cheeses with homemade biscuits was just what it should be. It almost goes without saying that excellent canapés were served before lunch and mouthwatering *petit-fours* afterwards.

The six-course dinner at Llangoed is about £32.50, but if you would like to pop in and see if it is worth saving up for this gourmet feast, then go between 3 and 5pm for afternoon tea in the elegant drawing room and choose from a selection of dainty sandwiches and delectable cakes, all served with the tea of your choice for just £7.50.

Fresh salmon is the speciality at the *Griffin Inn* at Llyswen, just over a mile away from Llangoed Hall, on the busy A470. The Griffin is a long-time favourite with the fishing fraternity. Travellers on the busy north-south road have now also discovered the fresh fish on the menu, not to mention the wide range of other beautifully cooked foods that won't break the bank. Lunchtime and dinner time are equally popular and you can stop off here at almost any time of day for excellent coffee.

It is a small, friendly pub which serves lunchtime meals in the bar and dinners, of much the same excellent fare, in the cosy restaurant. Salmon and trout are way and above the favourite choice here, but they do things like ratatouille *au gratin* and delicious puddings including treacle tarts, fruit pavlovas and sorbets. The Griffin is one of half a dozen or so really first-rate eating places in Wales with the exceptional advantage of being on a main route.

To continue with country house hotels,

here are two very special ones in lakeside locations, both built shortly after the turn of the century – the Lake Hotel at Llangammarch Wells and the Lake Vyrnwy at Llanwddyn. The *Lake Vyrnwy*, sitting at the end of the great lake that supplies water for the people of Liverpool, has probably the most breathtaking view in Wales, looking down the lake to the Gothic water tower that resembles a fairytale castle – it's magical on a still summer's day and quite daunting when the mists hug the hills and dark clouds hover overhead. I might not go out of my way for dinner here, but I would happily spend a weekend or more, for the hotel is a warm and friendly place with beautifully comfortable public rooms and bedrooms and the food is good, substantial fare if not *haute cuisine*. Prices, too, are very reasonable.

The *Lake Hotel*, at Llangammarch, is a deceptively large hotel and is always busy with fishermen, birdwatchers and townsfolk anxious to escape from the city. In the years that the present owners, the Mifsuds, have been there, the place has

The Lake Hotel, Llangammarch Wells

been transformed. There are less bedrooms but more suites and, despite the size of the public rooms, they are warm and welcoming as are the couple themselves. Here I enjoyed a particularly good fresh salmon and herb terrine set on a watercress and mixed-herb mayonnaise, followed by poached lobster and monkfish glazed with a saffron hollandaise sauce. A pudding of brandy snap with apricot and stem ginger, served with apricot sauce, was good and tangy.

The magnificently located Lake Vyrnwy

Further north are two more country house hotels: the long-established Minffordd at Talyllyn and the recently re-established Dolmelynllyn Hall at Ganllwyd near Dolgellau.

Jo Barkwith at *Dolmelynllyn*, and Jonathan Pickles at the Minffordd, both started their catering training at Westminster. Jo, however, went on to Switzerland which is probably why her menu is more for the adventurous than the traditional fare at the Minffordd. The Barkwith family came to Wales from Cornwall and find the people here much friendlier than in the south-west. Jo, the daughter, does all the cooking and hence the menu is short, but exceedingly good. The deep-fried venison sausage with redcurrant, orange and port sauce was delicious, followed by melon and ginger water ice and then a superb ragout of monkfish, scallops and prawns with a grape and vermouth sauce, served on a bed of rice. The fish was tender and sweet, the sauce delicate and tasty – an altogether nicely rounded course served with mangetout, beetroot and potatoes dauphinoise.

I didn't think Jo's sticky toffee pudding was as good as I have eaten elsewhere (it does seem to be a favourite pudding in Wales at present) but the peaches in white wine with cinnamon cream and hazelnut shorties were first-class, and the cheeses that followed, particularly the properly served Stilton, were also to be commended. Jon Barkwith, a cheery man who loves to chat with his guests, prides himself on his fine wine list and is always happy to recommend something appropriate, although you can't go wrong here with the house wines. As at the best hotels, they served coffee or a choice of teas after dinner.

The *Minffordd Hotel*, in its superb mountain location, is an all-round hotel geared to complete relaxation, serving good, fresh food. Jonathan Pickles's Welsh onion soup was an excellent starter, with the alternatives of avocados, prawns with mayonnaise or simply served Ogen melon. The roast loin of Welsh lamb with

The Minffordd Hotel, Talyllyn, stands beneath Cader Idris

Shrewsbury sauce was sweet and tender, though the freshly poached salmon could have done with a tastier sauce than the very plain béchamel I had with it, but there were nice big dishes of vegetables – leeks, cabbage and cauliflower and our own tureen of potatoes in cheese and cream followed by a choice of Jonathan's nursery puddings.

For me the meal was rather plain, but enjoyable nevertheless, in this low-beamed one-time coaching inn, now filled with comfy sofas and nice pieces of antique furniture, and with the Pickles family friendly and attentive to our every need. Again, another place where it would be rather nice to stay the week.

Rural Mid Wales is not without towns, so if during your country holiday you feel like some stylish downtown eating, then head for Dolgellau, the largest town in the Snowdonia National Park, which boast one of the best bistros in Wales. A young Welshman with a pigtail, Dylan Rowlands, who took over the long-established Petite Auberge three years ago, immediately gave it a Welsh name – *Dylanwad Da* (Dylan's good influence) – and introduced his own style of Welsh cuisine.

It was an immediate success with the local Welsh-speaking community, but, equally important for Dylan, tourists have returned repeatedly to enjoy his excellent meals at unbeatable prices. Twenty pounds will buy two people three good courses which might include beetroot and ham soup, pork with pear – slices of pork sautéed with dessert pear, flambéed in pear brandy, and finished with cream – to be followed by a mouthwatering choice of puddings or excellent Welsh cheeses and biscuits.

With its spartan pine tables with red paper cloths, adorned only by vases of fresh

Dolgellau is a good touring centre from which to explore the heights of Snowdonia

flowers, this is quite my favourite local restaurant. The menu, which changes about every six weeks, offers a choice of five starters and six or seven main courses, always including a vegetarian dish, fish, and steak served in various ways. My own favourite dish this year was the vegetarian pancakes – wholemeal herb pancakes, one filled with ratatouille, the other with spinach and cream cheese – served with a tomato and orange sauce. Dylan has done wonders in Dolgellau and brought local people out to eat who would have never considered doing so before.

Teas should always be a treat on holidays, and for tea, coffee and the best cream cakes this side of Offa's Dyke then there is no better place than Sue and Allan Griffiths's *Old Coffee Shop* at Aberdovey. Sue is expecting her first baby in 1991 so forgive the couple if there is a momentary lapse in standards around Easter time when Sue will have to stand back for a week or two at least, but I have no doubt that she will be keeping a watchful eye on the reputation she has worked so hard to establish. The coffee shop also serves excellent meals.

North Wales

Plas Bodegroes, near Pwllheli, has an outstanding reputation for its food

If you love to be in the mountains and by the seaside, and at the same time want all the benefits of country house living, then there's no better place than North Wales. In recent years this area of dramatic scenery and beautiful coastline has become a paradise for lovers of fine food and stylish living.

It was here that Chris Chown was to establish Plas Bodegroes, the winner of Taste of Wales's Best Restaurant Award in 1989, and in my view still the best restaurant in Wales. However, there are many chefs in pursuit of Chown's status and in North Wales alone he faces considerable competition from the restaurant at Tyddyn Llan, Llandrillo, the Bull's Head at Beaumaris and the Meadowsweet at Llanrwst. All are remarkably fine restaurants with chefs in the top league, who are using Welsh produce at its very best.

Chown describes *Plas Bodegroes* as a restaurant with rooms, placing the emphasis on the dining room rather than the bedrooms, for the bijou manor house has only five bedrooms while the dining room will accommodate 40. The five-course dinner served nightly, except Tuesdays, with four or five choices of each course is, as a friend of mine suggested, 'a poem of a meal' and certainly there are many who have waxed lyrical after eating here. Strangely, in most restaurants, perhaps months after I have eaten there, I can recall one course or another as being particularly outstanding. At Chown's it is the memory of a perfect meal, beautifully prepared, beautifully presented and perfectly balanced – no question of that heavy feeling in your tummy as you go happily to bed or begin a long drive home. I hate to be quite so fulsome in my praise, but I literally couldn't fault a thing in the elegant green dining room which displays some rather good paintings on the walls by a number of Welsh artists.

Perhaps I was unadventurous in choosing the fresh vegetable soup, but for me soup says a lot about a kitchen, and indeed it said what I had anticipated, that this was just the start of something good. My husband chose the smoked salmon parcel of crab meat with pineapple and avocado salad served on a bed of *lollo rosso*, with a delicate dressing. I am assured it tasted as good as it looked. Then came a mousseline of scallops with tomato and coriander, another delicious work of art, and a selection of grilled seafood with a mouthwatering lime hollandaise.

The main course offered roast duck, braised partridge, grilled fillet of beef, char-grilled kebab of lamb and sea bass (caught that morning). My husband chose the grilled fillet of beef with a mushroom and pepper crust in a port sauce, served with baby carrots, parsnips and potatoes dauphinoise. I couldn't resist the Welsh lamb, the quality of which was incredible throughout 1990. The tender chunks of meat were served with ratatouille and garlic cream. It was good to have the vegetables on the plates and totally complementary to the food. Not many restaurants do this. There was a cheese course – a fine selection of Welsh and French cheeses served with biscuits and home-baked walnut bread, or grilled goat's cheese with walnut and celery salad or mature Colston Bassett Stilton. I missed out on this but my husband sampled the grilled goat's cheese which was very good.

Maybe I should have foregone the pudding, too, but I much enjoyed the fresh figs mulled in port and orange with delicious homemade white chocolate and banana ice cream and I also had to try just a little hazelnut meringue of strawberries and cream with praline ice cream. Served by Chris's charming Scandinavian wife, we couldn't have wished for a better meal. From the pre-dinner nibbles to the after dinner sweetmeats, it was a treat not to be missed.

But North Wales is full of sweet surprises. At the *Old Bull's Head* at Beaumaris, Anglesey, I had quite the best

The Old Bull's Head, Beaumaris

The Isle of Anglesey is linked to mainland Wales by two road bridges

lamb I have ever tasted. Chef Keith Rothwell, who was cooking fine food in Wales long before it became fashionable to do so, said it had been a vintage year for lamb, but few could cook it, however good, the way he had. He offered fillets of lamb wrapped in leeks, coarse-grain mustard and a fine puff pastry. The meat was pink, juicy and tender and the finest flavour you could wish for.

The Old Bull's Head is a dream of an old-world inn, equally popular with the locals and those who jam at the bridges from the mainland on Fridays and Saturdays to eat at the upstairs restaurant, with its low oak beams and copper pots and pans. There's an excellent menu with daily specials of locally caught fish and game in season, and there's a comfy, chintzy lounge for residents and diners, but many prefer the cheery bar for pre-dinner drinks, reserving the comfort of the lounge for coffee. A cassoulet of local seafood with cream, white wine and saffron, and parcels of smoked salmon with yoghurt and dill dressing proved to be excellent starters. A vegetable terrine of broccoli, carrots and spinach served with the lamb was colourful and tasty – 'that's thanks to the excellent vegetables we get from Jones and Hunt in Upper Bangor,' says Rothwell, who is always reluctant to take the credit for his excellent food.

The inn is run on very professional lines by David Robertson, who looks after the administration. David and Keith met while training in Cheshire and set up business together at the Seahorses in Port Dinorwic, back in 1976. They bought the Bull's Head in 1987. There's real food in the bar at lunchtime and superb dinners in the upstairs restaurant.

But the Bull's Head isn't the only good pub in the area. Robert Cureton and his wife run a fine establishment at the *Queen's Head* in the tiny village of Glanwydden. There's a big and ever-changing menu which always includes good fresh fish, and a selection of puddings that would be the envy of many fine hotels. The atmosphere here is informal, and I'm sure the beer is good, but most customers come here for the food. It's always busy and you are lucky to get a table to yourself at lunchtime, even in midwinter when locals will find any excuse for a drive from Llandudno to this rather difficult-to-find spot. On a cold day try the liver in onion gravy or noisettes of Welsh lamb with a plum and port wine sauce, but when the sun shines, they serve superb salmon, crab and lobster to be followed perhaps by peach and passion fruit soufflé, chocolate fudge pie or even spotted dick with custard.

Llandudno is Wales's most beautiful seaside resort. Arguably it is Britain's best, but undoubtedly *St Tudno's* is the best seaside hotel on British shores. It offers all the benefits of a country house with all the thrill of being right on the seafront opposite the famous pier. This beautiful Victorian town house with its elegant lounge, pure cotton sheets and garden restaurant was started from scratch by Janette and Martin Bland on return from their honeymoon in 1972. A former convalescent home, the house had stood empty for years. The newlyweds scrubbed, cleaned and bought second-hand furniture to open for business within a few weeks. In those days Martin did the cooking, learning as he went along. From the word go they played to packed houses, in the days when the Brits took their annual seaside holidays along their own shores.

Much has changed since those early times. There is now a team in the kitchen headed by David Harding and it doesn't matter what time of day you might drop in at St Tudno's, there's always something good to eat, no question of it not being meal time. Martin doesn't cook any more and Janette doesn't serve or scrub, but they are both always busy seeing to the details that make this hotel so special.

St Tudno's, Llandudno, is a stylish seaside hotel

Llandudno's seafront, framed between two headlands

Dinner, naturally, is the main meal of the day in the green and yellow garden room. We enjoyed chilled galia melon served with blackberries and *can y delyn* liqueur which was served so beautifully it looked almost too good to eat, and an excellent curried parsnip and carrot soup with cream and croutons, followed by a tasty vegetarian dish of sweet red peppers filled with braised rice, celery and walnuts, and breast of chicken with leeks and vermouth sauce. Puddings were rich and delicious and there was a superb selection of Welsh farmhouse cheeses to follow.

Driving inland again you might like to have lunch or tea at *Bodnant Garden's* lovely new café and book dinner at the *Old Rectory*, owned and run by Wendy and Michael Vaughan. Although it's across the river, the house seems to sit on the doorstep of Conwy Castle, providing the ideal base for those who love superbly comfortable surroundings and fine food.

Conwy Castle looms above a picturesque quayside

The house has only four letting bedrooms, all of them beautifully appointed, and guests share the same elegant dinner table to enjoy Wendy's excellent cooking. There's an impressive set menu every evening although special dietary needs are always met. Unfortunately I didn't eat with the Vaughans, but I am assured the cooking matches the splendour of the

The Old Rectory, near Conwy

The Meadowsweet Hotel, Llanrwst

Georgian surroundings and that the Old Rectory is also open to non-residents. It's the ideal place for special dinner parties. The breakfast menu looks pretty good here with smoked haddock, trout or kippers, a Welsh grill, Welsh rarebit, Welsh cheese with boiled ham and, of course, freshly squeezed orange juice served in crystal glasses to match the old-world elegance and style of this delightful Welsh home that takes guests.

Following the Conwy valley southwards we came to Llanrwst and the imposing, if not altogether beautiful, *Meadowsweet Hotel* run and owned by John and Joy Evans. The couple are very conscious of the fact that the house is on the main road, but feel quite rightly that once they can lure guests over the doorstep they have won the battle. Inside it is a charming, comfortable house where guests are immediately made to feel at home by Joy while John, a self-taught chef, creates wonders in the kitchen.

When we went on a fine summer's night we enjoyed delicate canapés as we perused the short but exciting menu, choosing first of all gravadlax – John cures the salmon himself with brandy, sea salt and dill and presents it beautifully with fresh edible flowers and local scallops, cooked to perfection and served with a tasty Provençal sauce. For the main course we both had fillet steaks of Welsh lamb on garlic croutons with a rosé wine sauce. The meat was pink and tender, the sauce delicious. The vegetables were also a delight – a tiny tartlet of whipped parsnip, potatoes dauphinoise, broccoli and carrots. Sorbets and a wonderful selection of cheeses completed an excellent meal.

Despite its position on the main A470, the views from the front windows of the house look out on to a tranquil pastoral scene of sheep grazing on the fields of the Conwy valley. Being on the main route north the hotel is perfectly located for all parts of Snowdonia and the North Wales coast. The Evanses, who have four children of their own, now grown up, make youngsters particularly welcome, providing for all their needs.

All the restaurants I have talked about so far have been in the county of Gwynedd but my final choice in the north, and a particular favourite of mine, is in Clwyd. The restaurant in the lovely grey-stone country house of *Tyddyn Llan*, in the village of Llandrillo between Bala and Corwen, is not only one of the finest in the area, it is also one of the least expensive.

Tyddyn Llan, Llandrillo

When we went in September, a three-course dinner was just £17.50, a good £2 less than most of its rivals. Peter and Bridget Kindred, who opened the hotel back in 1984, go from strength to strength. They extended both the dining and sitting room areas in 1990 and created a beautiful Victorian verandah, ideal for their special afternoon teas or for summer's evening drinks. The new blue dining room, designed by Peter, formerly a television set designer, more than doubles the dining capacity and complements the extremely fine food at this beautiful hotel. I have dined here on a number of occasions and have never been disappointed, but an inspection meal I had there was the best to date.

It was a difficult choice to make from the extensive menu of six items at each course, but what stands out in my memory is the superb thinly sliced fillet steak served on a potato galette with garlic and a fresh tarragon sauce. My husband had the fillet of fresh local salmon and laverbread, wrapped in a filo parcel and served with a

Tyddyn Llan is located close to Bala Lake

prawn and lobster sauce, while our daughter chose the lamb cutlets, pan fried and served deliciously with a caramelized onion and a mint hollandaise. But I haven't mentioned the starters. The *moules mariniéres* were superb as was the smoked Tay salmon and fresh prawns with a tomato cognac sauce. Our nine-year-old, who has aspirations to becoming the youngest editor of the *Good Food Guide*, felt that the honey in a concoction of avocado pearls, Greek yoghurt and fresh mango wrapped in aired, dried Cumbrian ham, made the dish a trifle too sweet.

She also realized she had made a mistake with the Continental chocolate pots with Drambuie which she swapped for my strawberries and a light chocolate mousse. I actually preferred the lighter mousse, but the rich, sweet chocolate pots garnished with a strawberry and a kumquat were delicious, if a little rich for my palate. My husband was sensible for once and chose the excellent cheese board served with big black grapes and celery.

There were so many other restaurants I would like to have visited in North Wales, but I think I have managed to give you a little glimpse of what's on offer in this most dramatic of Welsh regions.

You'll travel through magnificent countryside on your tour of North Wales

Our butter is freshly churned from Welsh Cream. It's specially selected to carry the Welsh Country Foods symbol.

For more information on this and the other quality dairy products in our range, together with details of your nearest stockist, please ask the operator for Freephone 2376.

BECOMING A SUCCESSFUL CHEF

BRENDA PARRY

There are, as Richard Binns has remarked, many talented people working in hotel and restaurant kitchens throughout Wales. Welsh cuisine has been transformed over the last decade thanks to innovative, creative chefs making the best of fresh local produce.

Apart from a dedication to excellence, the leading lights of the Welsh cooking scene have little in common. Some are self-taught, others have served apprenticeships in the catering trade before setting up on their own. Some have been involved in cooking since their teens, others have come to it later in life. Offering career guidance to would-be professional chefs is therefore fraught with danger – there is no single road to success, as you will see when you read of the seven very different routes described in this chapter.

Sandra and Roger Bates at the Crown, Whitebrook

A woman chef who wants to be taken seriously

Sandra and Roger Bates are new to the hotel business, which could explain their enthusiasm and attention to detail. Roger, a former business executive with a retail chain, clearly enjoys his new role as host at this beautifully situated restaurant with rooms on the Gwent-Gloucestershire border near Monmouth; while Sandra is blazing a trail for women chefs in Wales with her fine haute cuisine-style French cooking.

She is a trained chef with exacting standards, but she feels frustrated that women chefs are not taken seriously. 'I get patronizing glances and positively disappointed looks when I tell guests that my wife does the cooking,' says Roger, although he is relieved that the praise is *anything but patronizing after dinner.*

Over the years, Sandra, mother of two teenagers, has worked in executive dining rooms and before taking over the Crown had a successful bed and breakfast business in the Cotswolds. But Roger wanted a change of direction and more time to spend with his wife and family. 'I certainly see more of my family now; whether I actually spend more time with them is questionable.' Running a hotel with little help from outside is a labour-intensive business, and as any successful restaurateur will tell it is the early years when the strain is the greatest. Roger and Sandra reckon they are lucky if they get to spend Monday afternoons together. When I dined there in August she was desperately seeking the right sous chef. 'Things have to be done my way which probably means I will have to train someone from scratch, but even finding someone with the right attitude is difficult,' she said.

At present it is those very exacting standards she sets herself and a burning ambition to be amongst the top chefs in Wales that keep her busy from dawn until almost midnight – a routine she presumably cannot keep up forever. She makes everything that is served in the charming pub-style restaurant as well as the ever-changing bar snacks.

The Crown, set in the gently undulating border country of the Wye valley, used to be a pub but changed to become a restaurant with rooms several years before Roger and Sandra took over what was a very run-down business. 'It was dreadful at first,' Sandra confesses. 'I used to spend all day in the kitchen preparing the menu and nobody came. We used to sit and look at one another wondering if it would ever come right.'

But news of fine food travels fast in these parts and Roger's associates, somewhat bemused by his new venture, came first to see what the Crown was like and now come back with their friends. 'Thankfully we now have quite a lot of regulars – refugees from Newport and Cardiff and others from much further afield seeking a rural retreat and good food,' says Sandra.

The Crown is open daily serving bar snacks, dinners and Sunday lunches, but don't expect Sandra to produce roast beef and two veg; even Roger has to go elsewhere should he fancy such simple fare.

I'm sure by now Sandra realizes that her efforts to produce such imaginative French-style cooking with first-class Welsh produce is more than appreciated in an area not overblessed with good eating places.

Mark Salter and Tom Ward at Llangoed Hall, Llyswen

A country house with professionals at the helm

Most of the best hotels are those run and supervised by their owners. Llangoed Hall, Wales's newest and grandest country house hotel, is a rare exception where the very best professionals to be found were brought in to run the show. Sir Bernard Ashley, chairman of Laura Ashley, spared no expense in renovating the beautiful old house designed by Clough Williams-Ellis back in 1913 and likewise money was no object when choosing the men who would launch it. Head chef, Mark Salter from Cromlix House in Scotland, at 28 has won more awards and appears to have more experience and style than many twice his age. And to cap it all he's grown a moustache to convince people he really is 28, for in truth he looks little more than 18.

A calm, seemingly relaxed young man who likes things to run smoothly in his superb new kitchen, he appreciated the opportunity to take up his post months before the hotel opened, ensuring that he could establish all the best supply lines and employ the right kitchen staff to assist him. He has taken on as many as he can from the local community, but one assistant he didn't have to look far for was a pastry chef. That post is filled by his girlfriend Ailsa Pears who came with him from Scotland. Ailsa is responsible for the mouth-watering teas served in Llangoed's elegant drawing room. Warm scones with jam and cream, brandy snaps filled with cream, strawberry tarts and banana and walnut cake are just a few of the delights you can expect to be offered. Mark is one of a growing band of chefs intent on winning awards for his own special brand of cooking and for his hotel.

At the helm is Scotsman Tom Ward, at 40 a veteran of the grand hotel circuit. An immaculate man of great charm, he is the perfect host in this magnificently restored mansion. He trained at the Bell Inn at Aston Clinton before beginning his career at the Commodore Hotel in Stonehaven, Scotland in 1970. He moved about in Scotland before going to the Blue Boar at Cambridge and then as the assistant manager to the domestic bursar's office at Emmanuel College, Cambridge before moving north again. Eventually he became general manager at Invery House, Banchory and from there he came for the first time to Wales to take up 'a very exciting challenge'.

Tom is one of those canny Scots who seems to know instinctively what is required and if he thinks Sir Bernard is getting things wrong, he doesn't hesitate to tell him, diplomatically, of course. For instance, he didn't insist but politely suggested that a hotel should always have wall-to-wall carpets in the bedrooms rather than exposed wooden floors, however beautiful. Wall-to-wall carpets have been ordered and the shaver points in the beautiful bathrooms were replaced because Tom considered them more suitable for a cheap hotel chain.

Which just goes to show that even with £3$^1/_2$ million to spend you can still get some things wrong. But I doubt that guests will find much to fault at Llangoed Hall, not while Tom Ward holds sway and Mark Salter heads the kitchen team. Arthur Miller, who dropped by during the Hay-on-Wye Literature Festival, conceded: 'A nice place!' I would go further – it's a very nice place.

Anne Churcher and Frances Roughley at Gelli Fawr, near Fishguard

The perfect partnership

Anne and Frances describe Gelli Fawr as 'pure self-indulgence', doing what they want in one of the most beautiful spots in Wales. Fortunately for the rest of us what they want seems to be what so many of us are seeking in the perfect holiday – a friendly relaxed atmosphere in a totally informal setting where the food is quite outstanding.

Dogs and cats flop around the place, a pony pokes his nose over the stable door and the chances are that in the summertime you will be served your meal by a student in shorts.

Things are so laid back it is hard to imagine the frantic activity that goes on in the kitchen preparing the treats from homemade ice cream to seafood experiences that make a visit here so memorable.

Frances is the chef and Anne looks after the administration of this charming greystone farmhouse hotel, which also has self-catering accommodation in the stone barns that surround the outdoor swimming pool. A long time ago Anne and Frances had been neighbours in a Hertfordshire village. Frances was then a lecturer in catering at a local college. Some years later Frances and her husband Rob were seeking a change of direction and met up again with Anne who had divorced and was looking for a new challenge. Almost on the spot they decided to look together for the right hotel.

Gelli Fawr wasn't at all what they had had in mind, but they fell in love with the beautiful and remote location and decided to take it on – self-catering barns and all. The barns which hadn't figured in their original plan have proved to be an outstanding success, because few guests who sample Frances's cooking want to do any self-catering which means the restaurant is always busy.

Within two years of taking over Gelli Fawr it was in the Good Food Guide and Les Routiers and was being talked of far beyond Offa's Dyke. There are no pretensions here, just a genuine effort to make you feel welcome and comfortable and to serve some of the best food in Wales.

'If anyone had told me three years ago I would be cooking dinner for 60, I would have died, but now I am able to cope and enjoy it,' says Frances, who also runs widely applauded cookery courses attended by professional and amateur cooks and enthusiastic housewives from all over Britain. 'They are great fun and have worked very well. I learn from the students and they hopefully from me – it is a true workshop atmosphere.'

One of the things Frances likes to cook most is the local fish and she loves to serve what she calls a 'Seafood Experience' of oysters, lobster, crab and prawns on a bed of red lettuce, garnished with red flowers from the garden and served with delicious salads and new potatoes. Such an experience, which can rarely be enjoyed in the British Isles, will set you back £25 and you must give 24 hours' notice. But it can be a shared experience – Frances is quite happy to serve it for two, and it's still more than ample.

Between them Anne and Frances make a wonderful team, backed up by Rob and their various offspring. They have made a deliberate effort to retain the remoteness of the hotel set in the foothills of the Preselis, refusing to install televisions and direct-call telephones in the bedrooms. 'People come here to get away from it all, so why should they want to tune in to the news on the hour every hour or even worse call the office,' says Anne, who these days has little desire to get back to the Madding Crowd.

Chris and Gunna Chown at Plas Bodegroes, near Pwllheli

Wales's premier chef

To many onlookers Chris Chown has reached the pinnacle of his career with the greatest of ease – his superb cooking seems to come naturally as does the slightly formal but still relaxed atmosphere created by his Scandinavian wife, Gunna, at Plas Bodegroes – the place of the rosehips.

But things that come easily are rarely appreciated and Chris and Gunna know only too well how much hard work they have had to put into their very risky venture and also the luck they have enjoyed on the way. Chris had trained in London and Switzerland and wanted to return to Wales. He took various jobs while looking for the right place and was catering for shooting parties on Anglesey when he first saw and fell in love with Plas Bodegroes, a bijou manor house set in many acres.

It was miles from any large centre of population and although relatively close to the affluent sailing and boating mecca of Abersoch, the couple had no way of gauging the potential patronage from the watersports fraternity or even of how many months in the year they could rely upon it.

But they were convinced Plas Bodegroes was the house they wanted for their great venture. Even when they had done the major work on the house it wasn't all easy going. 'I thought I knew it all, but I had always worked with a team and I was a fool to think I could do on my own what I had been doing with six other people in Switzerland. There were some panics in the kitchen and long delays in the dining room in those early days,' Chris admits.

Four years later he has his own team in Andrew Price, Barry Thomas and 'a very enthusiastic young woman' on a youth training scheme. 'I have been relatively lucky with staff and now thanks to my ratings in the Good Food Guide and winning the Welsh Restaurant of the Year Competition young chefs are actually keen to come and work here.

Chris, now 34, was brought up in Wales and learnt basic cooking skills from his Scottish mother who also taught him to appreciate the importance of using fresh produce. But he trained as an accountant before deciding to take up cooking as a career. 'I would be a richer man today if I had stuck with figures,' he laughs, but he doesn't give the impression of a man who would be happy with a calculator and a ledger for very long.

While a lesser chef might have decided that the remote situation of Plas Bodegroes precluded a regular supply of fresh foods, Chris turned it to his advantage, shopping at surrounding farms and waylaying fishermen before they could sell to foreign markets. It's difficult to define his cooking. Generally speaking it is modern classical and certainly not nouvelle cuisine, not only because nouvelle in no longer nouvelle, but because it has never been his style to present minute portions. He produces small courses that make up a perfectly balanced meal.

Having made such a success of Plas Bodegroes, the couple have no plans to move. 'Every day presents a new challenge and when people drive from London clutching the Good Food Guide we know we must live up to their expectations,' says Chris. The house and restaurant have been designed for the serious food brigade and although the tiny bar and sitting room have been rearranged to give a little more space, the elegant green dining room, painstakingly sponged by Chris and Gunna, is still where the main action takes place.

Worth noting here, the restaurant has a good and sensibly priced wine list that will not make the cost of dinner for two prohibitive, a policy Chris intends to maintain.

John and Joy Evans
at the Meadowsweet, Llanrwst

Taking up the challenge

Buying a hotel as a new venture is challenge enough for anyone, but taking over one that already has a reputation as one of the best eating places in North Wales, with no professional catering experience whatsoever, was awesome for John and Joy Evans. But that was all 12 years ago and today the Evanses have created their own enviable reputation. 'People who came to us in our first 18 months expecting the standards set by Stephen Bull were bitterly disappointed and many have never returned,' says John. It's time they did.

It took John a good two years to find his feet in the Meadowsweet kitchen and since then he has gone from strength to strength producing daily menus that could be served with pride at any of Britain's top hotels. 'It has been very much a case of trial and error – I have read books, watched television programmes, taken advice from other chefs and above all I have been in the kitchens almost every day since we took over. I think I have got it right now,' he says modestly.

A big jovial man who looks the perfect part

in his striped apron, John and his wife Joy have made the Meadowsweet very much their own and one of the ideal North Wales stopping points. The couple once both had their careers in banking – she with the Bank of England, he with the Midland. Subsequently Joy relinquished her job to bring up their children and John took over the management of a south-east supermarket chain. Always a keen amateur cook, he picked up many new skills from the supermarket's butchery department. During this time they lived in a village in the Essex countryside, frequently taking holidays in Wales.

They decided to buy a hotel and it was to Wales they looked for the right one, and in 1978 they moved with their four children to the Meadowsweet. It is probably the couple's love of their own family, now grown up, that helps to make the Meadowsweet a hotel where parents with babies and young children can relax and enjoy their holidays in the knowledge that their little ones will be properly provided for.

Re-establishing the Meadowsweet was not easy for the couple, for although it is in the heart of Snowdonia it is on the main A470 and therefore not so attractive as hotels set in their own grounds. Yet from the front rooms the scene beyond the road (which is not always busy) couldn't be more rural, with sheep grazing as far as the eye can see in the fields of the unspoilt Conwy valley.

'We really have to capture our guests. They look at the house and its position and drive on, but we believe that those who make the effort to come inside feel differently,' says Joy whose ready charm and friendly warmth dismiss any fears that the hotel's exterior tells the whole story. But it's not simply a case of comfort and friendliness that makes a stop here irresistible – the restaurant is one of the best for miles, serving excellent fresh fish, beautifully cooked meat with soups and sauces, and starters and puddings you might never expect from a man who has taught himself. He works single-handed in the kitchen but that does not prevent him from taking many extra hours to provide those enjoyable final touches of pre-meal canapés as well as sweet delights to have with coffee.

Joy cooks for the family, but never for the hotel. 'I am a very plain cook,' she says. John, on the other hand, is always learning new skills and trying out new recipes on the family with the superb produce he can mostly obtain locally or with the help of Vin Sullivan, that extraordinary Abergavenny supplier without whom the hotel business could hardly survive. Like all the best apprentices, the Evanses wanted to learn and now they can fairly be said to have graduated with honours.

CHRIS AND LYNDA KEENAN AT KEENAN'S, SWANSEA

A downtown restaurant without rooms

With 18 years cooking experience Chris Keenan remains as enthusiastic today as he was the day he started. He trained in Wales, went to London, worked in some of the capital's leading hotels and restaurants and found to his horror, when he returned to his native Swansea, that nobody wanted his experience and skills.

He hadn't planned on opening his own restaurant. It was something he had never really considered, but it rapidly became clear to him that that was the only way he could stay in Swansea. So with the support and encouragement of his wife Lynda he bought a disused amusement arcade in a terrace of eating places, which included an ice cream parlour, ethnic restaurant and a take-away, opposite the Roma Fishbar in Swansea's St Helen's Road.

The interior was a mess but within months, and in spite of restrictive fire regulations, Lynda had designed a beautiful downstairs restaurant and upstairs dining room that was to transform the place, and Chris designed his ideal kitchen. In the event both the restaurant and kitchen were rather smaller than they had planned to accommodate a fire exit. 'My kitchen was literally cut in half,' says Chris.

But at least from the diners' point of view it hasn't cramped his style. He describes his cooking as modern classical, but adds: 'I hope I have a recognizable individual style. There are many great dishes I could follow, but I like to produce my own. I want people to come here for my cooking, not for the way I reproduce other people's dishes.'

After quite literally being forced into buying his own restaurant, Chris lives and breathes it. His enthusiasm is infectious. 'I'm not only doing it for me, I'm doing it for Wales. Any remaining ideas that Wales is a culinary wilderness have got to be dispelled. So much has happened in recent years that I have no doubt we are at least as good as England and in many respect better – the Welsh food scene is bubbling over and it is up to Taste of Wales and its members to make sure that message is being broadcast throughout the world.'

Chris was a finalist in the 1989 Restaurant of the Year Competition and was disappointed not to win. 'But my day will come. I have every intention of becoming the best chef in Wales. It won't happen overnight, I've seen the competition, but I will get there.'

He loves his downtown Colonial-style peach-and-green restaurant and is delighted when old school friends and even old teachers come in and enjoy his food. But when he is off duty, or rather recovering on Sunday and Monday, he likes to drive into the countryside and have dinner with his wife at 'one of our growing number of country pubs. We drive out towards Carmarthen – there are lots of good eating places out that way,' he says.

A nice man, always ready to compliment others on their cooking, Chris couldn't resist a little one-upmanship. 'You do realize, we were the only restaurant in the Restaurant of the Year Competition – all the others were hotels.'

FRANCO AND ANN TARUSCHIO AT THE WALNUT TREE INN, NEAR ABERGAVENNY

BY GILLI DAVIES

An award-winning restaurant where Wales meets Italy

On 17 November 1963, just three days after their wedding, Ann and Franco Taruschio opened the Walnut Tree Inn near Abergavenny. Serving just one table, they began on a marriage of local flavours with Italian overtones, a combination that has proven unbeatable.

Now, after 27 years, the Walnut Tree has won more accolades for good food in Wales than any other restaurant, a result of the couple's commitment to maintaining a standard of quality that never falters. 'Some of our very first customers still come back to eat lasagne at the bar,' says Ann; others make a mighty pilgrimage to the Walnut Tree just to check that the reputation is as fine as ever. 'Last week, one family returned bringing the fourth generation to sample Walnut Tree food, although he was still in a carry cot!'

The quality and profusion of local

ingredients have helped in the Walnut Tree's the success story, and Franco is the first to agree that the choice of food he finds in Wales is now as great as anywhere. Apart from the deep winter, Franco serves Welsh lamb throughout the year. Local game such as pheasant, rabbit, hare, woodcock and even wild duck, together with salmon, pork, thick cream and Welsh farmhouse cheeses are featured regularly on the menu. Walnut Tree dishes also include an ever-increasing amount of local vegetables and fruit, even wild cherries.

Franco's cooking has many dimensions, but follows three main avenues. The menu is never without a rich Italian flavour developed from the Marche region of Italy where Franco was brought up. Ann has family roots in the Brecon area, and local ingredients bring out a Welsh flavour. But added to these two influences, Franco has developed a keen interest in the cuisine of Thailand, a flavour that very much suits their adopted daughter Pavinee. Needless to say, a meal at the Walnut Tree can set you spinning around the world.

With a staff of 26, Franco still runs the kitchen and nothing goes amiss under his watchful eye. Nigel Ramsbottom, Franco's second chef, is highly competent and has allowed Franco a small amount of freedom to pursue his hobbies. One of these is to keep up friendships with some of the other great British chefs.

Elizabeth David, a close friend, shares Franco's passion for gathering wild ingredients. On one of her visits, they walked over the Black Mountains in search of wild mushrooms, to return triumphant with 20 pounds of cepes. Truffles is another passion with Franco, and each autumn sees him return to Italy for the annual truffle hunt. Taking orders from many, he returns with his prizes so that lucky customers can sample slivers of his hidden gold while stocks last.

Ann is everywhere that a good hostess should be. Energy bursts from her and it is not surprising to learn that as well as running the restaurant she has time to follow a keen interest in journalism. She attends to every detail with staff and customers alike, and it is a credit to the Taruschios that their staff just stay and stay.

It is this double act of perfection that keeps then Walnut Tree Inn at the top. Whatever the occasion, every customer is guaranteed a courteous welcome, a wonderful meal with exceptional wines, and perhaps just a glimpse of a gentle, disarming smile from the chef himself.

KEY TO SYMBOLS

The following symbols are used throughout the Taste of Wales membership listings, which begin opposite.

NBB	Nightly bed and breakfast per person – with prices		Access credit cards accepted	·RAC	RAC 1 star
WBB	Weekly bed and breakfast per person – with prices	VISA	Visa credit cards accepted	:RAC	RAC 2 stars
	Restaurant has no smoking area		Diner's Club credit cards accepted	∴RAC	RAC 3 stars
V	Vegetarian dishes served	AMEX	American Express credit cards accepted	::RAC	RAC 4 stars
C	Children welcomed	·WTB	Wales Tourist Board 1 crown	⋮RAC	RAC 5 stars
	Dogs accepted	:WTB	Wales Tourist Board 2 crowns	·AA	AA 1 star
	Disabled facilities	∴WTB	Wales Tourist Board 3 crowns	:AA	AA 2 stars
	Number of bedrooms	::WTB	Wales Tourist Board 4 crowns	∴AA	AA 3 stars
	Number of bedrooms with bath/shower	⋮WTB	Wales Tourist Board 5 crowns	::AA	AA 4 stars
				⋮AA	AA 5 stars

TASTE OF WALES MEMBERSHIP COUNTY BY COUNTY
CLWYD

*Members are listed alphabetically, based on location.
Numbers on map relate to order of entry in gazetteer.*

- COLWYN BAY (2,3)
- HOLYWELL (5,6)
- RUTHIN (11)
- ROSSETT (9,10)
- WREXHAM (12-15)
- CORWEN (4)
- LLANGOLLEN (7,8)
- CHIRK (1)

The International Musical Eisteddfod, Llangollen

1 THE NATIONAL TRUST CHIRK CASTLE
CHIRK LL14 5AF

Vera Borrett, catering manager
Tel (0691) 777701

Licensed restaurant. Open March 28-Sept 29, 11am-5pm daily except Monday and Saturday, but open Bank Holidays. Oct 5-Nov 3, Saturday & Sunday only. Prices: Lunch £5-£8.

Half-mile west of Chirk village off A5.

Marcher fortress completed in 1310, commanding fine views over the surrounding countryside. Elegant state rooms with elaborate plasterwork, superb Adam-style furniture, tapestries and portraits; formal gardens with clipped yews.

2 EDELWEISS HOTEL OFF LAWSON ROAD
COLWYN BAY LL29 8HD

Nicola Woodcock
Tel (0492) 532314

Licensed hotel. Open 1-12. Serving times: Breakfast 8-9am, Bar Lunch 12-2pm, Lunch 12-2pm, Dinner 6.30-8pm. Prices: Lunch £11.50, Dinner £11.50.

Coming from east on A55, take Colwyn Bay turning, B5104.

An impressive 19th-century country house in its own grounds, with a large private car park. At the end of a secluded drive, and yet at the very heart of genteel Colwyn Bay.

The wonders of Wales

'Pistyll Rhaeadr and Wrexham steeple, Snowdon's mountain without its people, Overton yew-trees, St Winifred wells, Llangollen bridge and Gresford bells.' So are listed the traditional 'Seven Wonders of Wales', obviously by a North Walian, as they are mostly in Clwyd! You will appreciate line two if you have ever queued to ascend Snowdon in the summer.

St Winifred's Well in Holywell, often called the 'Lourdes of Wales', is still a place of pilgrimage, and many miracles have been attributed to its healing water. Winifred was a 7th-century girl, of royal descent, who was violated by Prince Caradog: he cut off her head, and the spring gushed from where her blood fell. There is a happy ending to the story – her uncle, St Beuno, came along and put her head back on again.

Pistyll Rhaeadr waterfall

3 THE OLD RECTORY
LLANRWST ROAD
LLANSANFFRAID
COLWYN BAY LL28 5LF

M. Vaughan, partner
Tel (0492) 580611 Fax (0492) 584555

Licensed country house. Open 2-12. Restaurant open to non-residents. Serving times: Breakfast 8-9am, Dinner one sitting 7.45pm. Specialities include Welsh lamb medallions, Welsh black beef, Conwy salmon. Children over 12 welcome. Egon Ronay, Good Food Guide listed, Wales Tourist Board highly commended.

On A470, half a mile south of junction with A55.

Georgian country house overlooking Snowdonia, Conwy Castle and estuary. Residents dine together, non-residents separately. Luxury draped beds, antiques and paintings abound. Harpist plays, mainly summer evenings.

🛏4 🛁4 [NBB] £52-£62 [V] [▲] [::WTB]

4 TYDDYN LLAN COUNTRY HOUSE HOTEL & RESTAURANT
LLANDRILLO
NR CORWEN LL21 0ST

Bridget & Peter Kindred, owners
Tel (049084) 264 Fax (049084) 264

Licensed hotel and restaurant. Open 1-12. Restaurant is open to non-residents. Serving times: Breakfast. 8.30-10am, Bar Lunch 12.30-2pm, Lunch 12.30-2pm Dinner 7-9.30pm. Prices: Bar Lunch from £3, Lunch £11.50, Dinner £18-£20. Specialities include: local Welsh lamb dishes and fresh fish. Egon Ronay, Good Food Guide listed.

Situated on the edge of Llandrillo on B4401.

A delightful 18th-century country hotel set amidst unrivalled beauty. An ideal centre for exploring North and Mid Wales and offering a variety of sporting activities ranging from fishing on our own stretch of the river Dee to croquet.

🛏10 🛁 10 [NBB] £33.50-£36.50
[WBB] £234.50-£255.50 [V] [C] [▲] [AMEX]
[::WTB] [:AA]

5 KINSALE HALL COUNTRY HOUSE HOTEL
LLANERCHYMOR
NR HOLYWELL CH8 9DT

Sean Boyle, director/general manager
Tel (0745) 560001 Fax (0745) 561298

Licensed hotel. Open 1-12. Restaurant open to non-residents. Serving times: Breakfast 7-9.30am, Bar Lunch 12-2pm, Lunch 12-2.30pm, High Tea 3-5pm, Dinner 6.30-10.30pm. Prices: Lunch £8-£12, High Tea £4.95, Dinner £10-£25. Specialities: two restaurants - our main one serving à la carte and the other a carvery/grill in the Victorian conservatory.

From the A55, take the Holywell turn and come down to the coast road.

The Hall is set in 100 acres of beautiful parkland, with panoramic views of Wirral and Dee estuary. The conference centre can accommodate from 4-300 delegates with excellent audio/visual facilities. Banquets/ weddings can be catered for.

🛏29 🛁29 [NBB] £22.50-£47.50
[WBB] £315-£665 [V] [C] 🐕 ♿ [▲] [VISA]
[⊙] [AMEX]

6 HOTEL VICTORIA
HIGH STREET
HOLYWELL CH8 7TW

Michael Boyle, manager
Tel (0352) 711684 Fax (0352) 711238

Licensed hotel/restaurant. Open 1-12. Restaurant open to non-residents. Serving times: Breakfast 6.30-9am, Bar Lunch 12-2.30pm, Lunch 12-2.30pm, Coffee 2.30-6pm, Dinner 7pm. Prices: Bar Lunch £3.95, Lunch £6.95, Dinner £9.95. À la carte menu. Good Food Guide listed.

In Holywell. Convenient for A55, A5026 and A548.

The Hotel Victoria is family owned, and has been restored to its former splendour. Furnishings and fabrics have been carefully chosen, all to a very high standard, and depict a true Victorian ambience.

🛏10 🛁10 [NBB] £17.50-£22.50 [V] [C] 🐕
[▲] [VISA] [::WTB]

7 BRYN HOWEL HOTEL & RESTAURANT
LLANGOLLEN LL20 7UW

John Lloyd, general manager
Tel (0978) 860331 Fax (0978) 860119

Licensed hotel and restaurant. Open 1-12.
Restaurant open to non-residents.
Serving times: Breakfast 7.15-9.30am,
Bar Lunch 12-2pm, Lunch 12-2.30pm,
High Tea 2.30-5.30pm, Dinner 7-10pm.
Prices: Bar Lunch from £1.50, Lunch £10,
High Tea £4.50, Dinner £15.
Specialities: Fresh produce, menu changes daily.

Situated on the main Wrexham to Llangollen road A539.

Set in eight acres with breathtaking views, this 19th-century country house hotel is internationally renowned for good food and wine. West End trained chef Dai Davies has brought his wealth of experience of working on the Continent back to his home country.

🛏37 ♦37 NBB £37 -£50. V C 🐕 ♿
▲ VISA ⬛ AMEX ∷WTB ∴RAC ∴AA

8 WEST ARMS HOTEL LLANARMON D.C.
NR LLANGOLLEN LL20 7LD

Tim Alexander, owner
Tel (069176) 665

Licensed hotel. Open 1-12. Restaurant open to non-residents. Serving times: Breakfast 8.30-9.30am, Bar Lunch 12.30-2pm, Lunch 12.30-2pm, Dinner 7.30-9pm. Prices: Bar Lunch £2.25-£8, Lunch £9.95, Dinner £17.50. Specialities include local game and local Ceiriog trout. Egon Ronay, Good Food Guide listed.

Take B4500 for 11 miles to Llanarmon D.C.

A 16th-century country inn of great charm offering traditional hospitality in a tranquil village setting at the head of the beautiful Ceiriog valley. Comfort, warmth and friendly service coupled with delicious food help to make a stay both memorable and enjoyable.

🛏14 ♦14 NBB £35-£40 WBB £245-£280
V C 🐕 ♿ ▲ VISA ∷WTB :RAC :AA

9 GOLDEN LION HOTEL CHESTER ROAD
ROSSETT LL1Z 0HN

Brian Bennett, manager
Tel (0244) 571020

Licensed hotel/restaurant. Open 1-12.
Serving times: Breakfast 7.30-9.30am,
Bar Lunch 12-2.30pm,
High Tea 2.30-6.30pm, Dinner 7-9.45pm.
Prices: Bar lunch £1.20-£4,
Lunch £3.50- £8, Dinner £6-£18.50.

5 miles from Chester on the A483.

17th-century inn set in three acres - beer garden, children's play area, golf practice net. 42-cover restaurant. Traditional beers and wines.

🛏4 ♦4 NBB £18.50-£20.
WBB £120-£140 V C ▲ VISA ⬛ AMEX
∷WTB

Owain Glyndŵr

'I am not in the role of common men' are the words Shakespeare put in the mouth of Owain Glyndŵr. Uncommon he certainly was, and elusive too. Descended from several of the princely houses of Wales, he spent time studying at the Inns of Court in London and served in the English army against Scotland. One of the gentry, with an estate around Glyndyfrdwy in the Vale of Dee, from where he took his name Glyndŵr, he hardly seemed the sort of man to make a determined effort to recapture the independence of Wales.

He proclaimed himself Prince of Wales, and held parliaments in Machynlleth. Norman castles fell all over Wales, and he finally made his headquarters at Harlech. As the poet says, 'The fabled Dragon banner flies once more above the Dee'. But it was not to be - Harlech fell and Owain disappeared. To this day, no one really knows what became of this enigmatic hero.

10 LLYNDIR HALL HOTEL
LLYNDIR LANE
ROSSETT LL12 0AY

Phillip Crowther, general manager
Jeniffer Williams, sales manager
Tel (0244) 571648 Fax (0244) 571258

Licensed hotel. Open 1-12. Restaurant open to non-residents. Serving times: Breakfast 7-9.30am, Bar Lunch 7.30am-9.30pm, Lunch 12-2pm, Dinner 7-9.30pm. Prices: Bar Lunch £2.50, Lunch £12-£25, High Tea £6-£9, Dinner £15-£25. Egon Ronay, Good Food Guide listed.

From Wrexham take A483 to Chester and then sign to Rossett.

38 individually designed bedrooms all with private facilities, conference/catering facilities up to 100 persons, leisure club containing swimming pool, jacuzzi, solarium, steam rooms, snack bar, à la carte. Two lounges.

⊨38 ♚38 [NBB] £37.50-£47.50 ⤫ [V] [C]
♿ ▲ [VISA] [⊙] [AMEX] ⁞⁞WTB ∴AA

11 BRYN AWEL FARM
BONTUCHEL
NR RUTHIN LL15 2DE

Beryl J. Jones, proprietor
Tel (08242) 2481

Unlicensed farmhouse. Open 1-12. Serving times: Breakfast 7-9am, Dinner at 6pm. Prices: Dinner £5-£7.50. WTB Farmhouse award.

B5105 out of Ruthin.

Farmhouse accommodation on a 35-acre working farm on the outskirts of the picturesque market town of Ruthin. Planned routes available for motoring and country walks, half-mile private fishing.

⊨3 ♚1 [NBB] £12-£13 ⤫ [V] [C]

12 BOD IDRIS HALL
LLANDEGLA
NR WREXHAM LL11 3AL

Robert Best, partner
Tel (097888) 434/479 Fax (097888) 335

Licensed hotel. Open 1-12. Serving times: Breakfast 7.30-9.30am, Bar Lunch 12- 2pm, High Tea 3-5pm, Dinner 7-9pm.

Prices: Bar lunch £7.50, Lunch £10, High Tea £5, Dinner £15. Specialities include: high-quality fresh cuisine with Continental touches.

2 miles east of Llandegla on A5104.

An ancient country house hotel in a unique and secluded rural setting. Spacious public rooms with log fires, a superb à la carte restaurant and very personal service from the owners.

⊨ 12 ♚9 [NBB] £38-£42.50
[WBB] £266-£290 ⤫ ▲ [VISA] [AMEX] ⁞⁞WTB
∴AA

13 Y DAFARN NEWYDD
MOUNTAIN STREET
RHOSLLANERCHRUGOG
WREXHAM LL14 1BT

Sioux & Geoff Hodgkinson
Tel (0978) 840471

Licensed restaurant/inn/pub. Open 1-12. Serving times: Bar Lunch 12-2pm, Dinner 7-10pm, bookings only. Prices: Bar Lunch £1.50-£3, Dinner £10-£15, à la carte bookings only. Specialities include curries, Welsh menu.

Halfway between Wrexham and Llangollen on A483.

It's a little off the beaten track, difficult to find but harder to leave. A tastefully decorated restaurant sited to friendly public house. Food at reasonable prices, a worldwide menu, a jewel for unsuspecting vegetarians.

⤫ [V] [C] ♿

14 THE NATIONAL TRUST ERDDIG
NR WREXHAM LL13 0YT

Gillian Pickering, catering manager
Tel (0978) 355314

Licensed restaurant. Open Good Friday - October 13, except for Thursday and Friday. Serving times: 11am-5.15pm. Prices: Lunch £5-£8.

2 miles south of Wrexham - signposted (N.T.) from A483 & A525.

Late 17th-century house with 18th-century additions, retaining most of its original furniture. The range of outbuildings includes kitchen, laundry, bakehouse, stables, sawmill, smithy and joiner's shop. Large walled garden restored to 18th-century formal design.

15 PANT-YR-OCHAIN HALL HOTEL
OLD WREXHAM ROAD GRESFORD NR WREXHAM LL12 8TY

Patrick Mauser, managing director
Tel (0978) 852646 Fax (0978) 853097

Licensed hotel/restaurant. Open 1-12. Restaurant open to non-residents. Serving times: Breakfast 7-10am, Bar Lunch 12-11pm, Lunch 12-2pm, High Tea 2-5pm, Dinner 7-10pm. Prices: Bar Lunch £3, Lunch £6, High Tea £3, Dinner £12.50. Specialities include catering for vegetarians, diabetics and gluten free.

Off A483 (Nantwich/Holt turning) on Chester/Wrexham by-pass.

Quality country house hotel with three acres of its own gardens and surrounded by 16 acres of parkland with lakes.

DENBIGH FARMHOUSE ICES

In 1774 Mrs Thrale, visiting Gwaenynog with Dr Johnson, wrote 'Ices were served as a dessert....'
Hopefully as good as today's from
DENBIGH FARMHOUSE ICES - HUFEN IA DINBYCH
Find us at the best places all over North Wales and at our Broadleys Farm Shop.

Gwaenynog Hall, Denbigh, Clwyd
Tel: (0745) 814053

The toast of North Wales

WREXHAM LAGER

UK champion draught lager 1990

Established since 1882

DYFED

*Members are listed alphabetically, based on location.
Numbers on map relate to order of entry in gazetteer.*

ABERYSTWYTH (2-4)
ABERAERON (1)
NEW QUAY (26)
TREGARON (34)
CARDIGAN (9)
LAMPETER (18,19)
LLANYBYDDER (24)
BONCATH (6-8)
LLANDYSUL (21-23)
FISHGUARD (11-13)
LLANDOVERY (20)
LLANWRDA (25)
ST DAVID'S (27-29)
SOLVA (31)
HAVERFORDWEST (14-16)
CARMARTHEN (10)
KILGETTY (17)
AMMANFORD (5)
SAUNDERSFOOT (30)
TENBY (32,33)

The magnificent Pembrokeshire coast

135

1 SELECTIONS
25 ALBAN SQUARE
ABERAERON SA46 0AJ

Janice Hughes, owner
Tel (0545) 570561

Licensed coffee shop. Open 1-12. Serving times: 9am- 6pm. Prices: From £1.25 to £8. Specialities include fresh local trout, welshcakes.

On A487 between Aberystwyth and Cardigan.

The coffee shop forms part of Selections Confectionery and Gift Shop. Tastefully decorated with seating for 24. All food is freshly prepared on the premises with baking to a very high standard.

2 CONRAH COUNTRY
HOUSE HOTEL
CHANCERY
RHYDGALED
NR ABERYSTWYTH SY23 4DF

John Heading, owner
Tel (0970) 617941 Fax (0970) 624546

Licensed hotel/ restaurant. Open Jan 1-Dec 23. Serving times: Breakfast 8-9.30am, Bar Lunch 12-2pm, Lunch 12-2pm, High Tea 3-5.30pm, Dinner 7-9pm. Prices: Bar Lunch £3.50-£7.50, Lunch £11.50-£12.50, Dinner £17-£18.50. Egon Ronay, Good Food Guide listed.

3 miles south of Aberystwyth on A487.

A favourite Welsh country house hotel set in 22 acres of gently rolling grounds. Modern Welsh menus using the very best of local and Conrah kitchen garden produce. Blissful, relaxed, country living in style.

22 20 NBB £32.50-£42.50
WBB £227.50-£297.50 V C VISA
AMEX ∴WTB ∴AA ∴RAC

DOUBLE DRAGON
"The National Ale of Wales"
FELINFOEL BREWERY (0554) 773357

3 GROVES HOTEL & RESTAURANT
NORTH PARADE
ABERYSTWYTH SY23 2NF

Steve Albert, partner
Tel (0970) 617623

Licensed hotel. Open 1-12, except Christmas. Restaurant open to non-residents. Serving times: Breakfast 8-9.15am, Bar Lunch 12-2pm, Dinner 7-8.30pm. Prices: Bar Lunch £1.50-£7.50, Dinner £9-£15. Specialities include *chicken wyddfa* (breast of chicken in wine and cream sauce).

In town centre.

Long-established family-run hotel in tree-lined avenue. All rooms en-suite with colour telvision, radio, tea/coffee facilities. The hotel restaurant is a noted eating place of the town and uses the best of local produce.

🛏11 ☕11 [NBB] from£24.25 [WBB] £135
[▲] [VISA] [AMEX] [⁑WTB] [:AA] [:RAC]

4 LLETY-GWYN HOTEL
LLAWBADARN FAWR
ABERYSTWYTH SY23 3SX

Tel (0970) 623965

Licensed hotel. Open 1-12. Restaurant open to non-residents. Serving times: Breakfast 8-9am, Bar Lunch 12-2pm, Dinner 6pm. Prices: Bar Lunch from £3, Lunch from £7.50, High Tea from £5, Dinner from £9. AA listed.

On A44 1½ from seafront.

Family-owned licensed country house hotel with gym, sauna, sun-bed, pool, table, Rooms all have colour TVs, clock-radios, tea/coffee makers. TV lounge, large dining room. Pleasant garden with swings for children.

🛏14 ☕8 [NBB] £15-£22 [V] [C] [🐕] [♿] [▲]
[VISA] [⁑WTB]

5 COBBLERS RESTAURANT
3 CHURCH STREET
LLANDYBIE
AMMANFORD SA18 3HZ

Margaret Rees, owner/chef
Tel (0269) 850540

Licensed restaurant. Open 1-12. Serving times: Bar Lunch 12-2pm, Lunch 12-2pm, Dinner 7-9.30pm. Prices: Bar Lunch £2.50, Lunch £3-£5.50, Dinner £17.50. Specialities include laverbread roulade with marinated salmon, noisettes of Welsh lamb stuffed with leeks in wholemeal hob rust. Full Welsh cheeseboard. Good Food Guide listed.

Between Ammanford and Llandeilo off A483.

Original village cobbler's shop - since 1981 has been run as a speciality restaurant. Award-winning 'Taste of Britain' 1988. Welsh Lamb Restaurant of the Year 1988. Appeared on many radio and television programmes in Wales. Also Floyd on Britain.

[V] [C] [♿] [▲] [VISA]

6 AWEL-Y-GRUG
BONCATH SA37 OJP

Carol & John Vaughton, owners
Tel (0239) 841260

Licensed guest house. Open 1-12. Serving times: Breakfast 8-10am, Dinner 6-8.30pm. Prices: Dinner £4.50-£9. Wales Tourist Board Farmhouse Award.

On B4332 in village of Boncath.

Rural guest house with pleasant dining room and TV lounge. Plentiful home cooking using local and home-grown produce. Games room and large garden with furniture.

🛏4 ☕2 [NBB] £13-£16 [WBB] £91-£115.50
[✗] [V] [C] [🐕] [▲] [VISA] [⁑WTB]

7 FFYNONN FACH BISTRO
FFYNONE ARMS
NEWCHAPEL
BONCATH SA37 6EH

Eric Homer, chef & partner
Tel (0239) 841235

Licensed inn/pub. Open 1-12. Serving times: Breakfast 8-10am, Lunch 12-2.30pm, Dinner 6.30-9.30pm. Prices: Lunch £3-£7, Dinner £6-£12. Specialities include traditional Welsh recipes such as lamb steak with port and rosemary sauce. Good Food Guide listed.

On B4332 on Cardigan coast.

A traditional stone-built country inn. Discover the dramatic Cardigan coast and walk the Preseli hills or enjoy flower-filled lanes around the inn.

[🛏]3 [NBB] £12.50-£15 [WBB] £85-£100 [V]
[C] [🐕]

8 FRON FAWR
BONCATH SA37 0HS

Fay Cori, owner
Tel (0239) 841285 Fax (0239) 841545

Self-catering cottages with farmhouse food delivered. Each cottage has three bedrooms. Dinner can be served any time. Cottage weekly rates £190- £429 + VAT according to season. Main course items average £3.30. Specialities include sweet lamb pie, fruit crumbles, homemade ice cream. Wales Tourist Board 5 Dragons grade.

Off the Cardigan to Tenby road, A478.

Nestling on a hillside with beautiful views for miles around (10 minutes' drive to the sea). The cottages offer superb self-catering accommodation plus the independence of ordering home-cooked meals delivered to the door.

[V] [C]

9 PENBONTBREN FARM HOTEL
GLYNARTHEN
CARDIGAN SA44 6PE

G.B. & M.M. Humphreys
Tel (0239) 810248 Fax (0239) 811129

Licensed hotel. Open 1-12. Restaurant open to non-residents. Serving times: Breakfast 8-9am, Dinner 7-8.15pm. Prices: Dinner £10-£14. Specialities include many adapted traditional Welsh dishes.

Travelling south on A487 take first left after Sarnau (signposted Penbontbren). Travelling north on A487 from Cardigan take second turning right after Tan-y-groes signposted Penbontbren.

Family farm buildings converted to modern hotel. In interesting countryside, only 2 miles from Cardigan Bay. Family rooms offer colour TV, bathroom en-suite, rural views. Varied menus with local Welsh specialities.

[🛏]10 [♦]10 [NBB] £23-£26 [WBB] £161-£182
[✂] [V] [C] [🐕] [VISA] [::WTB] [:RAC] [:AA]

10 PANTGWYN FARM
WHITEMILL
CARMARTHEN SA32 7ES

Tim Giles, proprietor
Tel (0267) 290247

Unlicensed farmhouse. Open 2-12. Serving times: Breakfast 7-8.30am, Dinner 7-8.30pm. Prices: Dinner £7-£9. Specialities include home produced honeyed lamb with redcurrants, fresh herb soups, elderflower syllabub with home-grown soft fruits.

Off A40 between Carmarthen and Llandeilo. 4 miles from Carmarthen.

A warm welcome awaits you at our beautifully restored 200-year-old farmhouse situated in hillsides above Towy river. Quiet location with acclaimed home-cooked food. Fishing, golf, riding and historic castles nearby.

[🛏]3 [♦]1 [NBB] £13-£17 [WBB] £85-£113 [✂]
[V] [C] [🐕]

11 BRYNGARW
ABERCASTLE ROAD
TREVINE
NR FISHGUARD SA62 5AR

R.W. & J.K. Gratton, owners
Tel (0348) 831211

Licensed guest house. Open 4-9. Serving times: Breakfast 8-8.30am, Dinner 6-7.30pm. Prices: Dinner £8.50. Specialities include Welsh breakfast of bacon and cockles, home preserves. Wales Tourist Board commended.

On coast road between St David's and Fishguard.

Peaceful with fantastic sea views. Wide choice of menus. Home-grown vegetables.

🛏5 🍽5 [NBB] £18 [WBB] £110 ✘ [V] [C]
[∴WTB]

12 GELLI FAWR
COUNTRY HOUSE
PONTFAEN
NR FISHGUARD SA65 9TX

Ann Churcher/Frances Roughley, owners
Tel (0239) 820343

Licensed hotel/restaurant. Open 1-12. Restaurant open to non-residents. Serving times: Breakfast 8.30-11.30am, Bar Lunch 12-2.30pm, Dinner 7.30-10pm. Prices: Bar Lunch £2.50-£7, Dinner £15-£17. Specialities include unusual bar food - delicious salads. 'Seafood experience' platter. Good Food Guide listed.

Off B4313 to Fishguard in Preseli hills above Newport.

Ancient site for historic farmhouse in idyllic setting. Hotel, restaurant, self-catering accommodation. Heated outdoor swimming pool, perfect for family holidays, superb food. Peaceful rural setting. Four miles from beach and coastal path.

🛏10 🍽5 [NBB] £20-£23.50
[WBB] £135-£160 [V] [C] 🐕 ♿ 🐕 ▲ [VISA]

The last invasion of Britain

'A still night, when all nature, earth and ocean wore an air of unusual serenity' - so Richard Fenton described the night of the last invasion of British soil, in 1797, near Fishguard. Four French ships disgorged 1500 men, with a plan to effect a peasant uprising, at a time when revolution was in the air.

The invasion turned into a French farce when the original plan of landing at Bristol was thwarted as the ships were driven north by the wind. Eight hundred of the French, a motley crew of soldiers and convicts, lost no time in getting drunk on looted alcohol and consequently mistook 400 Welsh women assembled on the clifftops dressed in red flannel for Redcoats. Surrender followed quickly; one of the women, Jemima Nicholas, even rounding up a dozen prisoners with a pitchfork. Serenity was soon restored, and is still a feature of picturesque Lower Fishguard. Mementos of the ill-fated invasion can be seen in the Royal Oak, an inn in the centre of Fishguard.

Fishguard harbour

13 TREGYNON COUNTRY FARMHOUSE HOTEL
GWAUN VALLEY
NR FISHGUARD SA65 9TU

Peter Heard & Jane Cox, owners
Tel (0239) 820531

Licensed farmhouse hotel and restaurant. Open 1-12. Restaurant open to non-residents. Serving times: Breakfast 8.30-9.30am, Bar Lunch by arrangement, Dinner 7.50-8.50pm. Prices: Dinner £11-£16.50. Good Food Guide, Ashley Courteney listed. AA selected, RAC acclaimed. Children by arrangement

From intersection of B4313 and B4329 take B4313 towards Fishguard.

Wales's award-winning, personally run, 16th-century farmhouse hotel nestles in Preseli mountains in Pembrokeshire Coast National Park. Magnificent views, trout ponds, forest, Iron Age fort, 200ft waterfall. Log fires in winter.

🛏8 8 NBB from £18.50
WBB from £129.50 V WTB

14 JEMIMA'S RESTAURANT
FREYSTROP
HAVERFORDWEST SA62 4HB

Ann Owston, owner
Tel (0437) 891109

Licensed restaurant. Open 1-12. Serving times: Lunch 12-2pm, Dinner 7-9pm. Prices: Lunch £6-£8, Dinner £12-£18. Good Food Guide listed.

2 miles south of Haverfordwest on Burton road.

Small, individual restaurant offering modern cuisine using fresh local produce. The emphasis is on freshness and natural tastes with meat from local farms, fish from Milford Haven.

V C VISA

SPECIALITY ICE CREAMS AND FROZEN DESSERTS

Windsor Creameries

Luxury Dairy Ice Creams
Sorbets
Purees
Knickerbocker Glories
Gateaux
Sundae Cups
Truffles

- AND A WHOLE LOT MORE

Windsor Creameries
- Wales biggest independent manufacturer of quality ice creams.

Call us now to arrange a tasting.

Windsor Creameries Mfg Ltd.
Pembrey Dyfed SA16 0HZ
Tel: 0554 890392

15 ROGESTON COTTAGES
ROGESTON
PORTFIELD GATE
HAVERFORDWEST SA62 3LH

John & Paula Rees, owners
Tel (0437) 781373

Self-catering cottages. Open 1-12. Cottages sleeping four from £136-£344. Granary apartment, sleeping six from £156-£430. Dishes serving 2/3 people from £6.50. Wales Tourist Board 5 Dragons grade.

6 miles west of Haverfordwest.

Rogeston has taken the catering out of self-catering. Gourmet meals which are prepared from local produce by our chef, Kate Scale, can be delivered to your cottage. 1985 Wales in Bloom award for landscaping. Rogeston Cottages are the first self-catering cottages in Wales to have received a RIBA commendation.

[V] [C] ♿

16 WOLFSCASTLE COUNTRY HOTEL & RESTAURANT
WOLFSCASTLE
NR HAVERFORDWEST

Andrew Stirling, owner
Tel (043787) 225

Licensed hotel. Open 1-12. Restaurant open to non-residents. Serving times: Breakfast 7.30-9.30am, Bar Lunch 12-2pm, Sunday Lunch 12-2pm, Dinner 7-9pm. Prices: Bar Lunch £1.60-£4.95, Dinner £11-£16. Specialities include Sussex beef with port and ale, spinach and mushroom roulade. Egon Ronay listed.

Just off A40.

A traditional country house offering a warm and relaxed atmosphere. Its situation in the beautiful Pembrokeshire countryside is well placed for visits to all parts of the National Park.

🛏16 ⌂16 [NBB] from£58 [WBB] £366 ⚔ [V]
[C] [🐕] [⛰] [VISA] [AMEX] [∴WTB] [∴AA] [∴RAC]

17 JEFFRESTON FARMHOUSE RESTAURANT
JEFFRESTON
KILGETTY SA68 0RE

Norman & June Williams, chef/owners
Tel (0646) 651291

Licensed restaurant. Open 1-12. Nightly Dinner, Bed and Breakfast £33.50. Restaurant open to non-residents. Serving times: Dinner 7-9pm. Prices: Dinner £14.50. Specialities include roast duckling with lemon, honey and mint sauce, savoury Welsh rarebit, homemade petit fours.

Off A477 in a tranquil village.

18th-century restaurant with fixed price. À la carte menu is changed regularly. Chef-owner June gives a true Taste of Wales with Glamorgan sausages, rack of Welsh lamb, homemade ices and sweets, Welsh cheeseboard.

🛏3 ⌂3 [NBB] £20 ⚔ [V] [C] [🐕] [⛰] [VISA]
[∴WTB]

18 BRYNCASTELL
LLANFAIR ROAD
LAMPETER SA48 8JY

Beti Davies
Tel (0570) 422447

Unlicensed farmhouse. Serving times: Breakfast 7.30-9am, Dinner 6-7.30pm. Prices: Dinner £6.50-£8.50. Specialities include Teifi trout in wine, fillets of lamb, cawl. Wales Tourist Board Farmhouse Award.

1 mile north-east of Lampeter.

Superior bungalow on 140-acre working farm, commanding panoramic views across the Teifi valley. Fishing, rough shooting, hillside walks, farm activities, water divining. Pony trekking, golf, tennis nearby.

🛏2 ⌂2 [NBB] £12.50-£15 [WBB] £84 -£98
[C] [∴WTB]

19 PENTRE FARM LLANFAIR CLYDOGAU LAMPETER SA48 8LE

Eleri Davies, owner
Tel (057045) 313

Unlicensed farmhouse. Open 4-10. Serving times: Breakfast 7.30-9am, Dinner from 7pm. Prices: Dinner £7. Specialities include Welsh lamb in various sauces, dairy puddings, bread and butter pudding with butterscotch topping. Wales Tourist Board Farmhouse Award.

4 miles north of Lampeter on B4343 - farm in village of Llanfair Clydogau.

Overlooking Teifi valley, 12 miles from Cardigan Bay coast. This 400-acre dairy/sheep farm offers friendly welcome and first-class country cooking. Large stone farmhouse features polished slate floors, inglenook fireplace, beams and Welsh dresser.

🛏3 🍴2 [NBB] £14-£15 [WBB] £95-£100 [V] [C] [∴WTB]

---

20 KING'S HEAD INN HOTEL MARKET SQUARE LLANDOVERY SA20 OAB

Mr & Mrs D. P. Madeira-Cole, owners
Tel (0550) 20393

Licensed hotel. Open 1-12. Restaurant open to non-residents. Serving times: Breakfast 8-10am, Bar Lunch 12-2pm, Lunch 12-2pm, Dinner 5.30-9.30pm. Specialites include King's Table (cold buffet), traditional Sunday roast beef lunch, steak, farmer's lunch (beef casserole). Egon Ronay, Good Food Guide listed.

On corner of market square, opposite town hall - off A40 and A483.

Inn of historical and architectural interest, nestling in beautiful Towy valley, centrally situated for exploration. Same owners successfully running the inn for 18 years. Weekend and midweek breaks.

🛏4 🍴4 [NBB] £18.50 [WBB] £85 [V] [C] [∴WTB]

---

21 BRONIWAN RHYDLEWIS LLANDYSUL SA44 5PF

Carole & Allen Jacobs
Tel (023975) 261

Unlicensed farmhouse. Open 1-12. Serving times: Breakfast 7.30-9am, Dinner 7-8pm. Prices: Dinner £7-£8. Specialities include organically grown produce from our large kitchen garden, cheese roulade with courgette/yoghurt filling. Wales Tourist Board Farmhouse Award.

5 minutes from A487 Cardigan/Aberystwyth; B4334 to Rhydlewis.

Small farm with glorious views of distant Preseli hills from charming Victorian farmhouse, 10 minutes from coast. All meals, including vegetarian, prepared with produce from large organic garden. Own meat, milk, eggs.

🛏3 🍴1 [NBB] from£13 [WBB] from £90 ✄
[V] [C] 🐕 [:WTB]

---

22 FARMHOUSE RESTAURANT CASTELL HOWELL PONTSIAN LLANDYSUL SA44 4UA

Lisa & Andrew Nunn, owners
Tel (054555) 209

Licensed restaurant within holiday centre. Ten cottages - rental per week £175-£525. Restaurant open to non-residents. Serving times: Bar Lunch12-2pm, Dinner 7.30-9pm. Prices: Bar Lunch £1.50-£6, Dinner £12-£15. Specialities include starters - Dyfed smokies (smoked fish in spicy cream sauce); main courses - salmon en papillote, best end of Welsh lamb in sherry and cream sauce.

Halfway between Carmarthen and Aberystwyth - 9 miles inland from Newquay on B4459.

A small friendly restaurant, open at weekends, serving dinner for holidaymakers and locals. The short à la carte menu features local produce. Other facilities include heated indoor pool, squash courts, horse riding and clay pigeon shooting.

🛏 23 [NBB] £14.50-£19 [V] [C] ♿ 🏊 [VISA]

23 HENDRE FARM LLANGRANNOG
LLANDYSUL SA44 6AP

Bethan Williams, owner
Tel (0239) 654342

Unlicensed farmhouse. Open 4-10. Serving times: Breakfast 8-9am, Dinner 6.30pm. Prices: Dinner £7-£9. Specialities include: Teifi salmon starter, turkey in cream, lamb with leek and walnut stuffing, welshcakes. Wales Tourist Board Farmhouse Award. AA Welsh winner of the best newcomer award 1990-91.

Off A487 at Pentregat on B4321.

Lovely 19th-century farmhouse offering friendly accommodation, just 2 miles from glorious coastline. Delicious home-cooked meals served using fresh local produce. Working farm with sheep and beef cattle.

🛏3 🍴1 [NBB] £12-£15 [WBB] £84 [WTB]

24 MINYLLAN LLANWENOG
LLANYBYDDER SA40 9UT

Mair Davies, owner
Tel (0570) 480378

Unlicensed guest house. Open 5-9. Serving times: Breakfast 8-9am, Dinner 6.30-7.30pm. Prices: Dinner £7-£9. Specialities include: cheesy leek and ham, rhubarb crunch, chocolate queen of puddings, own fresh garden produce.

6 miles from Lampeter on A475 Newcastle Emlyn road.

All bedrooms have washbasins. Good parking. Speciality meals.

🛏2 [NBB] £11.50-£13 [C] [WTB]

25 GLANRANNELL PARK HOTEL CRUGYBAR
LLANWRDA SA19 8SA

Dai & Bronwen Davies
Tel (0558) 685230

Licensed hotel. Open 4-10. Restaurant open to non-residents. Serving times: Breakfast 8.30-9.15am, Bar Lunch 12.30-1.30pm, Dinner 6.45-8pm. Prices: Bar Lunch £3-£8, Dinner £12.50-£18. Specialities include: home-produced lamb, local sewin, old-fashioned puddings.

10 miles west of Llandovery off A482.

Peaceful country house with its own farm and trout stream, overlooking lawns and ornamental lake. Ideal centre for a quiet holiday, yet centrally placed and within easy reach of the whole of West and Mid Wales.

🛏8 🍴5 [NBB] £20-£27.50 [WBB] £137-£163
[C] 🐕 [WTB] [AA]

26 PARK HALL CWM TUDU
NR NEW QUAY

Mr & Mrs McDonnell, owners
Tel (0545) 560306

Licensed country house. Open 1-12. Restaurant open to non-residents. Serving times: Breakfast 8.30-9.30am, Dinner 8pm. Prices: Bar Lunch £5, Lunch £5, High Tea £3.50, Dinner £14.50. Specialities include mackerel mariend, Welsh lamb in orange sauce. Wales Tourist Board Dragon Award. AA selected, RAC highly acclaimed.

Off A487 Cardigan to Aberystwyth road on coast.

A small country house run by Peter and Chris McDonnell. The emphasis is on personal service and a friendly atmosphere. Pony trekking, dry ski slope and beach are very close by.

🛏5 🍴5 [NBB] £19.50-£25 [WBB] £136-£175
[V] [C] 🐕 ♿ [VISA] [D] [AMEX] [WTB]

143

27 CWMWDIG WATER GUEST HOUSE
BEREA
NR ST DAVID'S SH62 6DW

Eifion & Elsie Evans, owners
Tel (0348) 831434

Licensed guest house. Open 1-12. Serving times: 8.30-9am, Dinner 7pm. Prices: Dinner £8.

On coast road between St David's and Fishguard.

Converted farmhouse and barns, 5 miles from St David's. Beautiful sea views from most rooms. Less than 1 mile from coast path. Resident owners. Log fires, TV lounge. High-quality home cooking.

🛏10 ☕2 NBB £14-£17 WBB £89-£104
V C 🐕 VISA AMEX :WTB

28 HARBOUR LIGHTS RESTAURANT
PORTHGAIN
NR ST DAVID'S SA62 5BW

Anne Marie Davies, owner
Tel (0348) 831549

Restaurant. Open 1-12. Serving times: Dinner 7-9.30pm. Prices: Dinner £17.50-£20. Good Food Guide listed.

Off A487.

Small harbour restaurant using fresh local produce - lobsters, crab, cray, etc. from the harbour - and locally grown vegetables. County Restaurant of the Year for 1991.

V C ♿

29 RAMSEY HOUSE
LOWER MOOR
ST DAVID'S SA62 6RP

Mac & Sandra Thompson, owners
Tel (0437) 720321

Licensed guest house. Open 1-12. Weekly bed, breakfast and dinner per person: £136.20-£156. Restaurant open to non-residents by prior arrangement. Serving times: Breakfast 8-8.30am, Dinner 7pm. Prices: Dinner £9.75. Specialities include 'Dragons' eggs', roast shoulder of Welsh lamb stuffed with pork sausage meat, fresh herbs and laverbread, suprême of salmon with cucumber sauce. AA listed, RAC acclaimed, Wales Tourist Board commended.

On road to Portlcais, half-mile from the centre of St David's.

Superior accommodation with all amenities standing in its own grounds half-mile from cathedral and spectacular coastal scenery. Within easy reach of sandy beaches. Welsh speciality menus, both traditional and innovative, changed daily.

🛏7 ☕2 NBB £13.80-£16.10 V 🐕
:WTB

30 ST BRIDES HOTEL
SAUNDERSFOOT SA69 9NH

Ian Bell, owner
Tel (0834) 8123021 Fax (0834) 813323

Licensed Hotel. Open 1-12. Restaurant open to non-residents. Serving times: Breakfast 8-10am, Bar Lunch 12-2pm, Lunch 12.30-1.30pm, Dinner 7-.30pm. Prices: Bar Lunch £3-£8, Lunch £9.50-£12.50, Dinner £14-£20. Specialities include fish and seafood.

A40 from Carmarthen A477 from St Clear's. A478 from Fishguard.

Cliff-top Tudor-style hotel in the unspoilt grandeur of Pembrokeshire Coast National Park. Restaurant features locally caught fish and seafood. Heated pool (mid-May to Sept). Five elegant suites including Lady Hamilton with four-poster bed.

🛏45 ☕45 NBB £42.50-£57.50 V C 🐕
♿ 🐕 VISA :WTB ∴AA ::RAC

144

WELSH QUALITY MEATS

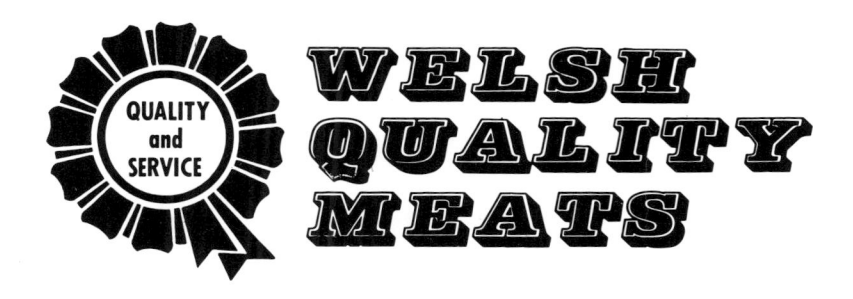

FOR QUALITY AND SERVICE SECOND TO NONE

CONTACT OUR HEAD OFFICE
ON NEYLAND (0646) 601816 (6 LINES)
OR FAX (0646) 601664

Unit 15
Great Honeyborough
Industrial Estate
Neyland, Dyfed
Tel: 0646 601816 (6 lines)
Fax: 0646 601664

Also at: Butchery Department
Dragon Cash & Carry
Dragon House, Penarth Road
Cardiff CF1 7UN
Tel: 0222 228424 (4 lines)
Fax: 0222 382712

GOLD MEDAL - AWARD WINNING WHOLESALE CATERING BUTCHERS
Welsh National Championships "CATERING BUTCHER OF THE YEAR"
for the third consecutive year 1987, 1988 and 1989

31 LOCHMEYLER FARM
PEN-Y-CWM
NR SOLVA SA62 6LL

Morfydd Jones, owner
Tel (0348) 837724/837705

Licensed farmhouse. Open 1-12. Restaurant open to non-residents. Serving times: Breakfast 8-8.45am, Dinner 7pm. Prices: Dinner £7.50. Wales Tourist Board Farmhouse Award, AA selected, RAC highly acclaimed, Wales Tourist Board commended. Children over 10 welcome.

From Fishguard follow the A487 St David's road to Mathry, turn left and follow road to the village of Llandeloy.

Working dairy farm centre on St David's peninsula, 4 miles from Solva harbour. 16th-century farmhouse, en-suite rooms, some with four-poster beds. All with TV, video, hair dryer, tea making facilities, electric blankets, telephones.

🛏6 🍽6 [NBB] £15 [WBB] £100 ✗ [V] 🐕
[▲] [VISA] [::WTB]

32 FOURCROFT HOTEL
CROFT TERRACE
TENBY SA70 8AP

P. L. Osborne, managing director
Tel (0834) 2886 Fax (0834) 2888

Licensed hotel. Open 3-11. Restaurant open to non-residents. Serving times: Breakfast 8.30-9.30am, Bar Lunch 12-2pm, Dinner 7-8.30pm. Prices: Dinner £13.50.

5 minutes from town centre overlooking harbour and Carmarthen Bay.

Private garden down to North Beach. Comfortable, spacious lounges, restaurant and conservatory. Bedrooms with every amenity. Lift, swimming and spa pools, sauna, multi-gym, snooker, pool, table-tennis, bowls.

🛏38 🍽38 [NBB] £31-£36 ✗ [V] [C] [▲]
[VISA] [::WTB] [:RAC] [:AA]

33 PENALLY ABBEY
PENALLY
NR TENBY

Mr & Mrs S.J Warren
Tel (0834) 3033

Licensed hotel. Open 1-12. Restaurant open to non-residents. Serving times: Breakfast 7-11am, Bar Lunch 1-2pm, Dinner 7.30-9.30pm. Prices: Bar Lunch £8, Dinner £16-£19.

1½ miles from Tenby.

In five acres of gardens. Quiet location overlooking golf course and bay. Eight four-posters, candlelit dinners, very warm pool, billiards. Local produce: fish, meats, veg. Excellent wine cellar.

🛏11 🍽11 [NBB] £28-£34 [WBB] £196-£238
✗ [V] [C] [▲] [::WTB] [:AA]

34 NEUADDLAS GUEST HOUSE
TREGARON SY25 6JL

Margaret Cutler, proprietress
Tel (0974) 298905

Unlicensed guest house. Open 1-12. Serving times: Breakfast 7.30-10am, Dinner 7-8.30pm. Prices: Dinner £7.50. Specialities include vegetarian, low fat diets.

On A485, 1½ miles from Tregaron.

In own grounds on the doorstep of the Cors Caron Nature Reserve, nestling under the Cambrian mountains. Central for the coast, golf, pony trekking and bird watching. Dining room and lounge.

🛏4 🍽3 [NBB] £14-£18 [WBB] £198-£252 ✗
[V] [C] 🐕 ♿ [::WTB]

MID, SOUTH & WEST GLAMORGAN

Members are listed alphabetically, based on location.
Numbers on map relate to order of entry in gazetteer.

Castell Coch, Tongwynlais

1 EGERTON GREY HOTEL
PORTHKERRY
NR BARRY CF6 9B2

Anthony Pitkin, owner
Tel (0446) 711666 Fax (0446) 711690

Licensed hotel. Open 1-12. Restaurant open to non-residents. Serving times: Breakfast 7.30-9.30am, Bar Lunch 12-2pm, Lunch 12-2pm, High Tea 5-7pm, Dinner 7-9.30pm. Prices: Bar Lunch £3-£10, Lunch £15-£21, High Tea £6, Dinner £21. Specialities include fresh sewin, loin of lamb. Egon Ronay, Good Food Guide listed.

Close to airport. Take slip-road from junction 33 off M4.

Luxurious former rectory in a secluded valley facing the sea, 20 minutes from Cardiff. One hour from the Gower peninsula and Brecon Beacons. Inexpensive two-day breaks.

⛌10 ⛌10 [NBB] £27.50-£55
[WBB] £165-£325 [V] [C] [&] [▲] [VISA] [◐]
[AMEX] [::WTB] [∴AA] [∴RAC]

2 GREAT HOUSE RESTAURANT
HIGH STREET
LALESTON
BRIDGEND CF32 0HP

Norma & Stephen Bond, proprietors
Tel (0656) 657644

Licensed restaurant. Open 1-12. Serving times: Bar Lunch 12-2pm. Lunch 12-2pm, Dinner 7-9.30pm. Prices: Bar Lunch £4-£5, Lunch £10.25, Dinner £17.50. Good Food Guide listed.

In Laleston village, 20 minutes from Cardiff-Wales airport. Close to M4.

In olde-worlde village close to Porthcawl and Bridgend. Aiming to please all tastes and pockets from excellent restaurant to lite-bites at lunch and evening bistro.

[V] [C] [&] [▲] [VISA] [◐]

BRAINS TRADITIONAL BEERS - THE REAL TASTE OF WALES

it's Brains you want!

3 ARMLESS DRAGON
**97 WYEVERNE ROAD
CATHAYS
CARDIFF CF2 4BG**

David Richards, owner
Tel (0222) 220136

Licensed restaurant. Open 1-12. Serving times: Lunch 12.30-2.13pm, Dinner 7.30-10.30pm. Egon Ronay, Good Food Guide listed.

In Cathays, Cardiff.

Small informal, friendly restaurant with a genuinely varied menu. The emphasis is on fresh seasonal produce (local where available), fish and game. Several original specialities.

| V | C | ▲ | VISA | ⦾ | AMEX |

4 BARDELL RESTAURANT
**ST BRIDES SUPER ELY
ST FAGANS
NR CARDIFF CF5 6EZ**

Jane Budgen, chef
Tel (0446) 760534

Licensed restaurant. Open 1-12. Serving times: Lunch 12.30-2pm, Dinner 7.30-9.30pm, later upon request, i.e., theatre dinners etc. Prices: Sunday Lunch £13.50, Dinner £17. Specialities include seafood platter, fresh fish daily, game in season. Good Food Guide listed.

5 minutes from St Fagans.

Country house restaurant, family run. Individual parties can select their own menus and can book restaurant exclusively for an evening or lunch. Ample parking.

| ⌿ | V | C | ▲ | ⦾ |

5 BISHOPS EMPORIUM & TEA ROOM
**28-30 HIGH STREET
LLANDAFF
CARDIFF CF5 2DZ**

Selyf Davies-Edwards, owner
Tel (0222) 552886

Licensed delicatessen and tea room. Open 1-12. Prices: Lunch £2-£6. Specialities include Welsh homemade cakes. Guide dogs accepted.

In the main shopping street of Llandaff

Purveyor of fine foods with a very friendly atmosphere. 1st-floor tea room serving light lunches and traditional Welsh homemade cakes.

| V | C |

6 CARDIFF INTERNATIONAL HOTEL
**MARY ANN STREET
CARDIFF**

Alistair Sandall, manager
Tel (0222) 341441 Fax (0222) 223742

Licensed hotel. Open 1-12. Restaurant open to non-residents. Serving times: Breakfast 7-9am, Bar Lunch 12-2.30pm, Lunch 12.30-2.30pm, High Tea 3-6pm, Dinner 6.30-10pm. Prices: Bar Lunch £5-£8, Lunch £10-£18, Table d'hote £11.50, High Tea £3.50-£5.50, Dinner £10-£20, Table d'hote £14.50. Guide dogs accepted.

Cardiff city centre, half a mile from station.

Cardiff's newest hotel. Each of the bedrooms is en-suite with tea/coffee making facilities, satellite TV, etc. Relax in the sumptuous surroundings of the 'Sportsman's' Bar and dine in the 'Gazebo' Restaurant.

| ⌁143 | ⬛143 | NBB | £63-£95 | ⌿ | V | C | ♿ |
| ▲ | VISA | ⦾ | AMEX | ∴AA |

WS WINES

At W S Wines we have discovered the three most important things that any wine merchant can provide for restaurateurs and hoteliers. They are, in order of importance:

1   SERVICE

2   SERVICE

3   SERVICE

If you feel that we can be of assistance to you in any of these areas why not contact us and hear what we call service!

236a Cowbridge Road East, Canton, Cardiff, CF5 1GY
Telephone (0222) 377850 (24 hours) Fax (0222) 227531

Gourmet Hampers

A selection of luxury food hampers, exclusively and creatively designed to suit every taste.

A wide delivery area

Special occasions catered for

Contact Gail
Tel: (0446) 772379

Ty-Bronudd, Nash,
Nr. Cowbridge, S. Glam.
S. Wales CF7 7NS

Gail Armytage
B.Tech., E.E.T.C., N.D.S.E.

Three sites in one

The High Victorian Dream of knights and ladies, of chivalry and of crusades, was the inspiration behind the magnificent 19th-century reconstruction of Cardiff Castle by the 3rd Marquess of Bute, and his architect, William Burges.

The castle began its days as a Roman fort, and it contains one of the finest Roman walls in Britain. In its second phase of development, Cardiff became the Norman headquarters of the Lordship of Glamorgan. The castle's extensive grounds contain a well-preserved medieval keep – one of Britain's finest – which crowns a tall, steep-sided earthen mound. But the castle as we now see it is mainly a product of the fertile imagination of the 'eccentric genius' William Burges. The castle's extravagant, no-expense-spared interiors also reflect the immense wealth generated by Cardiff's booming 19th-century coal-exporting docklands, which were controlled by the Bute family.

7 CELEBRITY RESTAURANT
(PART OF ST DAVID'S HALL - THE NATIONAL CONFERENCE & CONCERT HALL OF WALES)
THE HAYES
CARDIFF CF1 2SH

David Williams, restaurant manager
Gillian Nurton, catering manager
Tel (0222) 227211 for reservations
Tel (0222) 342611 Fax (0222) 383726

Licensed restaurant. Open 1-12, except Christmas Day, Sunday and Monday dinner. Serving times: Bar Lunch 12-2.15pm, Lunch 12-2.15pm, High Tea, Coffee Shop 10-4.30pm, Dinner 6-9.30pm (last orders 9.30pm). Prices: Bar Lunch £3, Lunch £6-£8.50, Dinner £7-£12. Specialities include Vale of Glamorgan pork and fresh West Wales trout. Guide dogs accepted. Arts Card.

Restaurant is part of St David's Hall complex in city centre.

Celebrity restaurant with a distinctive Welsh flavour. Shoppers' luncheon, speciality evening menus and show supper menus available.

8 CELTIC CAULDRON
47/49 CASTLE ARCADE
CASTLE STREET
CARDIFF

V. Bhagotra, owner
Tel (0222) 387185

Licensed restaurant. Open 1-12. Serving times: Bar Lunch 10-8pm, Lunch 10-8pm, High Tea 10-8pm, Dinner 10-8pm. Bar Lunch £1.50, Lunch £3.50-£5.50, High Tea from £2, Dinner £6-£8. Specialities include laverbread, authentic Welsh rarebit, Glamorganshire sausage. Guide dogs accepted.

Right opposite Cardiff Castle at the entrance of Castle Arcade.

This café/restaurant is situated in Cardiff's premier arcade. It boasts authentic Welsh fayre and a wide range of vegetarian dishes which can be eaten in the restaurant's relaxed and friendly atmosphere or taken away. Luncheon vouchers.

9 CHAMPER'S
61 ST MARY STREET
CARDIFF

Mr B.D. Martinez, proprietor
Tel (0222) 373363

Licensed restaurant. Open 1-12. Serving times: Lunch 12-3pm, Dinner 7-12.30pm. Prices: Lunch £5-£10, Dinner £10-£15. Specialities include shellfish, charcoal grills. Good Food Guide listed.

In Cardiff city centre, top of St Mary Street.

An authentic wine bar, with a genuine Spanish atmosphere, and a selection of over 100 Rioja, quality Spanish wines.

10 DE COURCEY'S
TYLA MORRIS AVENUE
PENTYRCH
NR CARDIFF CF4 8QN

Thilo & Patricia Thielmann, owners
Tel (0222) 892232 Fax (0222) 892232

Licensed restaurant. Open 1-12. Serving times: Lunch 12-2pm, Dinner 7.30-10pm. Prices: Lunch £15-£23.50, Dinner £23.50. Good Food Guide listed.

11 HOLIDAY INN CARDIFF MILL LANE
CARDIFF CF1 1EZ

Tracey Evans, sales manager
Tel (0222) 399944 Fax (0222) 395578

Licensed hotel. Open 1-12. Restaurant open to non-residents. Serving times: Breakfast 7-10.30am, Bar Lunch 11am-11pm, Lunch 12.30-2.30pm, High Tea 3-5pm, Dinner 7.30-10.30pm. Prices: Lunch £12.95, Dinner £15. Egon Ronay listed.

Close to city centre.

⌬182 ⌬182 NBB from £54
WBB from £333 V C ♿ VISA
⌬ AMEX WTB ::AA ::RAC

12 LA BRASSERIE 60 ST MARY STREET
CARDIFF

B. D. Martinez, proprietor
Tel (0222) 372164

Licensed restaurant/inn pub. Open 1-12. Serving times: Lunch 12-3pm, Dinner 7pm-12.30am. Prices: Lunch £3-£10, Dinner £10-£25. Specialities include game in season, i.e., pheasant, partridge, venison, suckling pig, pigeon, fresh salmon. Listed in Good Food Guide.

In Cardiff city centre, at the top of St Mary Street.

Has the theme of a typical French wine bar, with good fresh food and a very large selection of quality French wines.

V ⌬ VISA ⌬ AMEX

13 LE MONDE 60 ST MARY STREET
CARDIFF

B.D. Martinez, proprietor
Tel (0222) 387376

Licensed restaurant /inn/pub. Open 1-12. Serving times: Lunch 12-3.00pm, Dinner 7pm-12am. Prices: Lunch £5-£15, Dinner £10-£25. Specialities include sea bass, tiger prawns. Daily selection of fresh fish and shellfish, lobster, crabs and oysters. Good Food Guide listed.

In Cardiff city centre, at the top of St Mary Street.

Has an international theme, with an excellent selection of fresh fish and a large selection of French and Spanish wines, ports and champagnes.

V ⌬ VISA ⌬ AMEX

14 SANDRINGHAM HOTEL ST MARY STREET
CARDIFF CF1 2PL

T. M. Nolan, director
Tel (0222) 232161 Fax (0222) 383998

Licensed hotel. Open 1-12. Restaurant open to non-residents. Serving times: Breakfast 7.30-9.30am, Bar Lunch 11-3pm, Lunch 12-3pm, Dinner 6-10pm. Prices: Bar Lunch £2.55-£3.45, Lunch £6.75, Dinner £6.75-£9.50.

Centrally situated in Cardiff.

Privately owned 'friendly' hotel with 28 en-suite newly refurbished bedrooms. Grosvenor function room can accommodate 80 persons with private bar facilities. Sandy's Bar and Restaurant features comprehensive bar food menu, and 50-seater restaurant.

⌬28 ⌬28 NBB £22.50-£30
WBB £177.50-£187.50 V C 🐕 ⌬
VISA ⌬ AMEX

15 TRILLIUM RESTAURANT
40 CITY ROAD
ROATH
CARDIFF CF2 3DL

Kami & Debbie Soroush, owners
Tel (0222) 463665

Licensed restaurant. Open 1-12. Prices: Lunch £9-£12. Dinner £25-£35, including wine. Egon Ronay, Good Food Guide listed. Guide dogs accepted.

Within 5 minutes' walking distance of Cardiff centre.

Bar/lounge with leather armchairs, wood panelling. Library compared to a gentlemans' club. Restaurant with pink and white decor. Elaborate chandeliers, elegant drapes, oil paintings.

|V| |C| |▲| |VISA| |⊕| |AMEX|

16 YESTERDAY'S RESTAURANT
THE LODGE
SOPHIA CLOSE
CARDIFF CF1 9LJ

John & Wendy Wollen, proprietors
Tel (0222) 371420

Licensed restaurant. Open 1-12. Serving times: Business Breakfast 8-10am, Morning Coffee 10-12pm, Bar Lunch 12-2.30pm, Business Lunch 12-3pm, Afternoon Tea 3-5pm, Dinner 7-12pm. Prices: Morning Coffee £2.50, Bar Lunch £1.50-£4.50, Lunch £8.95, Afternoon Tea £2.50, Dinner £15-£20. Specialities include traditional Welsh and Japanese cuisine.

Close to Cardiff centre in Sophia Gardens.

The unique setting of this historic West Lodge building, situated at the edge of Cardiff Castle grounds, provides an exclusive dining venue for Yesterday's Victorian Orangery restaurant. Resident pianist provides evening entertainment. Party bookings welcomed.

|✂| |V| |C| |♿| |▲| |VISA| |AMEX|

Cariad
Welsh Table Wine
Gwin Da O Gymru

Cariad ... the only estate-bottled wine from Wales

Llanerch Vineyard, Hensol, Pendoylan,
Vale of Glamorgan CF7 8JU. Telephone: (0443) 225877

Cariad Wines

17 TREGENNA HOTEL
PARK TERRACE
MERTHYR TYDFIL CF47 8RF

Michael Hurley, owner
Tel (0685)723627 Fax (0685) 72951

Licensed hotel and restaurant. Open 1-12. Restaurant open to non-residents. Serving times: Breakfast 7-10am, Bar Lunch 12-2.30pm, Lunch 12-2.30 pm, High Tea 4-6pm, Dinner 7-10pm. Prices: Bar Lunch £3-£6, Lunch £4-£8, High Tea £3, Dinner £8-10. Good Food Guide listed.

Within easy reach of town centre.

Family run. Family rooms and four-bedroom holiday homes for larger families or groups. Brecon Beacons National Park 10 minutes away. 18-hole Morlais Castle golf course nearby.

21 21 NBB £23 V C & ▲ VISA
⊙ AMEX ::WTB :AA :RAC

18 NEATH COLLEGE PARAGON
RESTAURANT
DWR-Y-FELIN ROAD
NEATH

Wynne Edwards, lecturer
Tel (0639) 633276 ext 244
Fax (0639) 634208

Licensed restaurant. Open 9-6. Serving times: Lunch 12-1.30pm, Dinner 6-8pm. Prices: Lunch £5-£7, Dinner £7-£10. Speciality evenings are held frequently during the term. Guide dogs only accepted.

From the M4 take the A465 in the direction of Pontardawe.

A college training restaurant, run on traditional lines. The students are encouraged to produce 'new' and innovative dishes using fresh ingredients. All customers must book in advance for a reservation.

✂ V C &

19 CAPRICE RESTAURANT
THE ESPLANADE
PENARTH CF6 2AS

Eddie Rabaiotti
Tel (0222) 702424 Fax (0222) 711518

Licensed restaurant. Open 1-12. Serving times: Lunch 12-2.30pm, Dinner 7-11pm. Prices: Lunch from £8.95, Dinner from £16.95. Seafood specialities include fresh lobster, Dover sole, salmon, oysters.

On the seafront at Penarth.

Specialising in seafoods with fixed-price menu available daily. Four-course dinners. Available for wedding receptions, business functions etc. Extensive wine cellar.

V C ▲ VISA ⊙ AMEX

20 WHITE SPRINGS LODGE
RESTAURANT
PISTYLLGWYN FARM
GARNSWLLT ROAD
PONTARDDULAIS

Edward Vincent Lloyd, owner
Tel (0792) 885699

Licensed restaurant. Open 1-12. Serving times: Bar Lunch 12-2pm, Lunch 12-2pm, Dinner 7-9.30pm. Closed on Mondays. Prices: Bar Lunch £2.75-£4.50, Dinner £5.75-£10.50. Specialities include trout with prawn stuffing, pan fried trout etc. Guide dogs accepted.

M4 exit 48 from east, turn right half a mile.

Panoramic views of the countryside with three picturesque lakes in front of the restaurant. It also has a little animal farm for children.

✂ V C & ▲

21 LORELEI HOTEL
ESPLANADE AVENUE
PORTHCAWL CF36 3YU

Cameron Ellis, Tony Rogers, partners
Tel (0656) 772710 Fax (0656) 772712

Licensed hotel. Open 1-12. Restaurant open to non-residents. Serving times: Breakfast 7.15-10am, Lunch 12-2pm, Dinner 7.30-10pm. Prices: Lunch £3-£5, Dinner £12-£18. Specialities include fillet of salmon. RAC resaurant award of merit.

Off seafront in Porthcawl.

A Victorian double property offering a choice of two restaurants - Pinks (à la carte, AA Top 500 Restaurant Guide) and Planters Brasserie, informal and open seven nights a week. Real ales, friendly atmosphere.

⛌ 14 ⛌14 NBB £19.50 V C ▲ VISA
◐ AMEX ∵WTB

22 FAIRYHILL COUNTRY HOUSE
HOTEL & RESTAURANT
REYNOLDSTON
(GOWER)
SWANSEA SA3 1BS

Mr John Frayne, owner
Tel (0792) 390139

Licensed hotel. Open 1-12, except December 25, 26, 31, Jan 1. Restaurant open to non-residents. Serving times: Breakfast 7.30-9.30am, Lunch 12.30-1.15pm, Dinner 7.30-9m. Prices: Sunday Lunch £11.95, Dinner £20-£25. Specialities include deep-fried cockles, local mussels, sewin. Egon Ronay, Good Food Guide listed.

Take junction 47 off M4, follow directions to Gorseinon.

24 acres of woodland and parkland in the heart of the Gower peninsula, with half a mile of trout stream. A true haven of peace and tranquillity.

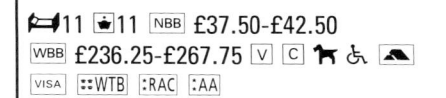

⛌11 ⛌11 NBB £37.50-£42.50
WBB £236.25-£267.75 V C 🐕 ♿ ▲
VISA ∵WTB :RAC :AA

23 KEENAN'S RESTAURANT
82 ST HELEN'S ROAD
SWANSEA SA1 4BQ

Chris & Lynda Keenan, owners
Tel (0792) 644111.

Licensed restaurant. Open 1-12. Serving times: Dinner 7-9.30pm. Prices: Dinner £15-£25 3 courses. Specialities include rack of Welsh lamb. Good Food Guide listed

Close to city centre and Swansea Bay.

A small restaurant of 26 covers, offering a menu of 5-6 choices at each course. All is complemented by an interesting wine list of 50 bins.

V C ▲ VISA

24 LANGLAND COURT HOTEL
LANGLAND
SWANSEA SA3 4TD

Colin Birt, owner
Tel (0792) 361545 Fax (0792) 362302

Licensed hotel. Open 1-12. Restaurant open to non-residents. Serving times: Breakfast 7.30-9.30am, Bar Lunch 12-2pm, Dinner 7-9.30pm. Prices: Bar Lunch £4-£5.50, Lunch £6.50-£8.50, Dinner £14.50- £18.50. Specialities include local seafood and Welsh cheeses. Egon Ronay, Good Food Guide listed.

A4067 to Mumbles, then B4593.

Tudor-style country house in own grounds overlooking Langland Bay and golf course. Within easy reach of countryside, coast and nearby Swansea. Folly's Wine Bar serves bar lunches, wines and ales.

⛌21 ⛌21 NBB £32-£34 WBB £224-£238
✂ V C ▲ VISA ◐ AMEX ∵WTB :AA
:RAC

Dylan's 'ugly, lovely' town

Dylan Thomas, the most famous 20th-century Welsh poet and writer, was born in Swansea, a city he once described as 'an ugly, lovely town'. The ugly duckling has turned into a lovely swan now, a return perhaps to its pre-industrial days as a fashionable resort when Georgian society flocked to its seashores

The magnificent sweep of Swansea Bay, which has been compared with the Bay of Naples, is enhanced by a new Maritime Quarter at the city end. This award-winning development, whose centrepiece is a 600-berth marina, has renewed Swansea's links with the sea in a most accomplished way. Along the quayside stands an excellent Maritime and Industrial Museum close to the Swansea Leisure Centre, one of Wales's top tourist attractions. Dylan Thomas is commemorated in the Maritime Quarter by a theatre named after him and a bronze statue surveying the new order.

Swansea's new Maritime Quarter

---

25 NICHOLASTON HOUSE HOTEL
NICHOLASTON (GOWER) SWANSEA SA3 2HL

Mr Lewis, partner
Tel (0792) 371317

Licensed hotel. Open 1-12. Restaurant open to non-residents. Serving times: Breakfast 8-9.15am, Bar Lunch 12-2pm, Dinner 7-9pm. Prices: Bar Lunch £3-£7, Dinner £8-£20.

On A4118, 10 miles from Swansea.

Country house hotel and restaurant enjoying one of the finest views in the country, overlooking Bristol Channel. As many local products as possible are used, creating a high standard of cuisine.

⌂11 ▪11 NBB from£25 WBB from£156
V C 🐕 ♿ ▲ VISA •WTB •AA •RAC

---

26 P.A.'S WINE BAR
95 NEWTON ROAD MUMBLES SWANSEA SA3 4BN

A. Hetherington, partner
Tel (0792) 367723

Licensed wine bar/restaurant. Open 1-12 (but closed October). Serving times: Lunch 12.30-2.30pm, Dinner 6-9.30pm. Prices: Lunch £2.25-£16, Dinner £3.25-£16. Good Food Guide listed.

On way out of the village towards Gower.

P.A.'s has an intimate, informal atmosphere and is popular with both locals and visitors. The constantly changing menu varies according to seasonal availability. Main courses make use of fresh fish from Swansea market.

V ▲ VISA

GWENT

*Members are listed alphabetically, based on location.
Numbers on map relate to order of entry in gazetteer.*

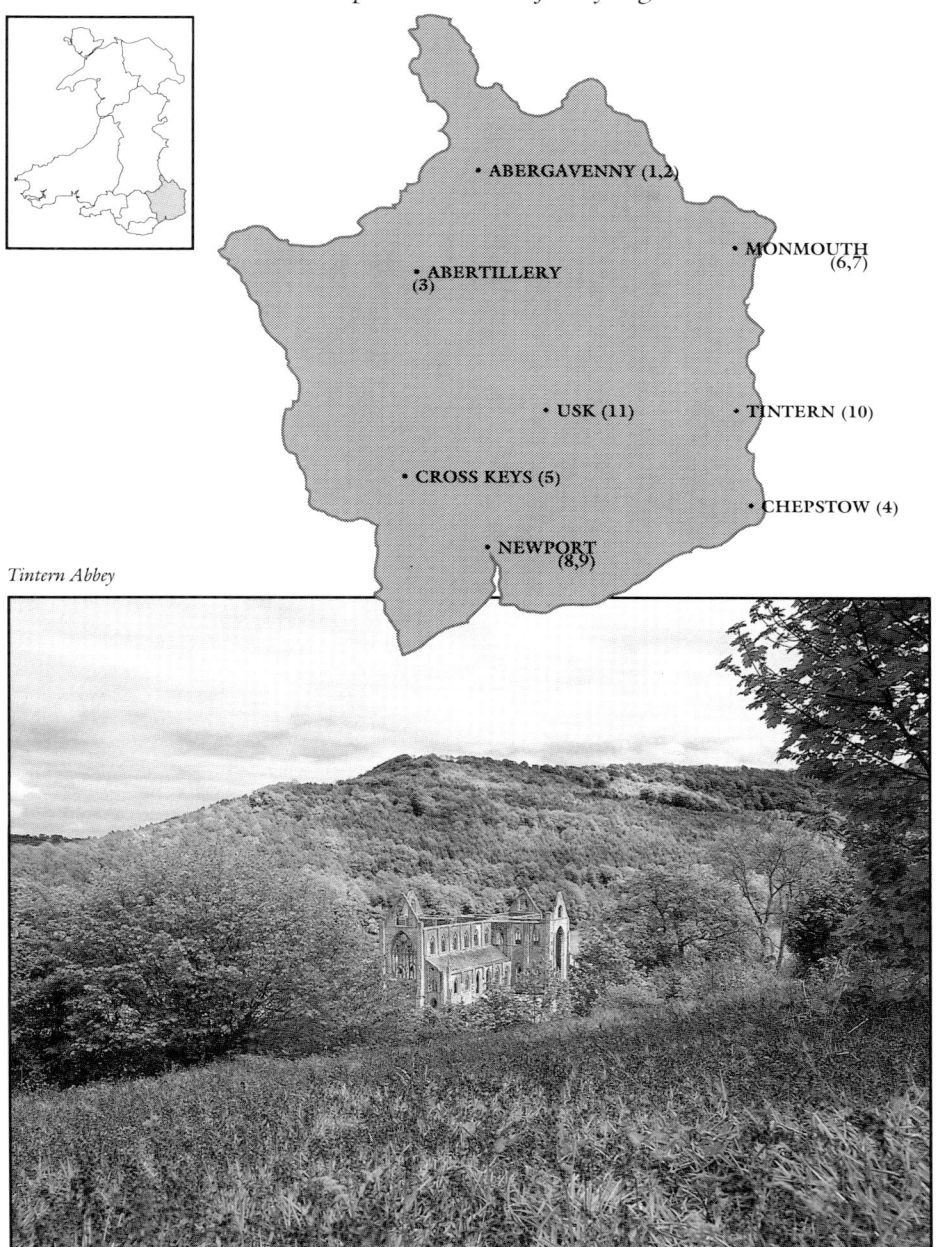

- ABERGAVENNY (1,2)
- MONMOUTH (6,7)
- ABERTILLERY (3)
- USK (11)
- TINTERN (10)
- CROSS KEYS (5)
- CHEPSTOW (4)
- NEWPORT (8,9)

Tintern Abbey

1 LLANSANTFFRAED COURT HOTEL
LLANVIHANGEL GOBION
NR ABERGAVENNY NP7 9BA

Mr & Mrs Alani
Tel (0873) 840678 Fax (0873) 840674

Licensed hotel. Open 1-12. Restaurant open to non-residents. Serving times: Breakfast 7-10am, Bar Lunch 12-2pm, Lunch 12-2pm, Dinner 7-9.30pm.

Between Abergavenny and Raglan on the B4598.

An elegant Georgian-styled country house hotel with origins going back to the 14th century. The restaurant is the oldest part. The main house is luxuriously furnished with a strong Georgian influence. Just 25 minutes' drive from the M4.

⌂21 ♨21 [NBB] £42.50-£60
[WBB] £175-£200 ✗ [V] [C] [🐕] [♿] [▲] [VISA]
[⊙] [AMEX] [∷WTB]

2 WALNUT TREE INN LLANDEWI SKIRRID
ABERGAVENNY NP7 8AW

Franco & Ann Taruschio
Tel (0873) 2797

Licensed restaurant. Open 1-12. Serving times: Lunch 12-2.30pm, Dinner 7-10.30pm. Egon Ronay, Good Food Guide listed.

3 miles north-east of Abergavenny on B4521.

Has been serving superb food in a relaxed country setting since the early 1960s. Taking full advantage of the finest ingredients in his area, Franco Taruschio produces a magnificent choice of real Italian combined with the best of Welsh.

[V] [C] [🐕] [♿]

3 OWLS END GUEST HOUSE
52-56 SOMERSET STREET
ABERTILLERY NP3 1DL

Astrid Hargreaves, owner
Tel (0495) 212553

Licensed guest house. Open 1-12. Prices: Dinner £7-£9. Specialities include roast honeyed Welsh lamb, leeks with ham in a cheese sauce. Wales Tourist Board listed.

Off A467 between Heads of the Valleys A465 and M4.

Friendly relaxed family atmosphere. Good home cooking, golf, fishing and many other attractions in this delightful area within easy reach. Five minutes from 1992 Garden Festival.

⌂4 ♨4 [NBB] £13.50 [V] [C] [▲]

4 AFON GWY RESTAURANT WITH ROOMS
28 BRIDGE STREET
CHEPSTOW NP6 5EZ

Rosemarie Jenkins
Tel (02912) 70158

Licensed restaurant with rooms. Open 2-12. Restaurant open to non-residents. Serving times: Bar Lunch 12-2pm, summer season only, Lunch as bar, Dinner 7-10pm. Prices: Bar Lunch £3-£5, Lunch £4-£9, Dinner £12-£15. Specialities include rack of Welsh lamb cooked in herbs and garlic and wrapped in filo pastry. Taste of Wales platter (laverbread, cockles and bacon, and Welsh cheeses), cawl. Good Food Guide, Ackermann/Martel listed.

150 yards past Chepstow Castle on the left-hand side.

A small family-run hotel/restaurant situated on the banks of the river Wye. It is in an area of outstanding natural beauty with superb views of the river. Gourmet weekends including a Wye boat trip.

⌂4 ♨4 [NBB] from £20
[WBB] from £126 ✗ [V] [C] [▲] [VISA] [∷WTB]

158

A Taste of Wales & so much more...

Exotic gardens, innovative displays, exciting rides and a kaleidoscope of events, from theatre and opera to pop concerts and laser shows, scientific demonstrations to nature parks, ancient legends to space age technology, in fact, something for everyone!

...all in the spectacular setting of
GARDEN FESTIVAL WALES
May to October 1992

Garden Festival Wales,
Festival House,
Victoria, Ebbw Vale,
Gwent. NP3 6UF

*Garden Festival Wales
Gŵyl Gerddi Cymru
Ebbw Vale 92*

WELSH CHEF OF THE YEAR

Andrew Jones, of the Celtic Manor Hotel, Newport is the winner of the Welsh Chef of the Year Award 1990.

All contestants used electric catering equipment in the final of the competition.

For free advice on all your electric catering requirements please contact Sally Trevett, South Wales Electricity.
Telephone: Cardiff (0222) 792111 Ext. 2462 or Judith McIntyre, Manweb. Telephone: Chester (0244) 377111 Ext. 2831.

South Wales ELECTRICITY
Trydan De Cymru
A POWER IN WALES
Head Office: St. Mellons, Cardiff CF3 9XW.

Manweb
ENERGY FOR Action
Head Office: Sealand Rd, Chester CH1 4LR.

CATERELECTRIC

5 YNYS HYWEL COUNTRYSIDE CENTRE
CWMFELINFACH
CROSS KEYS NP1 7JX

Nina Finnigan, manager
Tel (0495) 200113

Licensed hotel. Open 1-12. Restaurant open to non-residents. Serving times: Breakfast 8-9am, Lunch 12-2pm, Dinner 7.30-9pm. Prices: Lunch £6.50-£8.50, Dinner £7.50-£12.50. Specialities include welshcakes.

Off Junction 28 M4 to A467 then A4048.

Set in the Sirhowy Valley Country Park. Extended traditional Welsh Longhouse. Lounge Bar and restaurant themed on 'healthy living'. Conference/training rooms with audio-visual equipment. Also a traditional hill farm. Good for walkers and naturalists.

🛏9 ♦7 [NBB] £26.50 [WBB] £180 ✶ [V] [C] ♿ [∴WTB]

6 CROWN AT WHITEBROOK
WHITEBROOK
NR MONMOUTH NP5 4TX

Roger Bates, owner
Tel (0600) 860254 Fax (0600) 860607

Licensed restaurant with rooms. Open 1-12 except for three weeks in January. Restaurant open to non-residents. Serving times: Breakfast 8.30-9.30am, Bar lunch 12-2pm, Lunch 12-2pm, Dinner 7-9.30pm. Prices: Bar Lunch £2.25-£5, Lunch £12.50, Dinner £21.50. Specialities include Welsh lamb with redcurrant and brandy served with a red wine, mint and rosemary sauce, homemade ice creams and sorbets. Egon Ronay, Les Routiers and Good Hotel Guide listed.

5 miles south of Monmouth between the A466 and B4239.

French cuisine restaurant where everything is individually prepared to order from fresh local ingredients. This former inn dating back to 1679 is now a haven for lovers of good food, good wine, friendly and relaxing ambience.

🛏12 ♦12 [NBB] from £33 [WBB] from £231 ✶ [V] [C] 🐕 ⛰ [VISA] [⊙] [AMEX] [∴WTB] [∷AA] [∷RAC]

7 VILLAGE GREEN RESTAURANT & BRASSERIE
TRELLECH
NR MONMOUTH NP6 4PA

Bob Evans, owner
Tel (0600) 860119

Licensed restaurant/inn/pub. Open 1-12. Restaurant open to non-residents. Serving times: Bar Lunch 12-2pm, Lunch 12-2pm, Dinner 7-9.45pm. Prices: Bar Lunch £1.50-£8.75, Lunch three course £10.75, Dinner £10-£30. Egon Ronay, Good Food Guide listed.

4 miles south of Monmouth in Trellech.

Totally refurbished former coaching inn in the picturesque village of Trellech. Building is 450 years old, built in local stone with coach house accommodation at front.

🛏2 ♦2 [NBB] £20-£25 [V] [C] ♿ ⛰ [VISA]

8 CELTIC MANOR HOTEL
COLDRA WOODS
NEWPORT NP6 2YA

Tel (0633) 413000 Fax (0633) 412910

Licensed hotel. Open 1-12. Restaurant open to non-residents. Serving times: Breakfast 7-10.30am, Bar Lunch 11.30am-2.30pm, Lunch 12-2.30pm, Dinner 7-10.30pm. Prices: Bar Lunch £2-£8, Lunch £8-£18, High Tea £6, Dinner £12-£30. Specialities include: Welsh produce such as lamb, venison, pheasant, salmon. Egon Ronay, Good Food Guide listed.

Close to junction 24 on the M4.

Situated amidst 300 acres of hillside woodland and offering 74 air-conditioned rooms and two restaurants. Extensive banqueting and conference facilities to accommodate up to 300. Indoor swimming pool and leisure facilities.

🛏74 ♦74 [NBB] £49.50-£57.50 ✶ [V] [C] ♿ ⛰ [VISA] [⊙] [AMEX] [∴WTB] [∷AA] [∷RAC]

9 ELM TREE RESTAURANT & BISTRO
ST BRIDES WENTLOOGE
NR NEWPORT NP1 9SQ

Mike & Patricia Thomas, proprietors
Tel (0633) 680225

Licensed restaurant. Open 1-12. Serving times: Lunch 12-2pm, Dinner 7-10pm. Prices: Bar Lunch £5-£10, Lunch £10-£20, Dinner £10-£25. Specialities include seafood platters, fresh lobsters from tank. When in season all game dishes.

On the Old Lighthouse coast road, 3 miles from Newport

Our large spacious restaurant has an air of outstanding country elegance, the bistro a casual friendly ambience. We take pride in the originality and size of our menus - extravagant with fish and seafood in summer and game in winter.

| V | C | ▲ | VISA |

10 PARVA FARMHOUSE HOTEL & RESTAURANT
TINTERN NP6 6SQ

Dereck & Vickie Stubbs, proprietors
Tel (0291) 689411

Licenced hotel. Open 1-12. Restaurant open to non-residents. Serving times: Breakfast 8-9.15am, Dinner 7-8.30pm. Prices: Dinner £12.50-£15. Egon Ronay, Good Food Guide listed.

On the main A466 Chepstow to Monmouth road, 5 miles from M4.

17th-century farmhouse with all modern amenities, bedrooms newly refurbished, two four-poster rooms, lounge with leather chesterfields and log fires in winter. Inglenook restaurant with oak beams, interesting menu with varied dishes and plenty of choice.

🛏9　🍴7　NBB £19.50-£30　WBB £180-£250
V　C　🐕　∴WTB　∴AA

The viscount's parrot

Tredegar House, on the outskirts of Newport, Gwent, is regarded as Wales's finest 17th-century house. It has been meticulously restored by the local council and stands at the heart of a beautiful country park. The house was the seat of the Morgans for well over 500 years. This family included amongst its members a famous survivor of the Charge of the Light Brigade, and the equally famous Henry Morgan, the notorious pirate who became Governor of Jamaica.

The last Viscount Tredegar was Evan Morgan, dabbler and eccentric, whose extravagant house parties in the 1930s drew socialites like Nancy Cunard. This was despite his private menagerie of pets, which included a very rude parrot trained by Evan, and a snake who enjoyed sleeping on top of pelmets - much to the dismay of the maid who drew the curtains in the morning.

11 BUSH HOUSE OF USK
20 BRIDGE STREET
USK NP5 1BG

Steven Rogers, proprietor
Tel (02913) 2929

Licensed bistro. Open 1-12. Prices: Bar Lunch £3-£5, Lunch £3-£5, High Tea from £1.50, Dinner £9-£14. Specialities include a wide range of authentic Welsh and vegetarian dishes. Good Food Guide listed.

Middle of Main Street opposite town car park - pedestrian access.

Bistro offering breakfast, morning coffee, lunch, afternoon tea and dinner. A la carte and snack menu available. Informal relaxed environment.

| V | C | ▲ | VISA |

GWYNEDD

*Members are listed alphabetically, based on location.
Numbers on map relate to order of entry in gazetteer.*

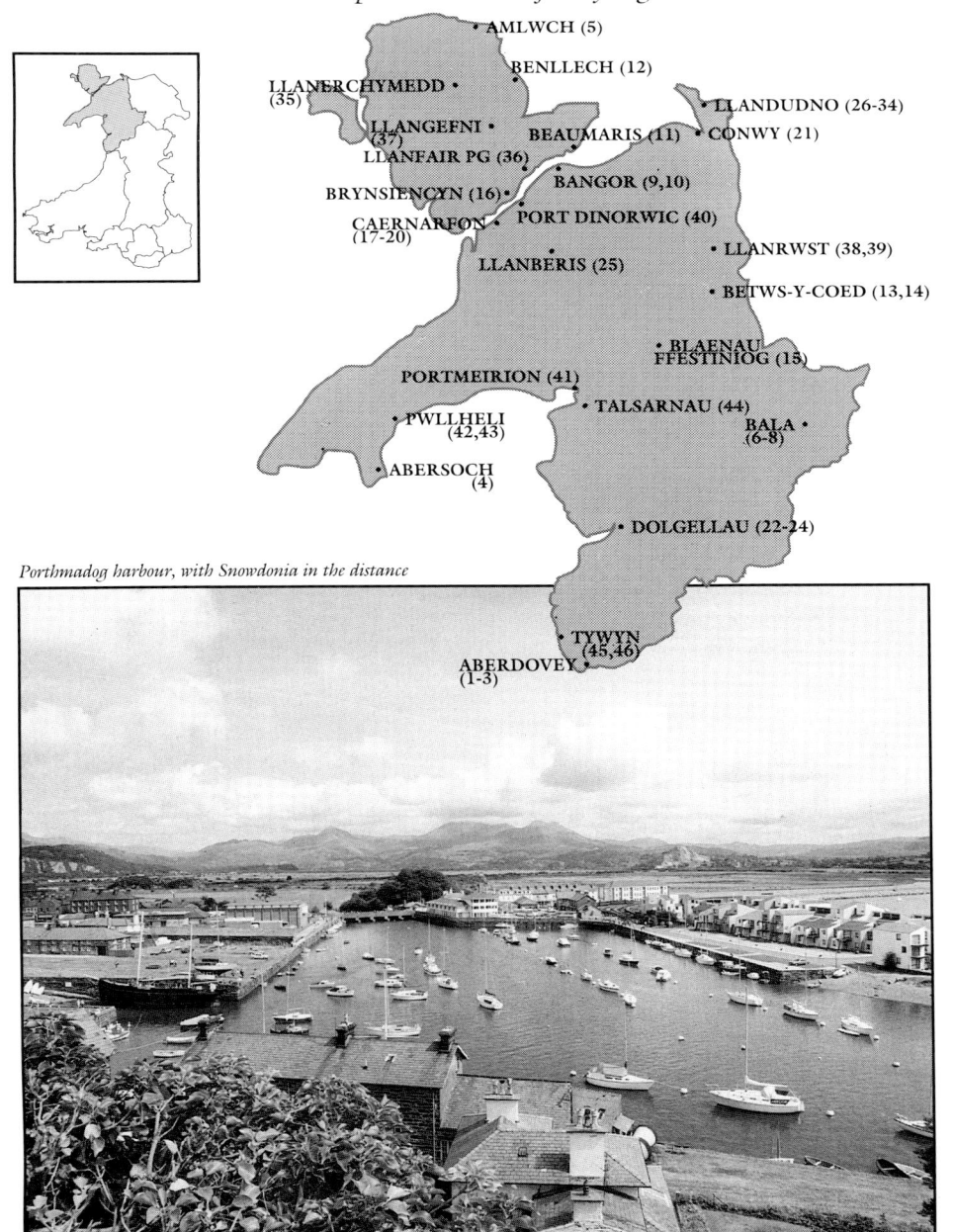

- AMLWCH (5)
- BENLLECH (12)
- LLANERCHYMEDD (35)
- LLANGEFNI (37)
- LLANFAIR PG (36)
- BEAUMARIS (11)
- LLANDUDNO (26-34)
- CONWY (21)
- BANGOR (9,10)
- BRYNSIENCYN (16)
- PORT DINORWIC (40)
- CAERNARFON (17-20)
- LLANBERIS (25)
- LLANRWST (38,39)
- BETWS-Y-COED (13,14)
- BLAENAU FFESTINIOG (15)
- PORTMEIRION (41)
- TALSARNAU (44)
- PWLLHELI (42,43)
- BALA (6-8)
- ABERSOCH (4)
- DOLGELLAU (22-24)
- TYWYN (45,46)
- ABERDOVEY (1-3)

Porthmadog harbour, with Snowdonia in the distance

163

1 OLD COFFEE SHOP
13 NEW STREET
ABERDOVEY LL35 OGH

Alan & Sue Griffiths
Tel (0654) 72652

Unlicensed restaurant. Open 1-12. Serving times: 12-2.30pm. Prices: Lunch £1.45-£5.25. Specialities include fresh salmon, patés, wholemeal quiches, sweets and pastries. Good Food Guide listed.

Off A493 Machynlleth to Tywyn road in Aberdovey village centre.

Food home cooked by Sue - sweets a speciality. Local produce, speciality teas and coffees, menu changes daily. Friendly welcome, character building, oak beams.

⌿ V C &

2 PENHELIG ARMS HOTEL & RESTAURANT
ABERDOVEY LL35 OLT

Robert or Sally Hughes, proprietors
Tel (0654) 72215

Licensed hotel. Open 1-12. Restaurant open to non-residents. Serving times: Breakfast 8.30-9.30am, Bar Lunch 12-2pm, Sunday Lunch 12.30-1.30pm, Dinner 7-9.30pm. Prices: Bar Lunch £1.50-£6, Sunday Lunch £8, Dinner £14. Good Food Guide listed.

Facing Penhelig harbour. Approach from Machynnlleth road.

Ideal location directly facing small picturesque harbour at the 'quieter' end of Aberdovey. Own car park. Beautiful walks on the doorstep. Menu changes constantly as we experiment with new ideas.

🛏10 🍴10 NBB from £25 C 🐕 🚗 VISA
∴WTB ∴AA

Terry Platt Wine Merchant
Ferndale Road
Llandudno Junction
Gwynedd
LL31 9NT
Telephone (0492) 592971
Fax (0492) 592196

TERRY PLATT
WINE MERCHANT

An independent family managed company, we offer the largest selection of fine wines available from any Wales based wine merchant.

Over 500 wines are shipped from country of origin, many exclusive to us.

We offer a specialist service to quality minded hotels and restaurants.

Please ask for a copy of our new list.

We look forward to hearing from you.

3 PLAS PENHELIG COUNTRY HOUSE HOTEL
ABERDOVEY LL35 0NA

David Richardson, director
Tel (0654) 767676 Fax (0654) 727783

Licensed country house hotel. Open 3-12. Restaurant open to non-residents. Serving times: Breakfast 8.30-9.30am, Bar Lunch 1-2pm, Dinner 7.30-8.45pm. Prices: Bar Lunch £3-£6, Lunch £9.50, Dinner £15.50. Egon Ronay listed.

Overlooking Dovey estuary.

An Edwardian country house with oak-panelled hall and log fires. Emphasis on country house atmosphere with all the service and comforts of a three-star hotel. Four acres of grounds and gardens including walled kitchen garden.

🛏11 🛁11 [NBB] £37.50-£40.50
[WBB] £270-£297 [✕] [C] [▲] [VISA] [AMEX] [∷WTB]
[∴AA]

4 RIVERSIDE HOTEL & RESTAURANT
ABERSOCH LL53 7HW

John & Wendy Bakewell, owners
Tel (075881) 2419/2818

Licensed hotel. Open 3-11. Restaurant open to non-residents. Serving times: Breakfast 8.30-9.30am, Bar Lunch 12-2pm, High Tea 5.30, Dinner 7.30-9pm. Prices: Bar Lunch £2.50, High Tea £4, Dinner £19. Specialities include walnut coated loin of Welsh lamb with minted bernaise. Egon Ronay, Good Food Guide listed.

Overlooking harbour on road from Pwllheli to Abersoch.

In idyllic position with substantial river frontage and lawns (canoes on the river for guests' use). Hotel has been family owned for 22 years and has a well-established reputation for fine food, wine and accommodation.

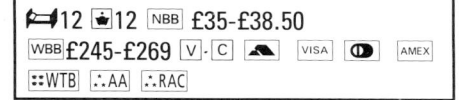

🛏12 🛁12 [NBB] £35-£38.50
[WBB] £245-£269 [V]·[C] [▲] [VISA] [◐] [AMEX]
[∷WTB] [∴AA] [∴RAC]

5 LASTRA FARM HOTEL & RESTAURANT
PENRHYD
AMLWCH LL68 9TF

Maurice Hutchinson & Adrian Parry, owners
Tel (0407) 830906

Licensed hotel/restaurant with function suite. Open 1-12. Restaurant open to non-residents. Serving times: Breakfast 7.30-9am, Bar Lunch 12-2pm, Lunch 12-2pm, Dinner 7-9.30pm. Prices: Bar Lunch £5.50, Lunch £6.50, Dinner £10-£13. Specialities include local lobster in season.

Rhosgogh Road near leisure centre.

A traditional farmhouse converted into modern family-run hotel and restaurant serving only the best of local produce. Refurbished to the highest standard.

🛏5 🛁4 [NBB] £16-£17.50 [WBB] £100-£110
[V] [C] [🐕] [▲] [VISA] [∷WTB]

6 NEUADD-Y-CYFNOD (OLD SCHOOL RESTAURANT)
HIGH STREET
BALA LL23 7PG

Miss N. Evans, manageress
Tel (0678) 520262

Licensed restaurant. Open 1-12. Serving times: Bar Lunch 12-9.30pm, Lunch 12-2.30pm, High Tea 3-5pm, Dinner 6-9.30pm. Prices: Bar Lunch £3.50-£6, Lunch £3.50-£4, High Tea £3-£5, Dinner £4.50-£12. Specialities include Welsh honey roast lamb in our own unique laverbread sauce. Guide dogs accepted.

On corner of A494 by-pass.

One of the oldest buildings in Bala. We cater for banquets, parties and weddings and specialize in traditional Welsh meals made from local fresh produce. Winners of Welsh Restaurant of the year 1987.

[✕] [V] [C] [♿] [·WTB]

7 PALÉ HALL LLANDDERFEL
NR BALA LL23 7PS

Tim & Jain Ovens, proprietors
Tel (06783) 285

Licensed hotel. Open 1-12. Restaurant open to non-residents. Serving times: Breakfast 7-11am, Lunch 12-2pm, Afternoon Tea all day, Dinner 7-9.30pm. Prices: Lunch £12.50, Afternoon Tea £2, Dinner £21. Children over 12 welcome. Egon Ronay, Good Food Guide listed.

4 miles from Bala off A494, near village of Llandderfel.

Victorian country mansion set in acres of parkland overlooking river Dee. Fine wines and food. Elegant accommodation. Golf, shooting, fishing, riding, archery, croquet.

⌁17 ⌁17 [NBB] £42.50-£77.50 ✈ [V] ♿
[▲] [VISA] [◉] [AMEX] [∷WTB]

8 WHITE LION HOTEL 61 HIGH STREET
BALA LL23 7AE

June Prescott or Karen Powell
Tel (0678) 520314

Licensed hotel. Open 1-12 except Christmas Day. Restaurant open to non-residents. Serving times: Breakfast 8-9.30am, Lunch 12-2.30pm, Afternoon Tea 3-5pm, Dinner 7-9.30pm. Prices: Lunch £7.25, Afternoon Tea £1.70, Dinner £9.50.

On A494 off the A5.

Family-run historic coaching inn (1759) in the lakeside resort of Bala with its wealth of sporting/leisure pursuits. Good food and wines in relaxed friendly atmosphere. Ideal for touring Snowdonia.

⌁26 ⌁22 [NBB] from £23 [WBB] from £160
[V] [C] [🐕] [▲] [VISA] [◉] [AMEX] [∷WTB] [:AA]
[:RAC]

9 GOETRE ISAF FARMHOUSE CAERNARFON ROAD
BANGOR LL57 4DB

Fred & Alison Whowell, proprietors
Tel (0248) 364541

Licensed farmhouse. Open 1-12. Serving times as required. Prices: Dinner £4.50-£8. Specialities include local produce, fish, meat, cheeses, honey.

2 miles outside Bangor on A4087.

The proximity of excellent butchers and a quayside source of fish is reflected in the menu. The house dates back probably to the mid 18th-century with original inglenook fireplace and incorporates an extension carried out in 1900.

⌁3 ⌁1 [NBB] £11-£12.50
[WBB] £77-£87.50 ✈ [V] [C] [🐕] [∷WTB]

10 THE NATIONAL TRUST PENRHYN CASTLE
NR BANGOR LL57 4HN

Tel (0248) 353084

Licensed restaurant. Open March 28-Nov 3, daily except Tuesday from 11am-5pm. Prices: Lunch £5-£8. Specialities include Welsh cheeses. Guide dogs acccepted.

1 mile east of Bangor at Llandegai on A5122.

A huge neo-Norman castle placed dramatically between Snowdonia and the Menai Strait. Fine pictures and furniture, industrial railway, doll museums and Victorian walled garden.

✈ [V] [C] ♿

11 YE OLDE BULL'S HEAD INN
CASTLE STREET
BEAUMARIS LL58 8AP

Keith Rothwell, David Robertson, owners
Tel (0248) 810329 Fax (0248) 811294

Licensed inn/pub. Open 1-12. Restaurant open to non-residents. Serving times: Breakfast 8-9.30am, Bar Lunch 12-2.30pm, Dinner 7.30-9.30pm. Prices: Bar Lunch £1.50-£9, Dinner £17-£22. Specialities include local bass, bream, grouse, hare. Good Food Guide listed, Wales Tourist Board commended. Children over seven welcome.

Town-centre location 100 yards for Beaumaris Castle.

Original coaching inn of the borough featuring prominently in the history of the town. Visited by Charles Dickens in 1859 and Dr Samuel Johnson. Hand-pulled real ales served in the oak-beamed bar. Many valuable antiques displayed.

🛏11 ♦11 [NBB] £31-£36.50 [WBB] £196 [V] [C] ▲ [VISA] [::WTB]

12 BRYN MEIRION GUEST HOUSE CATERING FOR THE DISABLED
AMLWCH ROAD
BENLLECH LL74 8SR

Christine Holland, owner
Tel (0248) 853118

Licensed guest house. Open 1-12. Restaurant open to non-residents. Breakfast 8.30-9.30am, Lunch 12-1.30pm, High Tea 2-4.30pm, Dinner 6-7pm. Specialities include scones, cakes, sandwiches, etc. Tea Gardens.

On A5025 to the north of Benllech.

We have a guest house fully adapted for the disabled, with en-suite rooms, ramps, etc. Castle Tea Gardens are open in the summer and cater for able-bodied and disabled. Gardens and castle ramped for wheelchairs.

🛏7 ♦6 ✗ [::WTB] [NBB] £15-£17 [V] [C] ♿

13 ROYAL OAK HOTEL
HOLYHEAD ROAD
BETWS-Y-COED LL24 0AY

F. Kavanagh, manager
Tel (0690) 710219 Fax (06902) 433

Licensed hotel. Open 1-12. Restaurant is open to non-residents. Serving times: Breakfast 7.45-9.30am, Bar Lunch 12-2pm, Lunch 12-2pm, High Tea 2-5.30pm, Dinner 6.45-8.30pm. Prices: Bar Lunch £4, Lunch £7.50, High Tea £5, Dinner £10.50.

On A5 in centre of village, within walking distance of station.

Former coaching inn overlooking river Llugwy. Ideal touring area. Luxury rooms with TVs and telephones. Elegant restaurant, grill open all day. Extensive menus use fresh local produce. Weekend and midweek breaks available.

🛏27 ♦27 [NBB] £25-£34 [WBB] £245-315
[V] [C] ▲ [VISA] [◐] [AMEX] [::WTB] [∴AA] [∴RAC]

14 TAN-Y-FOEL
COUNTRY HOUSE
CAPEL GARMON
NR BETWS-Y-COED LL26 0RE

Hazel & Barrie Michael, proprietors
Tel (0690) 710507

Licensed hotel. Open 2-12. Serving times: Breakfast 8.30-9.30am, Dinner 8pm – set time. Prices: Dinner from £17.50. Specialities include fresh local fish and lamb, home-produced fruit and vegetables. Children over 14 welcome. Egon Ronay, Good Food Guide listed.

2 miles north-east of Betws-y-coed via A470.

Relaxed informal and gently eccentric country house high on the hill overlooking the Conwy valley and the high peaks of Snowdonia. Superb food, congenial company make this the ideal hideaway.

🛏6 ♦6 [NBB] from £31 ✗ [V] 🐕 ♿ ▲
[AMEX] [::WTB] [::AA]

167

15 MYFANWY'S LICENSED RESTAURANT
4 MARKET PLACE
BLAENAU FFESTINIOG LL41 3NH

Roger & Barbara Kelly, owners
Tel (0766) 830059

Licensed restaurant. Open 2-12. Serving times: Lunch 11.45am-2.30pm, Dinner 6.30-10pm. Prices: Lunch £2-£15, Dinner £5.50-£15. Specialities – lamb, pork, chicken, sirloin steak, all served the delicious Myfanwy way.

In town, close to railway station and A470/A496 junction.

Five minutes' walk from the Ffestiniog Railway Station, with outstanding views of Victorian slate workings and the Moelwyn mountains. Myfanwy's offers the visitor an outstanding à la carte menu plus a lunch-time light-bite menu.

[V] [C] 🐕 ♿

16 ANGLESEY SEA ZOO
BRYNSIENCYN LL61 6TQ

Alison Lea-Wilson
Tel (0248) 430411   Fax (0248) 430213

Tourist attraction. Open 1-12, except 23-26 Dec and 1-6 Jan. Serving times: Bar Lunch 10am-4.30pm, Lunch 11am-2.30pm, High Tea 2.30-5.15pm. Prices: Bar Lunch £2-£3, Lunch £3-£5, High Tea £1-£2, Dinner £8-£12. Specialities include Anglesey oysters, mussels, local lobster to order.

Follow lobster signs from Britannia Bridge (A5) to zoo.

Award-winning sea zoo attracting 200,000 visitors per year. 100-cover restaurant specializing in home-cooked imaginative dishes. Seafood a speciality. Seafood shop on site. Evening parties by arrangement.

✂ [V] [C] ♿ 🏔 [VISA]

17 COURTENAY'S BISTRO
9 SEGONTIUM TERRACE
CAERNARFON LL55 2PN

Derek Norton & Cynthia Gilbey, owners
Tel (0286) 77290

Licensed restaurant. Open 1-12. Serving times: Lunch 12-2pm, Dinner 6.30pm. Prices: Lunch £5, Dinner £9. Specialities include Welsh lamb dishes.

At rear of main post office, Castle Square, Caernarfon.

Intimate 20-seat bistro producing home-cooked food at affordable prices. Welsh dishes are always available with a new menu choice each month. Vegetarian dishes at all times together with a good range of wines and 'tipple of the month'.

[V] [C] 🏔 [VISA]

18 PLAS TIRION FARM
LLANRUG
CAERNARFON LL55 4PY

Cerid Mackinnon, proprietor
Tel (0286) 673190

Licensed farmhouse. Open 5-9. Prices: Dinner £8. Specialities include: home-baked ham with madeira sauce, home-produced lamb and beef. Wales Tourist Board Farmhouse Award. AA listed.

1 mile outside village.

Working dairy farm with panoramic views of Caernarfon and Snowdonia range. Relaxed, comfortable surroundings. Start the day with our Welsh farmhouse breakfast and enjoy home-cooked dinners. Rough shooting on farm land.

🛏3 🍽3 [NBB] £16-£20 [WBB] £112-£140 [V]
[C] [❖WTB]

19 SEIONT MANOR HOTEL LLANRUG
CAERNARFON LL55 2AQ

H. John, Manager
Tel (0286) 673366 Fax (0286) 2840

Licensed hotel/restaurant. Open 1-12. Restaurant open to non-residents. Serving times: Breakfast 7.30-10am, Lunch 12-2.30pm, Dinner 7-10pm. Prices: Lunch £9.50, Dinner £14.50. Specialities include French cuisine and Welsh dishes. Egon Ronay listed.

Located between Llanberis and Caernarfon.

A deluxe hotel set within 150 acres of parkland, with its own leisure complex and helipad. The restaurant provides superb French cuisine and Welsh dishes using local produce. Ideally situated within easy reach of beaches and local tourist attractions.

🛏 28 🍽 28 [NBB] £42.50-£45
[WBB] £297.50-£315 ⌿ [V] [C] 🚗 [VISA]
[◐] [AMEX] [∴WTB] [∴RAC] [∴AA]

20 TY'N RHOS SEION LLANDDEINIOLEN
CAERNARFON LL55 3AE

Nigel & Linda Kettle, owners
Tel (0248) 670489

Licensed farmhouse. Open 1-12. Serving times: Breakfast 8.30-9am, Dinner 7-7.30pm. Prices: Dinner £12. Wales Tourist Board Farmhouse Award. Good Food Guide listed. Children over six welcome.

Off B4366 in the hamlet of Seion.

Set in 70 acres of farmland, Ty'n Rhos offers country house luxury but retains a friendly atmosphere with farmhouse-style catering using own and local produce. AA Farmhouse of the year for Wales in 1988. Close to Anglesey and Snowdonia.

🛏 11 🍽 11 [NBB] £18-£28 [WBB] £120-£176
⌿ [V] 🐕 ♿ [∴WTB]

21 LODGE TAL-Y-BONT
CONWY LL32 8YX

Barbara & Simon Baldon, owners
Tel (0492) 69766

Licensed hotel. Open 1-12. Restaurant open to non-residents. Serving times: Breakfast 8.15-9.15am, Saturday and Sunday 8.30-9.15am, Lunch 12-1.45pm, Dinner 7-8.45pm. Prices: Lunch £4, Dinner £11.50. Specialities: fish and seafoods. Vegetarian Good Food Guide listed.

5 miles from Conwy on the B5106.

A friendly, warm hotel where the guest comes first! Best-quality local produce used in our varied and wide menu. Majority of soft fruits and vegetables grown in our own gardens. Lovely comfortable restaurant. An unspoilt rural spot to be 'spoilt' in.

🛏 10 🍽 10 [NBB] from £22.50 ⌿ [V] [C] 🐕
♿ 🚗 [VISA] [∴WTB] [:AA] [:RAC]

22 BWYTY 'DYLANWAD DA' RESTAURANT
2 FFOS-Y-FELIN DOLGELLAU LL40 1YT

Dylan Rowlands, chef/proprietor
Tel (0341) 422870

Licensed restaurant. Open 3-1. Serving times: Dinner 7-9.30pm. Prices: Dinner £12.50-£15. Specialities include bacon amd mushroom baskets, lime and tarragon loin of lamb, *coron y tywysog* (meringue crown). Good Food Guide listed.

In town centre.

Small informal restaurant, with a friendly and relaxed atmosphere. Accent is on simple, well-prepared food from fresh ingredients at an affordable price.

⌿ [V] [C]

A tale of carnage

Harlech finds its place in the Mabinogion, those bardic stories of ancient Wales, as one of the courts of Bendigeidfran, King of Britain. The king's sister, Branwen, was one of the fairest maidens in the world, and Matholwch, the King of Ireland, came to ask for her hand in marriage. This was granted, but her half-brother Efnisien, upset at not being consulted in the matter, took his revenge by maiming Matholwch's horses. Though reparation was made, the seed of resentment was sown. For a year Branwen was held in high esteem in Ireland, then, on the birth of her son, Gwern, she was made to work in the kitchens as a scullery maid. She managed to get a message by means of a starling to Bendigeidfran, who proceeded with an army to avenge his sister. Matholwch made amends by making Gwern King of Ireland. But there was treachery in the air. Efnisien thrust Gwern into a blazing fire, and after the resulting battle, there were only seven survivors.

Fact or fiction, this legend makes bloody reading. In Harlech there is a bronze statue showing Bendigeidfran carrying the crumpled body of Gwern, a symbol of the futility of war.

Harlech Castle

POST BRENHINOL
ROYAL MAIL
1840-1990
CYNTAF YN Y BYD
FIRST IN THE WORLD

23 CLIFTON HOUSE HOTEL/ OLD COUNTRY GAOL RESTAURANT
SMITHFIELD SQUARE DOLGELLAU LL40 1ES

Rob & Pauline Dix, owners
Tel (0341) 422554

Licensed hotel and restaurant. Open 2-12. Restaurant open to non-residents. Serving times: Breakfast 8-9am, Lunch 12.30-2pm, Dinner 7-9.30pm. Prices: Lunch £3.50-£8, Dinner £7.50-£14. Specialities include marinated lamb with wild mushroom sauce, delicious desserts from homemade lemon ice cream in brandy snap basket to double chocolate and berry tart.

In centre of town.

A small well-appointed hotel personally run by proprietors Rob and Pauline Dix. All bedrooms have tea/coffee facilities, colour TV and hairdryer, most en-suite. The hotel's reputation is firmly based on Pauline's excellent cuisine in the comfortable cellar restaurant.

🛏7 🍴4 [NBB] £16-£22 [WBB] £98-£140 [V]
[C] [▲] [VISA] [∴WTB] [·AA] [·RAC]

24 DOLMELYNLLYN HALL HOTEL
GANLLWYD DOLGELLAU

Jon & Joanna Barkwith, owners
Tel (0341) 40273

Licensed hotel. Open 3-11. Restaurant open to non-residents. Serving times: Breakfast 8.30-9.30am, Dinner 7.30-9pm. Prices: Welsh Tea £3.50, Dinner £17. Wales Tourist Board commended. Children over nine welcome.

4 miles north of Dolgellan on the A470.

Period manor house above the river Mawddach in three acres of carefully tended gardens, surrounded by mountain and meadow. Elegantly refurbished to provide individually designed en-suite bedrooms. The relaxed atmosphere creates the perfect escape from the pressures of a busy life.

🛏11 🍴11 [NBB] £30-£40 [WBB] £210-£280
[✗] [V] [🐕] [▲] [VISA] [AMEX] [∷WTB] [∴AA] [∴RAC]

25 Y BISTRO
43-45 STRYD FAWR LLANBERIS LL55 4EU

Danny & Nerys Roberts, owners
Tel (0286) 871278

Licensed restaurant. Open 1-12. Serving times: Dinner 7.30-9.30pm. Prices: Dinner £18-£20. Specialities include local lamb, Torgoch and Welsh cheese. Egon Ronay, Good Food Guide listed.

On the main street of Llanberis, at the foot of Snowdon.

A long-established family-run restaurant having won many accolades over the years, including 'The Taste of Britain (Wales) Award.' Mentioned in all the current major food guides. We also have 'Y Bistro Bach' for lighter meals.

[✗] [V] [C] [▲] [VISA]

26 BRYN DERWEN HOTEL
34 ABBEY ROAD LLANDUDNO LL30 2EE

Stuart N. Langfield, owner
Tel (0492) 76804

Licensed hotel. Open 4-10. Restaurant open to non-residents. Serving times: Breakfast 8.30-9am, Dinner 6.30-7pm. Prices: Dinner £12. Children over five welcome.

Midway between the North and West Shore close to Great Orme.

Set in a tree-lined road, offering elegance in a relaxing atmosphere. Imaginative menus using only the highest-quality fresh produce. Chef/proprietor is a former Chef of Wales, catering lecturer and consultant to the Taste of Wales.

🛏10 🍴10 [NBB] £20 [WBB] £140 [✗] [V] [C]
[AMEX] [∴WTB]

27 GWESTY LEAMORE HOTEL
40 LLOYD STREET
LLANDUDNO LL30 2YG

Fred & Beryl Owen,
Tel (0492) 75552

Licensed hotel. Open Jan 4-Dec 20. Restaurant open to non-residents. Serving times: Breakfast 8.45-9.15am, Bar Lunch 1-2pm, Dinner 6-7.30pm. Prices: Bar Lunch £3.50, Dinner £8-£10.

In town close to pier.

Family-run hotel in our 21st year. Only a few minutes' walk to beaches, shops, pier and theatres. We will always be at your personal service throughout your stay. At Leamore you arrive as strangers but leave as friends.

🛏12 ♚7 [NBB] £15-£18 [WBB] £105-£119
 ⚤ [V] [C] [∴WTB] [·AA] [·RAC]

28 IMPERIAL HOTEL
THE PROMENADE
LLANDUDNO LL30 1AP

G.S. Lofthouse, general manager
Tel (0492) 77466 Fax (0492) 78043

Licensed hotel. Open 1-12. Restaurant open to non-residents. Serving times: Breakfast 7.30-10am, Bar Lunch 12.30-2pm, Lunch 12.30-2pm, High Tea 4.30-6.30pm, Tea 6.30-9pm. Prices: Bar Lunch from £4, Lunch from £9.50, High Tea from £6, Dinner £15.50-£25.

On the promenade in Llandudno.

Overlooking Llandudno Bay with a varied and interesting menu, offering the best local produce to achieve the highest standards of freshness and quality. The hotel facilities include health and fitness centre 'Mint Condition' and three theme bars.

🛏100 ♚100 [NBB] £37.50-£52.50
[WBB] £260-£330 [V] [C] [🐕] [⛰] [VISA] [⊙]
[AMEX] [∷WTB] [∴AA] [∴RAC]

29 INGLEBY HOUSE,
21 ST ANDREW'S PLACE
LLANDUDNO LL30 2YR

Shaun Bradley
Tel (0492) 77990

Unlicensed guest house. Open 1-11. Serving times: Breakfast 8.30- 9.30am, Dinner 6-7.15pm.

In town.

Non-smoking guest house offering a high standard to a group of six guests in a quiet residential part of Llandudno. Home-from-home and tastefully equipped. Choice of menu.

🛏5 ♚0 [NBB] £18-£21 ⚤ [V] [·WTB]

30 QUEEN'S HEAD
GLANWYDDAN
LLANDUDNO JUNCTION LL31 9JP

Robert Cureton, manager
Tel (0492) 546570

Licensed inn/pub. Open 1-12. Serving times: Bar Lunch 12-2.15pm, Evenings 7-9.30pm. Prices: Bar Lunch £4-£7. Specialities include organic wines. Local produce used. Children over seven welcome. Egon Ronay, Good Food Guide listed.

Off A470 turn right at the roundabout signed for Penryhn Bay.

Situated in a small rural village with a very quaint atmosphere. We strive for cosy pleasant surroundings and high-quality bar meals, using locally grown and produced food. A large menu with a selection of fine wines (some organic).

[V] [⛰]

31 ROSE TOR HOTEL
122/124 MOSTYN STREET
LLANDUDNO

Brenda Cotton, owner
Tel (0492) 870433

Licensed hotel. Open 1-12. Restaurant is open to non-residents. Serving times: Breakfast 7.30-9.30am, Bar Lunch 12-2.30pm, Dinner 6-9.30pm. Prices: Bar Lunch £2.40- £5.60, Dinner £6.25- £12.

In town on main shopping street.

A family-run hotel which has been tastefully decorated to give a calm and relaxing atmosphere. All bedrooms have colour TVs, central heating, hairdryers, etc.

🛏 25 🍽25 [NBB] £16.50-£20
[WBB] £115-£140 ✂ [V] [C] 🐕 [VISA]
[AMEX] ::WTB :AA

32 ST TUDNO HOTEL & GARDEN ROOM RESTAURANT PROMENADE
LLANDUDNO LL30 2LP

Martin & Janette Bland, proprietors
Tel (0492) 874411 Fax (0492) 860407

Licensed hotel. Open 1-12 except 1-16th Jan. Restaurant open to non-residents. Serving times: Breakfast 7.30-9.30am, Bar Lunch 12.30-1.45pm, Lunch 12.30-1.45, High Tea 5.30-6.15, Dinner 6.45-9.30pm (8.30pm Sunday). Prices: Bar Lunch £5-£10, Lunch £10.50-£13, Dinner £21-£25. Specialities include local fish, game, vegetables and Welsh cheeses. Egon Ronay, Good Hotel Guide, Good Food Guide listed.

In town on the promenade, opposite the pier and gardens.

A delightful, luxury seafront Victorian hotel and restaurant that has gained many awards for excellence. Heated indoor swimming pool, lift, three lounges and a car park.

🛏21 🍽21 [NBB] £30-£52 ✂ [V] [C] ♿ 🐕
[VISA] [AMEX] ::WTB :AA :.RAC

33 SPINDRIFT (PRIVATE HOTEL) 24 ST DAVID'S ROAD
LLANDUDNO LL30 2UL

Mr & Mrs Ogden, owners
Tel (0492) 76490

Unlicensed hotel. Open 3-10. Serving times: Breakfast 8.30am, Dinner 6.30pm. Prices: Dinner £7.50. Children over 10 welcome. RAC listed.

From seafront into St George's Place, St David's Road is on left.

This quality, 'no-smoking' small hotel is recommended not only for its delicious food but also for the very high standard of personal service, the utmost cleanliness and genuine hospitality. Guests may bring their own wine and we will chill.

🛏6 🍽1 [NBB] £14-£16 [WBB] £98-£112 ✂
[V] [C] ♿ :WTB

34 WEDGWOOD HOTEL DEGANWY AVENUE
LLANDUDNO LL30 2YB

Barry & Yvonne Cooper
Tel (0492) 78016

Licensed hotel. Open 3-12. Serving times: Breakfast 8.30-9am, Dinner 6-6.30pm. Prices: Dinner £5.

Central Llandudno. Easy walking to all amenities.

Good food. Choice of menu daily. Evening meal optional from day to day. Bedrooms superbly decorated, central heated, TVs, hairdryers, tea/coffee facilities, en-suites. Relaxed atmosphere of a quiet lounge or good company in a well-stocked bar.

🛏12 🍽9 [NBB] £16 [WBB] £112 ✂ [C] 🐕
:.WTB ·AA

35 LLWYDIARTH FAWR
LLANERCHYMEDD LL71 8DF

Margaret Hughes, owner
Tel (0248) 470321/470540

Unlicensed farmhouse. Open 1-11. Serving times: Breakfast 8-9am, Dinner 6.30-7pm. Prices: Dinner £7.50. Specialities include farmhouse fare. Wales Tourist Board Farmhouse award.

On the B5111, half a mile from the village of Llanerchymedd.

Secluded Georgian mansion standing in 850 acres of woodland and farmland with breathtaking views towards Snowdonia. Central heating, log fires. Personal attention and a warm Welsh welcome to guests who will enjoy the walks and private fishing.

🛏3 🍽3 [NBB] £17.50 [WBB] £122.50 ⚭ [C]
♿ [∴WTB]

36 THE NATIONAL TRUST
PLAS NEWYDD
LLANFAIR PG LL61 6EQ

Edna Clout, catering manager
Tel (0248) 714795

Licensed restaurant. Open March 23-September 29 daily except Saturday from 11am-5pm, then October 4-November 3, Friday and Sunday only 12-5pm. Prices: Lunch £5-£8. Specialities include Welsh cheeses.

Turn off A5 at west end of Britannia Bridge.

18th-century house by James Wyatt in unspoilt surroundings on the Menai Strait. Magnificent views of Snowdonia. Rex Whistler's largest wall painting; military museum with relics of 1st Marquess of Anglesey and Battle of Waterloo. Beautiful parkland.

⚭ [V] [C] ♿

37 TRE-YSGAWEN HALL
CAPEL COCH
NR LLANGEFNI LL77 7UR

Julian Peck, general manager
Tel (0248) 750750 Fax (0248) 750035

Licensed hotel. Open 1-12. Restaurant open to non-residents. Serving times: Breakfast 7-9.30am, Lunch 12-2.30pm, High Tea 2.30-5pm, Dinner 7-9.30pm. Prices: Lunch £8.50-£19, High Tea £1.75-£7.50, Dinner £15.95-£22. Egon Ronay, Good Food Guide listed.

On the outskirts of the village of Rhosmeirch.

This beautiful 19th-century manor house recently renovated to its former quality, is a special venue for conferences, board meetings and corporate entertainment and with private 3000 acres of shooting.

🛏19 🍽19 [NBB] £53.35 [WBB] £300 [V] [C]
🐕 ♿ ✈ [AMEX] [∷WTB] [∴AA] [∴RAC]

38 EAGLES HOTEL
LLANRWST LL26 OLG

Mr & Mrs Wainwright
Tel (0492) 640454 Fax (06902) 777

Licensed hotel. Open 1-12. Restaurant open to non-residents. Serving times: Breakfast 8.15-9.30am, Bar Lunch 12-2pm, Lunch 12-1.45pm, Dinner 7.15-8.30pm. Specialities include smoked Welsh lamb. Choice of 200 different sandwiches.

A470 5 miles from Betws-y-coed, 15 miles south of Llandudno.

Charming traditional, family-owned and run hotel in the heart of Snowdonia. Children's fun menu, vegetarian meals, Sunday lunches. Leisure breaks. Nearby dry ski slopes, climbing, fishing swimming and golf.

🛏12 🍽12 [NBB] £17.50 [WBB] £122.50 [V]
[C] 🐕 ✈ [VISA] [∴WTB] [:AA] [:RAC]

39 MEADOWSWEET HOTEL
STATION ROAD
LLANRWST LL26 ODS

John Evans
Tel (0492) 640732

Licensed hotel. Open 1-12. Restaurant open to non-residents. Serving times: Breakfast 8-9.30am, Dinner 6.30-9.30pm. Prices: Dinner £19.75. Specialities include local fish and lamb, cooked to traditional French recipes. Egon Ronay, Good Food Guide listed.

On A470 - 400 yards north of Llanrwst town centre.

A Victorian hotel overlooking meadowland towards the river Conwy. Ideally placed for Bodnant Garden, horse riding, forest and mountain walking. Open fires, the best breakfast in Wales, and one of the U.K.'s finest wine cellars.

🛏10 🍽10 [NBB] £25-£35 ✝ [V] [C] 🐕
▲ [VISA] [::WTB] [∴AA] [∴RAC]

40 TYDDYN PERTHI FARM
TAN-Y-MAES
PORT DINORWIC LL56 9UQ

Barbara Lewis
Tel (0248) 670336

Unlicensed farmhouse. Open 3-11. Restaurant open to non-residents. Serving times: Breakfast 7-8.30am, Dinner 6.30-7.30pm. Prices: Dinner £8. Wales Tourist Board Farmhouse Award.

Situated on Caernarfon side of Port Dinorwic, just off the A487.

We are a non-smoking establishment - small and very friendly offering comfortable accomodation and excellent meals. Situated between Caernarfon and Bangor, close to Anglesey, Snowdonia and many other wonders of this beautiful area.

🛏2 🍽0 [NBB] £14.50 [WBB] £157.50 ✝ [V]
[C] [∶WTB]

41 HOTEL PORTMEIRION
PORTMEIRION LL48 6ET

Robin Llywelyn, managing director
Menai Williams, manager
Tel (0766) 770228 Fax (0766) 771331

Licensed hotel. Open 1-12. Restaurant open to non-residents. Serving times: Breakfast 8-9.45am, Lunch 12-2pm, Dinner 7-9.30pm. Prices: Lunch £12.50, Dinner £22.50. Specialities include: Bardsey lobster, local seafood, Welsh lamb. Egon Ronay, Good Food Guide listed.

Off A487, signposted at Minffordd.

Situated at the heart of the Italianate village of Portmeirion and surrounded by woodlands and sandy beaches. The grounds are open to day visitors daily from 9.30-5.30. A carvery luncheon is served daily and table d'hote dinner is £22.50 per person for three courses and coffee.

🛏34 🍽34 [NBB] £32.50-£55 ✝ [V] [C] 🐕
♿ ▲ [VISA] [⊙] [AMEX] [::WTB] [∴AA] [∴RAC]

42 NANHORON ARMS HOTEL
FFORD DEWI SANT
NEFYN
NR PWLLHELI LL53 6EA

Angela Bennett, general manager
Tel (0758) 720203

Licensed hotel. Open 1-12. Restaurant open to non-residents. Serving times: Breakfast 7.30-9.30am, Bar Lunch 11.30-2.15pm, Lunch 12-2pm, High Tea 3-6pm, Dinner 6.30-9.30pm. Prices: Bar Lunch £1.50-£9, Lunch £7-£10, High Tea £1.95-£4.95, Dinner £13.50-£18. Specialities include *Bennin Cymraeg* (leeks with crab); *Teisan Hail* (Apricot Tartlet); seafish.

Off A499 west of Pwllheli.

After major refurbishment the hotel provides an exceptional standard of accommodation. Children welcome with their own special menu and safe, fully equipped play area. Golf/shooting breaks available.

🛏21 🍽21 [NBB] £21.50-£30
[WBB] £130-£160 [V] [C] 🐕 ▲ [VISA] [⊙]
[AMEX] [::WTB] [∴AA] [∶RAC]

43 PLAS BODEGROES
PWLLHELI LL53 5TH

Christopher Chown, managing director
Tel (0758) 612363 Fax (0758) 701247

Licensed restaurant with rooms. Open 3-12. Serving times: Breakfast 7.30-9.30am, Dinner 7.30-9pm. Prices: Dinner £19-£25. Specialities include warm salad of monkfish, Carmarthen ham and mushrooms. Vegetarian food by arrangement. Egon Ronay listed.

1 mile west of Pwllheli on A497 Nefyn road.

Georgian manor house (1780) in own six-acre grounds with formal gardens, woods and half-mile long beech avenue. People say the food's all right. Outstanding wine list.

[🛏5] [♦5] [NBB] £25-£35 [✂] [C] [🐕] [♿] [▲] [VISA] [::WTB] [:AA]

44 HOTEL MAES-Y-NEUADD
TALSARNAU LL47 6YA

June Slatter, partner
Tel (0766) 780200 Fax (0766) 780211

Licensed restaurant. Open 1-12. Restaurant open to non-residents. Serving times: Lunch 12.30-1.45pm, Dinner 7.15-9pm. Prices: Lunch £13.50, Dinner £23. Specialities: five-course meals, daily changing menu, using the best ingredients in season. Egon Ronay, Good Food Guide listed. Children over seven welcome.

3 miles north of Harlech, half a mile off the B4573.

Historical, beautifully located, granite and slate manor house, dating back to the 14th century. Most bedrooms have wonderful views of Snowdonia or Tremadog Bay. The food is superb, incorporating the best of local ingredients.

[🛏16] [♦16] [NBB] £45-£60 [WBB] £299-£399 [✂] [V] [🐕] [♿] [▲] [VISA] [⊙] [AMEX] [::WTB] [:AA] [:RAC]

45 HENDY FARM
TYWYN LL36 9RU

Anne Lloyd Jones
Tel (0654) 710457

Unlicensed farmhouse. Open 4-10. Serving times: Breakfast 7.30-9.30am, High Tea 5-6.30pm, Dinner 6-8pm. Prices: High Tea £5, Dinner £7.50. Specialities include freshly home-cooked meals. Special diets catered for on request.

Near Tywyn just off the A493.

A warm welcome awaits you at our working farm set amid beautiful scenic countryside. All bedrooms with washbasins, tea making facilities and colour TVs. Talyllyn railway nearby. Good farmhouse cooking.

[🛏3] [NBB] £11-£14 [WBB] £77-£98 [✂] [V] [C] [🐕] [:WTB]

46 MINFFORDD HOTEL
TALYLLYN
NR TYWYN LL36 9AJ

Bernard Pickles, owner
Tel (0654) 761665

Licensed hotel. Restaurant open to non-residents. Nightly dinner, bed and breakfast per person £39-£46. Weekly rate £258-£290. Serving times: Dinner 7.30-8.30pm. Prices: Dinner £14.75. Specialities include Welsh soups, Welsh lamb, river Dovey salmon, trout, traditional puddings. Good Food Guide listed. AA 1 Red Star, RAC 1 Blue Ribbon Star. Children over three welcome.

At junction of A487 and B4405.

Minffordd was once an 18th-century drovers' inn, set beneath the grandeur of Cader Idris mountain. The heart of Minffordd is found in the dining room, where guests enjoy the best of freshly prepared country cooking from the Aga.

[🛏6] [♦6] [✂] [V] [▲] [VISA] [⊙] [::WTB]

POWYS

*Members are listed alphabetically, based on location.
Numbers on map relate to order of entry in gazetteer.*

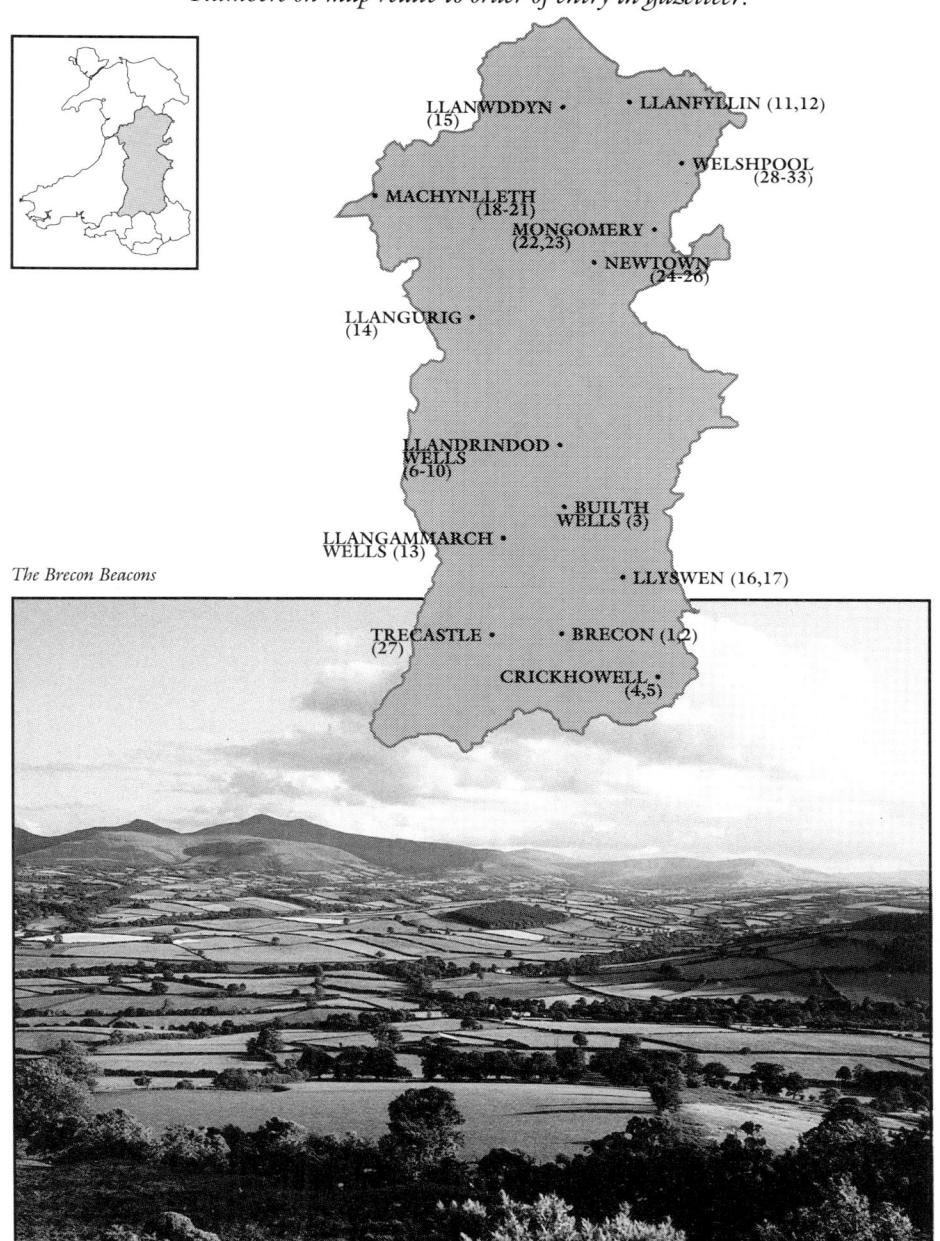

LLANWDDYN (15)
LLANFYLLIN (11,12)
WELSHPOOL (28-33)
MACHYNLLETH (18-21)
MONGOMERY (22,23)
NEWTOWN (24-26)
LLANGURIG (14)
LLANDRINDOD WELLS (6-10)
BUILTH WELLS (3)
LLANGAMMARCH WELLS (13)
LLYSWEN (16,17)
TRECASTLE (27)
BRECON (1,2)
CRICKHOWELL (4,5)

The Brecon Beacons

177

1 BEACONS GUEST HOUSE
16 BRIDGE STREET
BRECON LD3 8AA

Barbara & Belinda Cox, owners
Tel (0874) 3339

Licensed guest house. Open 1-12. Serving times: Breakfast 8-9.30am, Lunch 11.30-2.30, Dinner 6.30-7.30. Prices: Lunch £1.50-£4, Tea £2.50, Dinner £6.50-£7. Wales Tourist Board Farmhouse Award. AA listed.

West side of town centre, 100 yards over river bridge.

A Georgian guest house. Ideal location for local attractions and outdoor activities. Excellent home cooking with local produce and Welsh cheeseboard.

🛏10 ●7 NBB £13-£15 WBB £78-£90 ✕
V C 🐕 ▲ VISA AMEX ∴WTB

2 UPPER TREWALKLIN FARM
PENGENFFORD
TALGARTH
NR BRECON LD3 0HA

Meudwen Stephens, owner
Tel (0874) 711349

Farmhouse. Open 4-11. Serving times: Breakfast 8.30-9am, Dinner 7pm. Prices: Dinner £8. Specialities include home-made marmalades and preserves, puddings and deserts.

1 mile off A479 south of Talgarth.

Traditional farmhouse serving wholesome food. First-class produce, locally grown and from garden. Great care taken in presentation of food.

✕ V C ∴WTB

3 TY-ISAF FARM
ERWOOD
BUILTH WELLS LD2 3SZ

Nancy M. Jones, owner
Tel (0982) 560607

Unlicensed farmhouse. Open 1-12. Serving times: Breakfast: 8-9am, Dinner 7.30pm. Prices: Dinner £5-£7. Wales Tourist Board Farmhouse Award.

Just off A470 south of Erwood village.

Over looking Wye valley, 7 miles from Builth. Mixed working farm, milk pedigree charolais cattle. Tea/coffee making in all rooms. TV lounge, dining room, full central heating.

🛏3 NBB £10-£12 WBB £70-£77 V C
🐕 ∴WTB

4 BEAR HOTEL
CRICKHOWELL NP8 1BW

S Hindmarsh, owner
Tel (0873) 810408 Fax (0873) 811696

Licensed hotel. Open 1-12. Restaurant open to non-residents. Serving times: Breakfast 7-9.30am, Bar Lunch 12-2pm, Dinner 7.30-9.30pm. Prices: Bar Lunch £4.50, Dinner £10.50. Egon Ronay, Good Food Guide listed.

A 15th-century coaching inn, delightfully warm and friendly. Full of atmosphere and quaintness. Appointed Hotel Bar of the Year 1990. Open fires and delicious homemade food, together with an à la carte restaurant noted for excellent cuisine.

🛏24 ●24 NBB £21-£35 V C 🐕 ▲
VISA AMEX ∴RAC ∴AA

5 TY CROESO HOTEL
THE DARDY, LLANGATTOCK
CRICKHOWELL

Catherine & Peter Jones, owners
Tel (0873) 810573

Licensed hotel. Open 1-12. Restaurant open to non-residents. Serving times: Breakfast 7.30-10am, Bar Lunch 12-2.30pm, Lunch 10-2.30pm, Dinner 7-10pm. Prices: Bar Lunch £6-£14, Lunch £10-£18, Dinner £10-£18. Specialities include traditional and authentic Welsh dishes.

From Crickhowell bridge, take B road to Llangynidr/Talybont.

High above Usk valley with magnificent views. Originally the workhouse, now tastefully refurbished to a high standard. Log fires. Well-stocked bar including 30 plus malt whiskies.

🛏8 🍴6 [NBB] £20-£25 [WBB] £140-£175 [V] [C] [🛌] [VISA] [AMEX] [∴WTB]

6 BELL COUNTRY INN
LLANYRE
LLANDRINDOD WELLS LD1 6DY

Keith & Christine Price, proprietors
Tel (0597) 823959 Fax (0597) 825899

Licensed country house hotel. Open 1-12. Restaurant open to non-residents. Serving times: Breakfast 7.30-10am, Bar Lunch 12-2pm, Lunch 12-2pm, Dinner 6.30-10pm. Prices: Bar Lunch £4.50, Lunch £6.50, Dinner £12-£18. Specialities include Welsh products.

1½ miles north-west of Llandrindod Wells.

Discover the warmth of welcome at our charming, historic country inn. Set in rolling hills and offering every facility. Award-winning restaurant. Golf, walking, fishing, birdwatching and riding all close by. Courtesy car.

🛏10 🍴10 [NBB] £25 [V] [C] [♿] [▲] [VISA] [:AA] [::WTB]

7 CORVEN HALL
HOWEY
LLANDRINDOD WELLS LD1 5RE

R.G. Prince, owner
Tel (0597) 823368

Licensed guest house. Open 1-11. Serving times: Breakfast 8.30-9am, Dinner 7-8pm. Prices: Dinner £7-£7.50. Wales Tourist Board Farmhouse Award.

South of Llandrindod Wells off A483.

Victorian house of character with large grounds in peaceful setting, surrounded by beautiful unspoilt countryside. The house is centrally heated, comfortable and spacious. Traditonal cooking, homemade and freshly prepared. Ground-floor accommodation.

🛏10 🍴8 [NBB] £12.50-£14.50
[WBB] £119-£129 [✂] [V] [C] [🐴] [♿] [∴WTB]

8 FFALDAU COUNTRY HOUSE & RESTAURANT
LLANDEGLEY
LLANDRINDOD WELLS LD1 5UD

Mr & Mrs Knott, owners
Tel (0597) 87421

Licensed country house hotel. Open 1-12. Restaurant open to non-residents. Serving times: Breakfast 8.45-9.30am, Bar Lunch 11.30-1.30, Lunch 11.30-1.30, Dinner 7-9pm. Prices: Breakfast £3-£10, Lunch £14-£16, Dinner £14-£16. Specialities include smoked meats, Welsh lamb. Children over 10 welcome.

Set back from the A44 between Llandegley and Penybont.

The Ffaldau is a listed cruck-built long house c.1500 and has an excellent reputation for interesting food complemented by good wines. The menu ranges from delicious soups and unusual starters through to superbly prepared main dishes from fresh produce.

🛏3 🍴1 [NBB] £17.50-£18.50
[WBB] £75-£80 [V] [∴WTB]

9 METROPOLE HOTEL
TEMPLE STREET
LLANDRINDOD WELLS LD1 5DY

Denis Gardener, manager
Tel (0597) 2881 Telex 35237
Fax (0597) 4828

Licensed town hotel. Open 1-12. Restaurant open to non-residents. Serving times: Breakfast 8-9.30am, Bar meals from 10am, Lunch 12.30-2.15pm, Dinner 7-9pm. Prices: Lunch £9.50, Bar Lunch £1.20-£5, Dinner £15.

In centre of Llandrindod Wells on A470.

Victorian-style hotel offering a high standard of service and accommodation. Excellent restaurant with many Welsh dishes, and a fine wine list with wide variety. Indoor leisure complex includes 54ft swimming pool, sauna, steam room, jacuzzi and beauty salon.

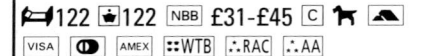

122 122 NBB £31-£45 C
VISA AMEX ::WTB ∴RAC ∴AA

Llywelyn the Last

Llywelyn ap Gruffydd holds a special place in Welsh history as the first and last native Prince of Wales, accepted by both the Welsh and by Henry III. Llywelyn's grandfather, Llywelyn the Great, had laid the foundation of Wales as a united country. This was a fragile unity, as much from the machinations of the Welsh themselves as from English opposition, which was finally shattered when Edward I came on the scene.

It was in 1282 that Llywelyn the Last was killed in a chance encounter with an English soldier on the banks of the Irfon river, near Builth Wells. At Cilmeri west of Builth there is a monument to him made from a block of stone from Snowdonia, the heart of his kingdom. Llywelyn was buried at Abbey Cwmhir, a religious settlement deep in the Mid Wales hills north of Llandrindod Wells.

10 THREE WELLS FARM
CHAPEL ROAD
HOWEY
LLANDRINDOD WELLS LD1 5PB

Ron, Margaret & Sarah Bufton
Tel (0597) 822484

Licensed farmhouse. Open 1-12. Serving times: Breakfast 8.30-9am, Dinner 6.30-7pm. Prices: Dinner £7-£8. Specialities include Welsh lamb. Wales Tourist Board Farmhouse Award. RAC highly acclaimed. AA listed. Children over 10 welcome.

1 mile from Llandrindod Wells on A483 south.

50-acre working farm overlooking fishing lake in beautiful countryside. Good food, spacious dining room, lounge, sun lounge, TV room, two bars. All bedrooms bath/shower en-suite, TV, coffee making facilities, central heating.

14 14 NBB £14-£19 ::WTB

11 BODFACH HALL
COUNTRY HOUSE
LLANFYLLIN SY22 5HS

Ian Gray, proprietor
Tel (069184) 272

Licensed country house hotel. Open 3-11. Restaurant open to non-residents. Serving times: Breakfast 8.45-9.30am, Bar Lunch 12-1.30pm, Sunday Lunch 12.30-1.15pm, Dinner 7.15-8.30pm. Prices: Lunch £8.75, Dinner £13.50. Specialities include Pembrokeshire mutton pie and roast leg of lamb with apricot and walnut stuffing.

Half a mile west of Llanfyllin on A490.

An exceptionally attractive country house, secluded in four acres of mature garden. Good homely fare, complemented by interesting wine list. Ideal centre for touring.

9 9 NBB 27.50-£28.50 V C
VISA AMEX ∴WTB :AA :RAC

12 CYFIE FARM LLANFIHANGEL-YNG-NGWYNFA LLANFYLLIN

George & Lynn Jenkins
Tel (069184)) 451

Farmhouse. Open 1-12. Serving times: Breakfast 8-9.30am, Dinner 6.30-7.30pm. Prices: Dinner £8. Specialities include dishes served with local and home produce. Wales Tourist Board Farmhouse Award.

8 miles north-west of Welshpool.

Beautifully kept, in magnificent setting. Provides a true farm-life atmosphere. Superb stable suite. Individual cosy bedrooms with TV, radio, private facilities, beverage trays. Log fired lounges, delicious cuisine. Noted walks from farm close to Lake Vyrnwy.

🛏3 🍴3 [NBB] £13-£18 [WBB] £70-£100 [V]
[C] [∺WTB]

13 LAKE COUNTRY HOUSE HOTEL LLANGAMMARCH WELLS LD4 4BS

Jean-Pierre Mifsud, owner
Tel (05912) 202 Fax (05912) 457

Licensed hotel. Open 1-12. Restaurant open to non-residents. Serving times: Breakfast 8.30-9.45pm, Bar Lunch 12.30-2pm, Lunch 12.30-2pm, Dinner 7.30-9pm. Prices: Bar Lunch varied, Lunch £11.50, High Tea £3.50, Dinner £21.50.

6 miles west of Builth Wells.

Set in 50 acres of grounds, the hotel now holds an AA rosette for food and AA and RAC awards for bedrooms lounges and our restaurant. Clay-pigeon shooting available. Three-acre stocked lake with trout and salmon fishing.

🛏19 🍴19 [NBB] £42.50-£55 ⨯ [V] [C] 🐕
♿ ▲ [AMEX] [∺WTB] [∴AA] [∴RAC]

14 THE OLD VICARAGE LLANGURIG SY18 6RN

Anna Rollings, proprietor
Tel (05515) 280

Licensed guest house. Open 3-11. Restaurant open to non-residents. Serving times: Breakfast 8-8.45am, Dinner 7-7.30pm. Prices: Cream Tea £1.50, Dinner £8-£10. Specialities include homemade scones. AA listed, Wales Tourist Board highly commended.

100 yards from centre of village on A470/A44.

Spacious Victorian vicarage in peaceful location in Llangurig (the highest village in Wales). All rooms tastefully furnished. Two guest lounges with large library and log fires in winter. Dining room with separate tables.

🛏4 🍴2 [NBB] £14-£17.50
[WBB] £94.50-£119 ⨯ [V] [C] 🐕 [∺WTB]

15 LAKE VYRNWY COUNTRY HOUSE & SPORTING HOTEL LLANWDDYN SY10 0LY

Jim Talbot, general manager
Tel (069173) 692 Fax (069173) 259

Licensed country hotel. Open 1-12. Restaurant open to non-residents. Serving times: Breakfast 8.30-9.30am, Bar Lunch 12.30-1.45pm, Lunch, 12.30-1.45pm, Tea 3-6pm, Dinner 7.30-9.15pm. Prices: Bar Lunch £1.25-£5.50, Lunch £8.75, Dinner £16.75. Specialities include game and fish dishes, fresh from the estate. Egon Ronay listed.

On B4393, 10 miles from Llanfyllin.

A Victorian lakeside retreat surrounded by 24,000 acres of the beautiful Vyrnwy estate over which sole sporting and fishing rights are held. Panoramic views can be enjoyed including those from the restaurant. A cosy country lodge atmosphere.

🛏30 🍴30 [NBB] £27.50-£55 [V] [C] 🐕 ▲
[VISA] [⊙] [AMEX] [∺WTB] [∴AA] [∺WTB]

BARCLAYS IS PLEASED TO BE ASSOCIATED WITH THIS GUIDE

+++ *YOU'RE BETTER OFF TALKING TO* BARCLAYS

16 GRFFIN INN
LLYSWEN LD3 OUR

Richard Stockton
Tel (0874) 754241

Licensed hotel. Open 1-12. Restaurant open to non-residents. Serving times: Breakfast 8.15-9.30am, Bar Lunch 12-2pm, Lunch 12-2pm, Dinner 7-9pm. Prices: Bar Lunch £3-£10, Lunch £3-£10, Dinner £10-£17.50. Specialities include fresh fish, game in season. Egon Ronay, Good Food Guide listed.

On A470 Builth Wells road.

In the beautiful upper Wye valley, an old and long-established sporting inn. The inn is owned and managed by the Stockton family who ensure the hotel maintains its reputation for traditional hospitality, good food and comfortable accommodation.

🛏8 7 [NBB] £24.50-£27.50 [V] [C]
[VISA] [AMEX] [••WTB] [:AA] [:RAC]

17 LLANGOED HALL
LLYSWEN LD3 OYP

Thomas Ward, general manager
Tel (0874) 754525 Fax (0874) 754545

Licensed country house hotel. Open 1-12. Special winter rates available inclusive of dinner. Restaurant open to non-residents. Serving times: Breakfast 7.30-10.30am, Lunch 12.15-2.15pm, Afternoon Tea 3-5pm, Dinner 7.15-9.30. Prices: Lunch £12.50-£19.50, Afternoon Tea £7.50, Dinner £23.50-£34.50. Specialities include pigeon, red mullet and lobster. Egon Ronay listed. Children over eight welcome.

9 miles west of Hay on Wye.

Recently restored and refurbished into one of the leading country house establishments in Wales. We are a 23-bedroom old manor house set in 10 acres of garden and parklands, offering a warm welcome, luxurious surroundings and excellent service.

🛏23 23 [NBB] £57.50-£114.50
[V] [C] [VISA] [AMEX] [::AA] [::RAC]

18 CRWYBR RESTAURANT
CORRIS CRAFT CENTRE
MACHYNLLETH SY20 9SP

Marit Withers, owner
Tel (0654) 761437

Licensed restaurant. Open 1-12. Prices: Lunch under £5. Specialities include lamb casserole, homemade cakes.

Between Machynlleth and Dolgellau on A487.

Within the craft centre, which has a large car and coach park and is open seven days a week from 10am. Adventure playground. 'The best coffee and bara brith in Mid Wales.'

[V] [C] ♿

19 TY BWYTA'R HEN FAIL
FURNACE
MACHYNLLETH

Mair Nutting & Gwen Davies, owners
Tel (0654) 74225

Licensed restaurant. Serving times: Lunch 12-2.30pm, Dinner 7-9pm (Wednesday to Saturday). Prices: Lunch £1.50-£6.50, Welsh Cream Tea £1.50, Dinner £5.50-£12.50. Specialities include many Welsh traditional dishes.

12 miles north of Aberystryth towards Machynlleth.

A traditional Welsh restaurant developed on the site of an old smithy and farm buildings, encompassing the Welsh language, culture and custom. Dovey Furnace and Watermill, waterfalls, Artists' Valley, RSPB reserve are all within walking distance.

[V] [C] ♿ [VISA]

20 WHITE LION COACHING INN
HEOL PENTRERHEDYN
MACHYNLLETH SY20 8ND

Malcolm & Jacqueline Quick, proprietors
Tel (0654) 703455 Fax (0654) 703746

Licensed hotel. Open 1-12. Restaurant open to non-residents. Serving times: Breakfast 8.30-9.30am, Bar Lunch 12-2.30pm, Dinner 6-9pm. Prices: Bar Lunch £2.25, Lunch from £3, Dinner from £7. Specialities include Dovey salmon, Welsh lamb.

On the T junction of A487 and A489.

Re-established inn set in historical Machynlleth. Ideally situated for golfing, fishing, walking. Comfortable and friendly atmosphere, superb fresh food cuisine with personal hospitality. Midweek and weekend breaks a speciality.

🛏9 🍴6 [NBB] £18.50-£26 ⚔ [V] [C] 🐕
[▲] [VISA] [⦿] [AMEX] [∷WTB] [∴RAC]

21 YNYSHIR HALL
EGLWYSFACH
MACHYNLLETH SY20 8TA

Bob & Joan Reen
Tel (0654) 781209

Licensed hotel. Open 1-12. Restaurant open to non-residents. Serving times: Breakfast 8.30-9.30am, Bar Lunch 12.30-1.30pm, Lunch 12.30-1.30pm, Dinner 7-8.30pm. Prices: Bar Lunch from £5, Lunch £18-£20, High Tea from £4, Dinner £18-£20. Egon Ronay, Good Food Guide listed. Children over nine welcome.

11 miles from Aberystwyth and 6 miles from Machynlleth.

An elegant Georgian manor house once owned by Queen Victoria, nestling amidst mountain scenery and the Dovey estuary in its own 12-acre landscaped gardens and surrounded by the famous Ynyshir bird reserve. Art courses.

🛏9 🍴9 [NBB] £40-£60 [WBB] £280-£420 ⚔
[V] [🐕] [♿] [▲] [VISA] [AMEX] [∷WTB] [∴AA] [∴RAC]

22 DREWIN FARM
CHURCHSTOKE
MONTGOMERY SY15 6TW

Mrs Ceinwen Richards, owner
Tel (0588) 620325

Unlicensed farmhouse. Serving times: Breakfast 8-8.30am, Dinner 6-7pm. Prices: Dinner £7-£8. Specialities include Welsh lamb, creamy chicken casserole, trout and almonds. Wales Tourist Board Farmhouse Award. AA listed.

Take B4385 signs for Pantglas.

17th-century farmhouse with oak beams. Two pleasant bedrooms with tea/coffee facilities. Overlooking panoramic views. Games room with snooker table available, Offa's Dyke footpath runs through the mixed farm.

🛏2 [NBB] £13-£14 [WBB] £78-£98 [V] [C]
[∷WTB]

23 LITTLE BROMPTON FARM
MONTGOMERY SY15 6HY

Gaynor Brigh, proprietor
Tel (0686) 668371

Unlicensed farmhouse. Open 1-12. Prices: Dinner £7. Specialities include orange and ginger chicken, special summer pudding. Wales Tourist Board Farmhouse Award. Dogs by arrangement. AA listed.

2 miles east of Montgomery on B4385.

A 17-century charming house on working farm. Many animals, fine ale tumblers in many rooms. En-suite and private bathrooms available. Good traditional cooking. A very warm welcome to all our guests

🛏3 🍴2 [NBB] £12.50-£15 ⚔ [V] [C] [∷WTB]

24 COURTYARD RESTAURANT
SEVERN STREET
NEWTOWN SY16 2AH

Hugh Davys Jones, owner
Tel (0686) 624944

Licensed restuarant. Open 1-12. Serving times: Lunch 12-2.30, Dinner 6.30-9.30. Guide dogs accepted.

Centre of Newtown.

Completely renovated property. The building dates from Tudor times with a Georgian facade added at a later date. Courtyard between the buildings which is used in fine weather. Blackboard menu changes every evening.

[V] [C] [♿] [▲] [VISA] [AMEX]

25 HIGHGATE FARM
NEWTOWN SY16 3LF

Linda Whitticase, owner
Tel (0686) 625981

Licensed farmhouse. Open 3-11. Serving times: Breakfast 8-9am, Dinner 6.30pm. Prices: Dinner £7-£8. Wales Tourist Board Farmhouse Award.

2 miles north of Newtown on B4389.

15th-century listed, half-timbered farmhouse with wealth of oak and inglenook fireplaces. Centrally heated throughout. Historic priest's hole. Mixed working farm. Breeders of Shire horses. Offers fishing, shooting and riding.

🛏3 🍴3 [NBB] £15-£17 [WBB] £98-£112 [V] [C] [🐕] [∴WTB]

26 LOWER-GWESTYDD
NEWTOWN SY16 3AY

Mrs I. Jarman, proprietor
Tel (0686) 626718

Unlicensed farmhouse. Open 1-12. Serving times: Breakfast 8-9am. Dinner: 6-7pm. Prices: Dinner £6-£6.50. Specialities include own lamb and beef, home-grown fruit and vegetables. Wales Tourist Board Farmhouse Award.

Just off B4568 north of Newtown.

Beautiful, half-timbered 17th-century listed farmhouse. Full of character, centrally heated. Easy day trips. Lovely views from this 200-acre mixed farm with country walks. A warm welcome to all.

🛏3 🍴2 [NBB] £13.50-£14 [WBB] £84 [C] [∴WTB]

27 CASTLE HOTEL &
RESTAURANT
TRECASTLE LD3 8UH

Clive & Corinne Marshall, owners
Tel (087482) 354

Licensed country hotel. Open 1-12. Restaurant open to non-residents. Serving times: Breakfast 8-9.30am, Bar Lunch 12-2pm, Lunch 12-2pm, Dinner 7.30-9pm. Prices: Bar Lunch £2-£10, Dinner £6-£18. Egon Ronay listed.

On A40 west of Brecon.

A Georgian building which dates from the 16th century. A warm relaxed atmosphere is the key to an enjoyable visit. People travel from far to sample the imaginative food and comfortable beds.

🛏9 🍴4 [NBB] £17.50-£25 [WBB] £122.50-£175 [V] [C] [🐕] [▲] [VISA] [∴WTB]

185

28 EDDERTON HALL
FORDEN
WELSHPOOL SY21 8RZ

Warren Hawksley, owner
Tel (093876) 339 Fax (093876) 452

Licensed country house hotel and restaurant. Open 1-12. Restaurant open to non-residents. Serving times: Breakfast 8.30-9.30am, Lunch 1-2pm, Dinner 8-10pm. Prices: Lunch £9.95, Dinner £16.95.

A490 Montgomery road, 2 miles from Welshpool.

Taste of Wales Restaurant of the Year for the Powys region in a beautiful Georgian residence, restored sympathetically. Overlooking the Severn valley and Powis Castle, with four-poster beds.

🛏8 🍴8 [NBB] £27.50-£42.50 [V] [C] 🐕
[▲] [VISA] [⦿] [AMEX] [::WTB] [:RAC] [:AA]

29 GUNGROG HOUSE
RHALLT
WELSHPOOL SY21 9HS

Mrs Eira Jones, owner
Tel (0938) 553381

Unlicensed farmhouse. Open 4-10. Serving times: Breakfast 8-9am, Dinner 6.30-7pm. Prices: Dinner £8. Wales Tourist Board Farmhouse Award.

On A483, 2 miles from Welshpool.

A spacious traditionally furnished 16th-century farmhouse standing in an elevated position giving magnificent views of the Severn valley. The 21-acre farm is run in conjunction with a farm produce business.

🛏3 🍴2 [NBB] £14-£15 [WBB] £90-£100 🍴
[V] [C] [:•WTB]

30 LION HOTEL
BERRIEW
NR WELSHPOOL SY21 8PQ

Mr & Mrs Thomas, owners
Tel (0686) 640452/844

Licensed country hotel and restaurant. Open 1-12. Restaurant open to non-residents. Serving times: Breakfast 8-9.30am, Bar Lunch 12-2pm, Dinner 7-9.15pm. Prices: Bar Lunch £4-£7, Lunch £7-£8.50, Dinner £12.50-£15. Specialities include Welsh lamb, Ty Mawr Pie, Welsh smoked meats and cheeses.

1 mile off A483 between Welshpool and Newtown.

17th-century inn situated in one of Mid Wales's prettiest villages. River Rhiew and Montgomery Canal nearby. Beautiful countryside surrounding the village. Fishing, shooting, golf, pony trekking all available.

🛏7 🍴7 [NBB] £27.50-£30
[WBB] £192.50-£210 [V] [C] [▲] [VISA] [::WTB]

31 MOAT FARM
WELSHPOOL SY21 8SE

Gwyneth Jones, owner
Tel (0938) 553179

Unlicensed farmhouse. Open 4-10. Serving times: Breakfast 8-9am, Dinner 6-7pm. Prices: Dinner £8. Specialities include leg of lamb boned and stuffed with apricot and walnut stuffing. Wales Tourist Board Farmhouse Award. AA listed.

On A483 south of Welshpool.

Dairy farm in the beautiful Severn valley with a 17th-century house offering comfortable accommodation. Fine timbered dining room with Welsh dresser. Tennis and croquet in garden. Good touring centre. Beach one hour away.

🛏3 🍴2 [NBB] £14-£16 [WBB] £98-£112 🍴
[V] [C] [:•WTB]

32 THE NATIONAL TRUST POWIS CASTLE
WELSHPOOL SY21 8RF

Diane Henry, catering manger
Tel (0938) 554336

Licensed restaurant. Open March 28-November 3, daily except Monday and Tuesday from 11am-5pm; July and August daily except Monday. Prices: Lunch £5-£8. Specialites include Welsh cheeses.

1 mile south of Welshpool on A483. Pedestrian access from High Street.

Medieval castle containing the finest country collection in Wales. Built around 1200 by Welsh princes. The gardens are of the highest horticultural and historical importance. Clive Museum.

[V] [C]

33 TYNLLWYN FARM
WELSHPOOL SY21 9BW

Freda Emberton
Tel (0938) 553175

Licensed guest house. Open 1-12. Serving times: Breakfast 8-8.45am, Dinner 6.30-7.30pm. Prices: Dinner £7. Dogs by arrangement. Wales Tourist Board Farmhouse Award.

1 mile from Welshpool on the A490 north.

Stands on a hillside with beautiful views. All bedrooms have colour TV, tea and coffee facilities. All home cooking, licensed bar, out of season bargain breaks available.

5 [NBB] £12 [V] [C] [:WTB]

The glories of Powis Castle

Powis Castle, the great border fortress near Welshpool, is one of the most glorious of all Welsh castles. It was built of red sandstone by the last of the Welsh princes of Powys in the 13th century. In 1587 it was bought by Sir Edward Herbert whose descendants became Earls of Powis. The title still continues, though the castle is now owned by the National Trust.

The magnificently appointed building has a splendid long gallery - an essential feature of an Elizabethan great house - and a grand staircase. This grandeur is almost eclipsed by the castle's surroundings, made up of Italianate terraced gardens, sweeping parklands and groves of ancient trees. Back in the castle, the ballroom contains Clive of India's famous collection, and that of his son. One of the most outstanding Indian collections in Britain, it includes personal relics of Tipu Sahib, the notorious 'Tiger of Mysore'.

INDEX

GENERAL

General index includes places and subjects of interest and locations of hotels, restaurants and food shops. References in italics indicate photographs.

Aberaeron	25, 41, 136	Centre for Alternative		Freystrop	96, 140
Aberdovey	103, 164, 165	Technology	25, *25*, 42, *42*	Furnace	42, 183
Abergavenny	35-6, *36*, 126	Chancery	136		
Abersoch	165	cheese and cheesemaking	20,	Ganllwyd	102, 171
Abertillery	158	21, 23, 25, 28		Glanwydden	106
Aberystwyth	40, 41, *41*, 137	Chepstow	158	Glynarthen	138
Anglesey	27, *106*	Chepstow Castle	*12*	Glyndŵr, Owain	15, 132
Anglesey Sea Zoo	43, 168	Chirk	130	Gresford	134
		Churchstoke	184	Grosmont Castle	*13*
baking	20-1, 26-7, 29-30	Coedkernew	37	Gwaun valley	140
Bala	44, 165, 166	Colwyn Bay	45, *45*, 130		
Bangor	44, 166	confectionery	22, 25, 27	Harlech	170
Barmouth	42	contemporary chefs	11, 113-27	Harlech Castle	*170*
Beaumaris	43, *43*, 104, 105,	Conwy Castle	108, *108*	Haverfordwest	38-9
167		cookery books	16	Hay-on-Wye	41
beer and cider	22, 24, 27	coracles	23	history of Wales	12-15, 132,
Benllech	167	Cowbridge	36-7	139, 150, 162, 170, 180,
Berea	144	Criccieth	43	187	
Berriew	186	Crickhowell	89, 178	Holyhead	31
Bethania	41	Crugybar	143	Holywell	130, 131
Betws-y-coed	167	culinary tradition	16-17	Howey	179, 180
Blaenau Ffestiniog	168	Cwm Tudu	93, *93*, 143		
Boncath	137, 138	Cwm-cou	40	Jeffreston	141
Bontuchel	133	Cwmfelinfach	161		
Borth	29, 42, *42*			Lake Vyrnwy	*101*
Brecon	30, 36, *36*, 98, 178	dairy farming	23, 26	Laleston	148
Brecon Beacons	20, *177*	Denbigh	45	lamb	24-5, 30-1
Brynsiencyn	43, 168	Dolgellau	42, 103, *103*, 169,	Lampeter	39, 40, 141
Builth Wells	40, 98, 180	171		language, Welsh	12, 19
Bwlch y Groes	*18*			laverbread	21
		Eglwysfach	184	Llanarmon D.C.	132
Caerleon	12	Erddig	134	Llanberis	44, 171
Caernarfon	43-4, 168	Erwood	178	Llandaff	149
Caernarfon Castle	*14*			Llandderfel	166
Capel Coch	174	Felin Crewi	25, 42	Llandegla	133
Capel Garmon	167	Felin Geri Watermill	40	Llandegley	179
Cardiff	34, 35, 37, 90, *90*, 92,	Felin Isaf Watermill	27	Llandewi Skirrid	158
149, 151-3		Ffostrasol	39	Llandovery	40, 142
Cardiff Castle	*13*, 21, *21*, 150	fish farms	21, 27	Llandrillo	104, 110, 131
Cardigan	39	Fishguard	39, *39*, 94, 118,	Llandrindod Wells	25, 41, *41*,
Carmarthen	38, *38*	139, *139*		179, 180	
Castell Coch	*147*	fishing industry	23, 25, 27, 31	Llandudno 27, 107, *107*, 171-3
Castle Morris	39	Flint	45	Llandudno Junction	44-5, 172
Cenarth	23	Forden	186	Llandybie	137

Llanerchymedd	174	
Llanerchymor	131	
Llanfair Clydogau	142	
Llanfair PG	174	
Llanfyllin	180, 181	
Llangammarch Wells	101, 181	
Langattock	89, 179	
Llangefni	43	
Llangollen	45, *45*, *129*, 132	
Llangrannog	143	
Llangurig	181	
Llanidloes	40	
Llanrug	168, 169	
Llanrwst	44, *44*, 104, 109, 122, 174, 175	
Llansanffraid	131	
Llanvihangel Gobion	158	
Llanwddyn	101, 181	
Llanwenog	143	
Llanyre	179	
Llyswen	100, 116, 183	
LlYwelyn the Last	14, 180	
Mabinogion	170	
Machynlleth	25, 40, *40*, 42, 183, 184	
Mamhilad	37	
map of Wales	8	
maps and map reading	18-19	
market gardening	22, 26	
markets		
Mid Wales	40	
North Wales	43	
South Wales	34, 35	
West Wales	38	
Marloes Sands	*22*	
Merthyr Tydfil	154	
Milford Haven	23, 31, 38	
mineral waters	22, 24, 27, 29	
Mold	45	
Monmouth	35	
Montgomery	184	
Mumbles	156	
Narberth	38	
Neath	154	
Nefyn	175	
Newcastle Emlyn	39	
Newchapel	138	
Newport (Dyfed)	39	
Newport (Gwent)	34, 161, 162	

Newtown	40, 41, 42, 185	
Nicholaston	156	
Offa's Dyke	12-13	
organic farming	23, 25, 29	
Pembroke Castle	15	
Pembrokeshire	*135*	
Pen-y-Bont	39	
Pen-y-cwm	146	
Penally	146	
Penarth	37, *37*, 154	
Penclawdd	21, *21*	
Penegoes	42	
Penrhyd	165	
Penrhyn Castle	166	
Penrhyndeudraeth	43	
Pentrefoelas	27, 44	
Pentyrch	90, 151	
pick-your-own farms	26, 37	
Pistyll Rhaeadr waterfall	*130*	
placenames	19	
Pontarddulais	154	
Pontfaen	94, 139	
Pontsian	142	
Port Dinorwic	175	
Port Penrhyn	44	
Portfield Gate	141	
Porthcawl	155	
Porthgain	95, *95*, 144	
Porthkerry	148	
Porthmadog	43, *163*	
Porthyrhyd	40	
Portmeirion	43, 175	
Powis Castle	187, *187*	
Pwllheli	43, 120, 176	
regional produce		
Mid Wales	24-5	
North Wales	26-7	
South Wales	20-2	
West Wales	22-4	
Reynoldston	155	
Rhallt	186	
Rhayader	40	
Rhosllanerchrugog	133	
Rhydlewis	142	
Rossett	132, 133	
Rowen	44	
Ruthin	45	

St Brides Wentlooge	162	
St David's	96, *96*, 144	
St Dogmael's	40	
St Fagans	29, 37, *37*, 149	
St Winifred's Well	130	
Saundersfoot	144	
Seion	169	
sheep farming	24-5, 26	
shellfish	21, 27, 31	
Snowdonia	26	
speciality food shops		
Mid Wales	40-2	
North Wales	43-5	
South Wales	34-7	
West Wales	38-40	
Swansea	35, *35*, 87, *88*, 88-9, 124, 155-6, *156*	
Tal-y-Bont	169	
Talgarth	178	
Talsarnau	176	
Talyllyn	102, 176	
'Taste of Wales' campaign	17	
Tenby	38, 146	
Thomas, Dylan	156	
Tintern	162	
Tintern Abbey	*157*	
Tongwynlais	*147*	
Trecastle	185	
Tredegar House	162	
Tregaron	40, 146	
Tregroes	40	
Trellech	161	
Trevine	139	
Trofarth	27	
Tywyn	25, 42, 176	
Usk	162	
watermills	24, 25, 27, 29, *40*, 44	
Welsh Folk Museum	29-30, 37, *37*	
Welshpool	40, 186, 187	
Whitebrook	87, 114, 161	
Whitemill	138	
wines and spirits	22	
Wolfscastle	141	
Wrexham	27, 45, 134	
Wye valley	*88*	

Index of Recipes

References in italics indicate photographs.

almonds, Bryngarw semolina
   almond slice   81
Anglesey eggs   52, *52*
apple and elderberry soufflé with
   port   70
apricot and Armagnac pudding   79
asparagus, lamb with   66

bacon
   laverbread with   46
   trout wrapped in   56, *58*
bara brith   *80*, 82
blackberry bread pudding   75
Blas ar Gymru venison   63, *63*
bread
   bara brith   *80*, 82
   Gelli Fawr loaf   *17*, 81
   quick wholemeal   84
   sesame bread buns   84
Bryngarw semolina almond slice   81

cakes and pastries
   Bryngarw semolina almond
     slice   81
   chocolate delight   83
   pikelets   83
   welshcakes   *80*, 83
   yoghurt cake   82
cheese   *17*, 28, *28*
   cucumber and cream cheese
     mousse   50
   escalope of pork Pantysgawn   64
   leek and goat's cheese
     parcels   48, *49*
   Nevern cheese and red wine
     pâté   54
   yoghurt cheese with fresh
     herbs   51
chestnut and mushroom pâté   47
chicken St Fagans   67
chocolate delight   83
Clwydian medieval lamb   60
crab, Gelli Fawr   54, *54*
cucumber and cream cheese
   mousse   50

desserts
   apricot and Armagnac
     pudding   79
   blackberry bread pudding   75
   crumble toppings   71
   elderberry and apple soufflé
     with port   70
   hazelnut and honey syllabub   70
   ice cream with fresh peaches   71
   Monmouth pudding   78
   muesli   78
   spiced plum tart   74
   sticky toffee pudding   74

   strawberry roulade   73, *73*
   tarten driog (treacle tart)   75

eggs, Anglesey   52, *52*
Eileen's raised game pie   55
elderberry and apple soufflé with
   port   70
escalope of pork Pantysgawn   64

fish   31
   mackerel and gooseberry
     sauce   50, *50*
   trout with lemon, butter
     and caper sauce   57, *58*
   trout wrapped in bacon   56, *58*
fruit
   apricot and Armagnac
     pudding   79
   blackberry bread pudding   79
   elderberry and apple soufflé
     with port   70
   gooseberry sauce for
     mackerel   50, *50*
   ice cream with fresh peaches   71
   spiced plum tart   74
   strawberry roulade   73, *73*

game
   Blas ar Gymru venison   63, *63*
   Eileen's raised game pie   55
Gelli Fawr crab   54, *54*
Gelli Fawr loaf   *17*, 81
gooseberry sauce for
   mackerel   50, *50*

ham cooked with cider   *17*, 67
hazelnut and honey syllabub   70, *79*
honey and hazelnut syllabub   70, *79*

ice cream with fresh peaches   71

lamb   30-1
   with asparagus   66
   Clwydian medieval lamb   60
   pâté   60
   Pembrokeshire lamb pie in
     hot water crusty pastry   59
   potted lamb lemonato   59
   rack of lamb with
     rosemary   66, *79*
   steaks with rosemary   60
laverbread   21
   with bacon   46
   roulade   46
leeks
   crackers   51
   and goat's cheese parcels   48, *49*
   and potato pie   48
lovage soup   52, *53*

mackerel and gooseberry
   sauce   50, *50*
Monmouth pudding   78
muesli   78
mushrooms
   and chestnut pâté   47
   with white wine and rosemary   47
mussels in a savoury choux
   pastry case   *61*, 62

Nevern cheese and red wine pâté   54
nutty crumble topping   71

pâté
   chestnut and mushroom   47
   lamb   60
   Nevern cheese and red wine   54
peaches, fresh with ice cream   71
Pembrokeshire lamb pie in hot
   water crusty pastry   59
pies
   Eileen's raised game   55
   leek and potato   48
   Pembrokeshire lamb pie in
     hot water crusty pastry   59
pikelets   83
plums, spiced plum tart   74
pork, escalope of pork
   Pantysgawn   64
potato and leek pie   48
potted lamb lemonato   59

quick wholemeal bread   84

saucepan oaty crumble   71
sesame bread buns   84
shellfish   31
   Gelli Fawr crab   54, *54*
   mussels in a savoury choux
     pastry case   *61*, 62
soup, lovage   52, *53*
sticky toffee pudding   74
strawberry roulade   73, *73*

tarten driog   75
treacle tart   75
trout   23
   with lemon, butter and
     caper sauce   57, *58*
   wrapped in bacon   56, *58*

venison, Blas ar Gymru   63, *63*

welshcakes   *80*, 83

yoghurt
   cake   82
   cheese with fresh herbs   51

*The publishers wish to thank the
Development Board for Rural Wales,
Wales Tourist Board and Welsh Rarebits
for supplying photographs for use in
this book.*

*The publishers also wish to thank
Pencoed Organic Growers,
Poppy Products (Abernant, Carmarthen),
Vin Sullivan (Abergavenny)
and the Welsh Folk Museum for supplying
food and assistance in respect of the front cover photography.*